AIR WAR OVER EUROPE

AIR WAR OVER EUROPE

1939–1945

CHAZ BOWYER

LEO COOPER

First published in 1981 by William Kimber & Co. Ltd.

Published in this format, 2003, by
Leo Cooper
an imprint of
Pen & Sword Books Limited
47 Church Street
Barnsley
South Yorkshire
S70 2AS

ISBN 0 85052 937 9

A CIP catalogue record of this book is available from
the British Library

Printed in England by
CPI UK

Contents

		Page
	Introduction	13
1	Now thrive the armourers	15
2	Before the holocaust	33
3	Blitzkrieg	50
4	Clash of eagles	64
5	Death by night	80
6	Seek and destroy	93
7	Around the clock	107
8	Aces all	118
9	Reaping the whirlwind	132
10	They also served	150
11	Day of the robots	165
12	Overture and beginners	176
13	Dawn of victory	194
14	Aftermath	209
	Bibliography	223

List of Illustrations

PLZ P.IIs of NO 122 Squadron of the Polish Air Force.

The notorious Junkers JU 87 *Stuka* dive-bomber.

A *Ratte* of Messerschmitt Bf 109Bs.

Amiot 143 bombers of the *Armèe de L'Air* in early 1940.

Morane-Saulnier MS 406 fighters.

Hawker Hurricanes of the Belgian Air Force, at Schaffen-Diest airfield.

Fairey Battle L5540, JN-C, of 150 Squadron RAF.

Messerschmitt Bf 110 flying along the English Coast in 1940.

Spitfire of 602 Squadron being re-armed for combat.

Air Chief Marshal Sir Hugh Dowding the architect of the RAF's victory in 1940.

The Vickers Wellington – or 'Wimpy' as it was dubbed.

Pilots of No 85 Squadron RAF, in early 1941.

North American B-25C 'Mitchell' (FV985) of 98 Squadron RAF.

Short Stirling.

A Handley Page Halifax during a daylight raid at Wanne-Eickel.

The twin-engined Manchester, precursor of the Avro Lancaster, which saw operational service from 1941-42.

Avro Lancaster NG347, QB-P, 'Princess Pat'.

Air Chief Marshal Sir Arthur Harris who commanded RAF Bomber Command from 1942-45.

A Lancaster over Germany gets a direct hit by flak.

How some came back. Lancaster C-Charlie of No 101 Squadron RAF which crash-landed at Ludford Magna airfield.

Focke Wulf Fw 190A-4 of II/JG2 at dispersal.

Lieutenant Joseph 'Sepp' Wurmheller, *Staffelkapitän* of 9/JG2 and his Focke Wulf Fw 190.

Adolf Galland with other Luftwaffe *Experten* fighter pilots.

Boeing B-17G Fortress of the 524th BS, 379th BG, 1st Air Division USAAF, based at Kimbolton in 1944.

Consolidated B-24J-145-CO Liberator based at Hethell in late 1943-early 1944.

'Little Friend'. Republic P-47C-5 Thunderbolt at Kingscliffe in 1943.

North American P-51D and P-51Bs – the Magnificent Mustangs.

Box bombing over Germany in 1943.

Precision bombing over the Focke Wulf aircraft assembly plant in 1943.

Victim. B-24H Liberator, 'Little Warrior' gets flak in its fuel tank over Quakenbrück.

Battle souvenir. A cheerful Bf 109G-5 pilot with a 'souvenir'.

Two 'Ton-Up' Lancasters.

An ammunition depot receives the attention of Halifaxes and Lancasters.

Beaufighters of 236 Squadron, RAF Coastal Command, with full complements of 3-inch rockets.

Nachtjäger – Messerschmitt Bf 110G-4b/R3.

Four German night fighters with the Luftwaffe commander-in-chief Hermann Göring.

Dornier Do 217 J-2 nightfighter of 4/NJG3, based at Svlt, in October 1943.

Air Chief Marshal Sir Arthur Tedder, supreme air commander of the Allied air forces.

Loading a Typhoon of No 247 Squadron RAF with 3-inch rockets.

The scene at Pforzheim on the night of 23/24 February 1945.

The notorious target of the Dortmund-Ems canal, a constant objective for the RAF.

Some of the USAAF's highest-scoring fighter aces, 56th FG, 1944.

'Black Nan', a B-24L Liberator receives a direct hit over Northern Italy.

Messerschmitt Me 262A-1a *Schwalbe* ('Swallow') twin-jet fighter.

Messerschmitt Me 163 *Komet* was a rocket propelled fighter designed to intercept the Allied bomber formations.

Heinkel He 162 *Volksjager* ('People's Fighter') twin-jet fighter.

Heligoland Bight under bombardment by a Lancaster force on 18 April 1945, viewed from 19,000 feet.

A Mosquito 'A-Apple' of No 143 Squadron strafing targets at Sandefiord, Norway.

Mercy Bomber. Eighth Air Force dropping food supplies to Dutch civilians.

'There is many a boy here today
who looks on war as all glory
– but, boys, it is all Hell.'

GENERAL SHERMAN, 1880
Columbus, Ohio

Introduction

The world war of 1939-45 is now almost sixty years in the past, yet many of its lessons are already forgotten; just as the lessons to be derived from that even bloodier war of 1914-18 were apparently lost upon the mentalities of the world's elder statesmen during the brief respite between those two global cataclysms. In particular, the aerial warfare of 1914-18 – the world's first conflict in the clouds – provided an ominous pointer to the future potential of air power; while the infinitely grimmer air war of World War Two put a seal on the awesome effect of death and devastation from the skies. The crucial need for establishing and wielding the weapon of air power was proven in undeniable form throughout 1939-45, and those relatively few prophets of the future domination of the air as the key to ultimate supremacy in war were wholly vindicated in fearful manner by the spring of 1945.

In this book I have attempted to trace the broad pattern of the use and effect of air power during 1939-45 over the European theatre of war alone, though patently this was but one portion of the overall aerial conflict of those years. In the Mediterranean and Far East operational zones, air power proved equally decisive in forging ultimate victory and, if only indirectly, contributed to the European struggle. Within the European parameters of my text three main air services dominated the air war: the Royal Air Force and its integrated Commonwealth partners, the American air forces based in Britain, and the German Luftwaffe. Thus my account concentrates primarily upon these giant warrior forces. In doing so it is by no means implied that other air services engaged in the war were of no importance, or that their efforts and sacrifices were in vain. Nevertheless, the duel between the two major Allied forces and the Luftwaffe was the crucial factor. Inevitably perhaps, to proscribe such a vast subject in a single volume forces the omission of a myriad of events and subjects which played small but vital roles, and such will be most evident in this account. Instead, the following pages are intended to offer a wide, general chronology and description of the

11

air war; a skeletal framework to which may be appended the flesh and sinews of details and data. Those readers seeking in-depth knowledge of specific aspects and events omitted or merely mentioned in passing herein are commended to the select bibliography provided at the end of my text.

War was once defined by a complacent statesman as 'The ultimate means of a community to impose its will upon others'; a view which merely reflects the utter failure of the world's politicians to achieve permanent harmony between nations by reasoned debate or 'diplomatic' entente. It should be borne in mind that it is the politician who creates and declares a state of war, *not* the military 'servants' of a nation. In the simpler cliché, 'Old men make wars, young men then have to fight them'. The professional serviceman has no illusions about war, taking the pragmatic view that 'War is not a matter of who is right - but who is left'. In the present era of aeronautical progress with its armoury of unimaginably destructive aerial weaponry, the aerial struggle of 1939-45 may seem 'small beer' to those who never witnessed the aftermath of Hamburg, Dresden and Hiroshima. Such patronising views should be set against the possibilities of nuclear conflict in the air, and then considered in the context of '. . . who is left'.

Thus, the European air war of 1939-45 may well now be a part of history, but its lessons still apply. The ironmongery of aerial warfare may have altered beyond recognition in the years since that conflict, but the principle of air supremacy as the prime guardian of peace remains unshaken. In the words of General Jan Smuts in 1917, at the height of the world's first-ever aerial struggle, 'It is important that we should not only secure air predominace, but secure it on a very large scale; and having secured it . . . we should make every effort to maintain it for the future'.

Chaz Bowyer
Norwich, 2003

CHAPTER ONE

Now Thrive the Armourers

On 10 January 1920 the Versailles Treaty's prohibitive and short-sighted terms for an utterly defeated Germany came into force. Among the myriad of clauses forbidding any forms of military forces were express restrictions on any aerial formations, even the handful of police air patrol squadrons then still in being for internal security duties. As a result, just three months later, on 9 April 1920, the German army Chief of Staff, General Hans von Seeckt ordered the disbandment of the few extant air units, which order was effective from 6 May. The closing words of the latter disbandment order read:

> We shall not abandon hope of one day seeing the Flying Corps come to life again. The fame of the Flying Corps engraved in the history of the German armed forces will never fade. It is not dead, its spirit lives on!

This hope for a revitalised German air arm was destined to wait only a relatively brief period in time before the seeds of such an air force were discreetly sown and patiently nurtured.

Architect of a new German air force was von Seeckt – though Nazi propaganda in the following decade inaugurated the false legend that Hermann Göring was the 'father' of the new Luftwaffe – and von Seeckt wasted little time in preparing the ground for the future air arm. Following a trade agreement between Germany and Russia in May 1921, the two countries concluded another treaty at Rapallo in April 1922, furthering the establishment of trade and diplomatic relations. Von Seeckt, with his immense foresight and shrewdness, regarded the Rapallo Treaty as the first concrete stepping stone to possible rebuilding of Germany's military forces; in particular a new air force, based initially for its working-up training outside Germany's borders in Russian territory. After prolonged, at times difficult, negotiations, such a base was agreed to by Soviet authorities, at Lipezk, some 250 miles south-west of Moscow. Here the first cadet training course for German airmen commenced early in 1925, using a batch of various Fokker biplanes already purchased by the German Ministry of Defence. By then, within Germany, further orders for new designs of aircraft intended for the future air arm of the German Reich had been placed in conditions of great secrecy with several aircraft manufacturers, such as Ernst Heinkel at Warnemünde.

Lipezk was to remain the clandestine Luftwaffe's main flying base on Russian soil from 1924 until 1933, well removed from the probing eyes of any Allied Control Commission investigators and inspectors. There the latest generation of German air crews were instructed in most facets of military or naval aviation, covering all forms of pilot and navigational training, bombing, mock combat, and the latest theories on tactics. Prior to attending the 'school' in Russia, a percentage of would-be air crews had received some *ab initio* instruction at the several civil flying schools slowly burgeoning inside Germany. Apart from flying instruction, however, the Lipezk base proved ideal for testing the steady flow of new and experimental aircraft designs built specifically for the future air force; all were produced by a wide variety of subterfuges and 'camouflage' methods either within Germany or close to its borders in defiance of the restrictive Versailles Treaty imposed limitations.

The use of Lipezk for such testing of the latest available German aircraft designs was to continue until 1933, by which time many of the fighters and bombers destined to equip the *Staffeln* of the eventual official Luftwaffe had received their initial trials at the Russian airfield – thereby affording the Russians with ample opportunities to observe and even fly the fresh designs during the occasional joint air exercises of 1932 and 1933. By 1930, the Allied restrictions on German aviation had gradually been relaxed to a point where the German Ministry of Defence could transfer air observer training to German flying schools, albeit still under the guise of training navigators for civil commercial air lines.

With Hitler's seizure of power, however, all links with Russia were ordered to be severed, and by September 1933 the Lipezk base had been evacuated for good. Nevertheless it had accomplished all that had been hoped for it, having trained some 450 air crew members and an equal number of skilled maintenance men; a readily available core of expertise and experience on which could be built any future military air arm. Moreover, the very latest fighters and bombers had been thoroughly tested under near-ideal circumstances and now stood as the basis for standardisation in production as soon as the German aircraft industry could throw off the lingering chains of Allied restrictions on manufacture of military aircraft.

In 1932 specific and greatly detailed instructions were issued by the German High Command in relation to the formation of a first-line operationally-fit air force within the parameters of a peacetime army i.e. subservient to the army (or navy, as appropriate) during peace-time and therefore simply an adjunct to the two senior services. In the following year, however, first steps were taken to separate the still-secret Luftwaffe-in-being from both army and navy, possessing its own Ministry under the overall aegis of the recently appointed Air Minister Hermann Göring. Implementation of Göring's personal desire to establish proper fighting units for the new force came on 1 April 1934 when the first fighter squadron, *Jagdstaffel* 135, was officially formed at Döberitz, near Berlin. This unit was quickly followed by the creation of 19 more squadrons of all types of operational roles. The year 1935 was the turning point. By Hitler's decree of 26 February, the newly-acknowledged air force was titled *Reichsluftwaffe* – his personal choice of title – but common usage and eventual official recognition reduced this title to simply Luftwaffe. Aircraft production was planned to create a total of 4,021 aircraft by October 1935, though in the event only about half of this number was actually produced by the end of the year. Nevertheless 1935 saw the Luftwaffe virtually treble in size, with a total of 48 squadrons by August alone.

For its initial equipment the Luftwaffe was forced to rely on existing biplanes and, to a lesser extent, monoplane designs little better than contemporary aircraft in other countries' air services, but 1935 also saw the initial trials of such modern concepts as the Messerschmitt Bf 109 fighter, at that time showing promise of surpassing any other fighter in the world in terms of speed and armament, and eventually selected as the Luftwaffe's standard fighter design for mass production. In general terms the newly-created air force in Germany, unlike most of its contemporary air services in Britain, France *et al*, was in a unique position to equip from scratch in the context of the very latest ideas and technology in aviation. Its manufacturing support industries were not clogged with long-standing, out-dated machinery, aircraft on order, or bound by inherited traditional methods of production or design. In addition, the overall massive direction of labour and infusion of finance and resources only possible in a totalitarian dictatorship ensured a minimal risk factor for aircraft firms wishing to experiment or invest in possibly unprofitable lines of research. In addition, by the direction of Hitler, progress rates in every facet of Germany's expanding rearmament programme were intensified to the highest practical pace.

Ever conscious of the value of opulent propaganda, Hitler and Göring proceeded to display the proud new Luftwaffe on every possible occasion, instigating a growing legend of invincibility and qualitative superiority which undoubtedly impressed – and fooled – many foreign spectators who witnessed such displays of Teutonic might and precision. In the period 1935–39, however, much of the extravagant claim made for the Luftwaffe was sheer bluff. Difficulties in development of new aircraft designs, a lack of finalised policy for the future of the air arm, and internal wrangling between various status-seeking hierarchies all contributed to slowing the planned re-equipment and enlargement of the Luftwaffe to its desired strength and capability. At that time the force was regarded almost wholly as a tactical formation; no provision had been seriously considered for home defence fighters – defence of the Reich from air assault being allocated virtually solely to the anti-aircraft artillery forces – while tentative ventures into the field of long-range strategic bomber design were relatively short-lived.

The opportunity for true testing of the Luftwaffe's mettle came in 1936, when General Franco appealed to Hitler for military aid to his Nationalist cause in Spain. Such aid was afforded in July 1936 by the provision of Junkers Ju 52 air transports to ferry thousands of soldiers and considerable freight and weaponry to Franco's forces from Spanish Morocco. By the end of 1936 Germany had despatched its own combat formation to Spain, the Condor Legion, initially equipped with some 42 aircraft. During the following two years of operations, the Luftwaffe was able to combat-test its latest standard aircraft types – the Heinkel He 111, Dornier Do 17 and Junkers Ju 87 bombers, and, particularly, the early versions of the Messerschmitt Bf 109 fighter. This latter quickly established itself as the best fighter in the Spanish Civil War, and gained lasting air supremacy for the Nationalist forces. Many of the German air crews detached to Spain for combat experience were later to lead Luftwaffe *Staffeln* and *Gruppen* into action during the European war. One of the prime benefits of the Spanish experience to emerge was the testing of close support tactics for ground forces, especially dive-bombing attacks against pin-point targets, a ploy which was to be fully exploited during 1939–40. Another important facet of that aerial conflict had been the ultimate testing of the Messerschmitt Bf 109 – air combat against opposing fighters and bombers. With minimal losses, the Condor Legion air crews accounted for 277 of the 335 enemy aircraft destroyed in the air between 1936 and 1938.* More significantly, aerial tactics were modified and improved and became standard from 1939.

On 4 February 1938 Hitler assumed supreme command of the entire German armed services. In the same year he ordered the annexation (i.e. invasion and occupation) of Austria, occupied the Sudetenland, and then brought the whole of Europe to the brink of war by demanding military occupation of the whole of Czechoslovakia. Personally convinced that Britain would not intervene, Hitler ordered mobilisation of the army and the Luftwaffe for an armed invasion of the Czech homeland. Matters came to a perilous head in mid-September 1938, with Hitler openly declaring to the British Prime Minister, Neville Chamberlain, that he was prepared to risk a world war if he could not have his way over Czechoslovakia. Both Britain and France pursued a policy of appeasement, resulting in the notorious Munich Agreement of 29/30 September 1938, a document which gave Hitler a bloodless victory for his demands.

Six months later German troops began military occupation of Czechoslovakia, but in the same month, March 1939, Hitler turned his eyes towards Poland, and sent demands to the Polish government for the free city of Danzig to be restored to German sovereignty, and for the construction of a German extra-terrestrial road and rail linkage across the Polish Corridor to East Prussia. On 26 March, however, the Polish government rejected Hitler's demands, while five days later the British Prime Minister announced a pledge of full British support should Polish independence be threatened. France immediately issued a similar pledge for support of Poland. Hitler's bluff had finally been called.

Undeterred, Hitler immediately ordered full-scale preparation for an armed invasion of Poland, detailed plans for which were completed by 22 June; two days later Germany signed a non-aggression pact with Russia, thereby avoiding any possible interference from the Soviets. Events over the following eight weeks moved irrevocably towards war – to the private dismay of Göring in particular and the Luftwaffe and Army general staffs. The Luftwaffe though ostensibly strong in quantity of aircraft and personnel was nevertheless in a transitionary stage of full development to its planned potential

---

* The remainder were shot down by Condor Legion anti-aircraft artillery.

establishment – which could not be achieved before 1942 on contemporary conditions. Serious deficiencies, especially in aero engines,
pure armament, and raw material supplies, boded ill for the Luftwaffe should it undertake any prolonged operations of war at that
time. From its genesis the Luftwaffe had been built up as a purely
tactical force, able to nullify and smother all opposition by sheer
weight in numbers and by rapid deployment in the field. Little or no
emphasis had been placed on long-term training or sustained
operational roles over any number of years. All of this was, in
simplified terms, parallel to Hitler's own view of war – a lightning
(*Blitzkrieg*) assault in avalanche-like proportion which would guarantee
rapid solution. It is true that Hitler, noting Britain's somewhat frantic
build-up of its armoury at the time of Munich, had called for a
five-fold increase in Luftwaffe strength. Yet even this plan was more
a desire to 'trump' any opponent's strength by an ability to display
a stronger hand of military 'cards'; actual war with Britain was
still not entirely a convincing possibility in Hitler's mind then.

In the early hours of 1 September 1939, Germany invaded Poland,
spearheaded by a total of almost 2,000 Luftwaffe aircraft, nearly half
of which were bombers. By 27 September the Polish campaign was
concluded. It had apparently proved the 'invincibility' of the Luftwaffe, which had completely overwhelmed the poorer-armed and less
modern Polish Air Force, had given copy-book support to the German
ground forces, and had clearly been the supreme factor in such a
quick victory. Yet the cost had not been light. Against fierce but
hopeless opposition in the air and from the ground, the Luftwaffe
had lost at least 750 men and nearly 300 aircraft, with a further 279
aircraft counted as overall strength losses due to serious damage. The
Polish Air Force, with less than 800 aircraft on 1 September, had
sustained a loss of 333 aircraft in action. Considering that the gross
strength of the Luftwaffe at the end of August 1939 was hardly more
than 4,000 aircraft of all types – perhaps only half of which could
be truly regarded as firstline 'attack' machines – the loss rate during
some three weeks of the Polish campaign, against ill-prepared and
inferior opposition in the context of aircraft, gave serious pause in
the minds of the more perceptive Luftwaffe heads of staff. Replacement of such casualties quickly was virtually impossible; such resources
were simply not available immediately. With France and the Low
Countries already designated as 'next' on Hitler's agenda for conquest,
the querulous doubts in many Luftwaffe chiefs' minds prior to the
Polish venture now assumed a level of deep concern.

This concern was exacerbated by the knowledge that Germany now had Britain and France as declared enemies. Only men like Göring or other Hitler-sycophants could believe that the Luftwaffe was fully prepared for any long-term aerial assault or struggle; the force was still in its adolescence, and had been built on the narrow platform of tactical air power. Its aircraft were too standardised in role to be capable of undertaking every possible task that would present itself during any sustained aerial conflict. The quality of its air and ground crews was never in question; all were peacetime-trained and thoroughly professional, while among the *Staffeln* and staffs was a hard core of combat-tested veterans of both the Spanish Civil War and the Poland campaign. Its aircraft presented a mixed picture. The standard fighter was the angular Messerschmitt Bf 109, on a par or clearly superior to almost any other fighter in the world in 1939. Its stablemate Bf 110 two-seat *Zerstörer* ('destroyer') was the apple of Göring's eye for the moment, but within a year would demonstrate forcibly its unsuitability for the 'escort fighter' role imposed upon its unfortunate crews. Of the frontline bombers, the already notorious crooked-wing Junkers Ju 87 dive-bomber was basking in the limelight of apparently deserved fame for its large contribution to recent operations, yet it too would reveal its feet of clay when faced with determined fighter opposition in the months ahead. Of the other bombers the porcine Heinkel He 111 and slender Dornier Do 17 predominated, both twin-engined, medium-range designs of relatively mediocre performance, and poorly armed for self-defence. Only the emerging Junkers Ju 88 offered slight hope of improved bomber performance, although even this excellent design was not intended for long range operations. The one great omission from the Luftwaffe's offensive air strength was a truly heavy, long range bomber. The only design projected for filling this gap was the troublesome Heinkel He 177, which was conceived in 1938 but did not commence operations until August 1942.

Notwithstanding the eventual failure of many of the 1939 Luftwaffe's operational aircraft types, the *contemporary* morale of the German air crews and their upper echelon staffs was very high. The rapidity with which Poland had been vanquished appeared to suggest that the *Blitzkrieg* tactical war was a sure-fire key to victory, an opinion echoed in the staff rooms of many of the Allied services of the period. If there were doubts about the future efficacy of the Luftwaffe they existed mainly in the minds of individual senior officers and strategists; no such gloomy thoughts pervaded the ranks of the firstline *Staffeln*. The high casualty rate against relatively 'soft' air opposition during the Polish *Blitzkrieg* was mostly attributed to inexperience on the part of younger air crews, a modicum of sheer bad luck, or simply the exigencies of war. There lingered no lack of confidence in men or machines. If there were any queries among the Luftwaffe crews these pertained to how they might fare against the French air force and, especially, the British Royal Air Force when the inevitable first clashes occurred over the Western Front. Led or commanded by veterans who had fought the Allies in the air during the 1914–18 war, all the young Luftwaffe crews had been trained and inculcated with the fighting traditions created by the now-legendary names in German aviation annals. Inbred in that tradition was an almost unconscious respect for the fighting qualities of the *Engländer* – would they now acquit themselves against the contemporary generation of RAF fliers with the same courage and honour as their forebears . . . ?

North-westwards across the narrow strip of water pompously referred to in all British geography schoolbooks as the 'English Channel', the objects of the Luftwaffe's silent thoughts, the RAF air crews, were equally confident and curious about the forthcoming joining of air forces in mortal combat in French skies. Like their German counterparts, the 1939 RAF air crews were very professionally trained in peace-time, but at that moment were far from fully equipped with the latest aircraft available. RAF Fighter Command, inaugurated in 1936 and progressively built up by its overall commander, Hugh Dowding, as primarily a home *defence* force for the United Kingdom, could boast an overall total of 1,099 aircraft on 1 September 1939. Of these the firstline units actually had 747 aircraft on strength, spread among 37 squadrons, including no less than 14 hastily-mobilised squadrons of the Auxiliary Air Force. The quality of modernity among the operational fighters on strength, however, was reflected in the mixture of outdated biplanes – Gloster Gauntlets and Gladiators – and modified Bristol Blenheim 1F 'fighters', which accounted for some thirty per cent of the frontline squadron equipment. The balance comprised totals of 347 Hawker Hurricanes and 187 Spitfires at the 'sharp end', with mass production of both monoplane types by then well under way giving promise of ample quantities of each for the near future.

Bomber Command was also in a state of virtual transition in the context of first-line operational strength and aircraft. At the outbreak of the war the command possessed some 53 squadrons overall, though only 33 of these were designated as 'operational'; the rest were classified as reserve or Group pool units. All were equipped with one or other of five types of bomber :

Fairey Battle .... 15 squadrons
Bristol Blenheim .... 10 squadrons
Vickers Wellington .... 10 squadrons
Handley Page Hampden .... 10 squadrons
Armstrong Whitworth Whitley .... 8 squadrons

All were at least six years old in conception, and excepting the Battle, all were twin-engined, medium range bombers. Four-engined, heavy, long-range bomber designs were already well advanced for eventual replacement as the command's offensive spearhead – the Short Stirling, Handley Page Halifax, and Avro Manchester III, later retitled Lancaster – but the first of these to enter the operations' lists, the Stirling, would not do so before 1941. The bomber crews, though well trained to peacetime standards of pure flying, were surprisingly lacking in such vital facets as night navigation and, indeed, in actual use of their aircraft for the prime *raison d'être* of a bombing formation – bombing. Very few Bomber Command crews had ever undertaken night-bombing sorties prior to the outbreak of war, and even less had even practised take-offs and landings with a full warload of 'live' bombs. Such glaring omissions from the routine training and daily practice of RAF bomber crews were directly attributable to the decades of Treasury parsimony and governmental uninterest in the post–1918 era. Prophets of offensive air power, like Hugh Trenchard and John Salmond, fought doggedly for years to establish a strong, high quality RAF, yet it was not until 1934 that the British government was reluctantly persuaded to take heed of such counsel, and in the following year agreed to a reasonable expansion programme for the UK air formations. Part-instigation for such a hasty reversal of long-standing policy was the overt build-up of Germany's new Luftwaffe. In March 1935 Hitler told Anthony Eden and Sir John Simon – at an 'arms limitations' discussion – that Germany already had frontline parity with the RAF, and would shortly outnumber the French. It would be no exaggeration to state that this claim – actually untrue at that moment, but soon to be justifiable – threw the British Cabinet into mild panic.

Even then the various schemes mooted and revised for expansion and updating of the RAF were only put into effect at a less than urgent pace. In 1935 a 'Scheme C' programme set out to provide for a UK-based RAF of 70 bomber and 35 fighter squadrons by 1942, a bias towards bombers which reflected the contemporary opinion at higher levels that any future aerial conflict would be primarily a bomber-versus-bomber battle of attrition, with fighters employed in the main as watchdog guards over the bomber bases. The inherent administrative and operational control difficulties of Scheme C led directly to a wide reorganisation of the RAF almost immediately, and in mid-1936 the force was basically divided into four separate commands – Bomber, Fighter, Coastal and Training. The new Bomber Command at that time comprised a total of 32 squadrons of the regular RAF, with a further 12 squadrons of the Auxiliary Air Force or Special Reserve. Without exception all were equipped with biplane aircraft; none could have carried out an effective bombing sortie against any target within the German borders.

Planned re-equipment of the RAF's bomber arm included several twin-engined, monoplane designs, and these began to reach the squadrons shortly after. Nevertheless, the need for truly heavy bombers, capable of delivering significant bomb loads on European targets, had already been acknowledged, and specifications were being drawn up which would eventually bear fruit with the four-engined 'heavies' which later undertook the strategic bombing offensive against Germany in the 1942–45 years. It was on this latter premise – to aim towards an all-heavy bomber force by 1942–43 at latest – that the Air Ministry based its forward planning for what they regarded as Britain's best form of defence i.e. *offensive* air power. The Air Ministry proposals immediately ran into a huge obstacle when a report by Sir Thomas Inskip to the Cabinet, in pursuance of his recently created post as Minister for Co-ordination of Defence, stated baldly that the projected expansion scheme ('Scheme J') was too costly, and then further recommended that bomber forces should be reduced, not enlarged, development of twin-engined medium bombers intensified, and much more emphasis given to building a strong metropolitan fighter defence force. Inskip's basic reasoning was that any German bombing attacks would best be countered *over Britain* (italics are the author's) rather than by attempting to bomb German bases and back-up industries. This completely negative view of air power was accepted by the Cabinet in December 1937, resulting in a drastic reduction in the proposed financial budget allocated to RAF expansion. The Air Ministry, though greatly dismayed, could at least find some comfort in the retention of the long-term plan to re-equip Bomber Command with four-engined heavy aircraft designs, albeit at a slower rate of progression. Clearly this extraordinary Cabinet decision indicated abandonment – at best, postponement – of any attempt to achieve parity with the burgeoning Luftwaffe. Instead efforts were concentrated on the latest priority: enlarging RAF Fighter Command and its many ancillary defence organisations and formations.

Unquestionably the over-riding fear in the government circles and, indeed, among the British public at large during the period 1936–38 was of an initial overwhelmingly strong air assault by Germany against England in the event of war. The RAF's overt weakness, in fighter defence and possible bomber counter-offensive strength and capability, was described by Sir Kingsley Wood as ' . . . positively tragic' at the time of the Munich Crisis in September 1938, a factor which loomed largely in British politicians' minds and led to Britain's acquiescence to Hitler's demands for possession of Czechoslovakia. Paradoxically, Hitler at that time had no contingency plans for any form of air attack on Britain, while his Luftwaffe was in no state to deliver any worthwhile assault against the United Kingdom in any significant strength. British intelligence of the period seriously over-estimated the extant potency of the Luftwaffe throughout the years prior to the outbreak of war, a view enhanced by the exaggerated claims for German air strength by such political figures as Winston Churchill, and no less a tribute to the effectiveness of German deliberate bluff propaganda about the new air arm in the late 1930s. Nevertheless, with the advantage of hindsight, it remains a moot point whether the 1938 RAF could have withstood any sustained aerial onslaught by the contemporary Luftwaffe, had the Munich crisis actually resulted in the 'open war' which Hitler had declared himself willing to undertake in default of acceptance of his demands over the Sudetenland.

In one other area Britain, as an island, was extremely vulnerable. Relying to a huge extent on imported goods and raw materials for normal domestic and industrial existence, Britain was – and still is – ultra-dependent on her mercantile shipping lanes from sources all over the globe. Blockade by sea preventing the smooth uninterrupted flow of such imports would clearly reduce the United Kingdom's ability to maintain any extended warfare in any form; hence the centuries-old reliance upon the Royal Navy to rule the waves. The advent of air power hardly altered that basic concept but did introduce a new dimension in sea warfare. The ability of aeroplanes to destroy capital ships had been amply demonstrated in the post–1918 years, and was to be tragically amplified throughout World War Two. Additionally, the relatively recent introduction of the submarine as an offensive weapon of war boded ill for merchant shipping convoys in the event of war – as was exemplified in 1916–17 when German U-boats had almost succeeded in achieving a virtual blockade of Britain from the sea.

Countermeasures to the greatly improved German U-boats of the 1930s remained primarily a matter for the Royal Navy, but to this traditional safeguard could now be added aircraft of the Navy's Fleet Air Arm and the RAF's newly-created Coastal Command. The latter, by 1939, lagged well behind other RAF commands in terms of modern aircraft designed for the specific maritime roles, and was ill-equipped in the context of anti-shipping and anti-submarine war-fare. In pure aircraft strength, on 3 September 1939 Coastal Command could muster a gross total of perhaps 450 aeroplanes, but no more than half of these could truly be regarded as in any war sense operational. The command's actual armoury of available weaponry for tackling underwater opponents was dismal, relying – rather hopefully – on the airborne torpedo as its chief anti-shipping (surface) 'antidote', but forced to use obsolete types of pure aerial bombs of RAF type for anti-submarine attacks. These latter GP (General Purpose) bombs had no penetrative power against metal hulls and were, frankly, useless against any submerged submarine. It was to be several years before effective anti-submarine weapons became available, and even these were to include what amounted to modified naval depth charges.

Had Germany given real priority to the construction of U-boats in the pre-1939 years, Britain's position as a totally dependent nation on her imports might easily have been exploited very early in the war, but the personal indifference to all naval matters by Hitler played a large part in the neglect of such a   build-up of underwater 'killer' strength, and in September 1939 Germany possessed a mere 56 submarines of which roughly half were incapable of extended operations in the deep water of the Atlantic Ocean. Even so, the early successes of these few U-boats forced Hitler to change his view and in subsequent years submarine production and quality was greatly enlarged. Such successes were due in no small measure to the intrepid daring and skill of certain individual German submarine commanders, but were no less the result of Coastal Command's lack of long-range aircraft to protect shipping convoys far from Britain's coastal waters, and too few aircraft with which to provide any aerial 'umbrella' around the United Kingdom's lengthy coastline. From the very beginning of the war with Germany, Coastal Command recognised the prime role for its aircraft as an air deterrent, rather than simply an anti-submarine formation; the latter role was still looked upon as chiefly a matter for the Royal Navy. The mere presence of an aircraft above or near any convoy was more than often sufficient to make any U-boat commander remain submerged and ineffective.

Thus, poised on the brink of war with Germany in September 1939, the Royal Air Force presented a mixed face. All operational commands were lacking in truly adequate numbers of aircraft to fulfil their designated roles, and even the existing firstline designs were by no means all of updated modernity. The air crews and ground technical staffs were nevertheless highly trained professionals, all volunteers, and supremely confident in their prospects. Higher command was in the hands, mainly, of men who were veterans of the 1914–18 war, with practical (if outdated) experience of aerial warfare; while behind the RAF was an increasingly urgent aircraft manufacturing industry just beginning to produce in quantity the much-needed volume of aircraft and weaponry. Volunteers for air crew training were never lacking at any period of the RAF's history, and in 1939 increased to numbers with which a peacetime-based administration was unable to cope initially. Future four-engined heavy bombers for a strategic air offensive were already off the drawing boards in prototype form, faster, better-armed fighters were in embryo, and the ever-expanding volume of back-up American-designed aircraft was giving promise of ample quantitative superiority over the Luftwaffe in the nearish future. To the unblooded RAF crews in that fateful autumn that future seemed bright. . . .

What of the other European air forces whose mettle would soon be sorely tested against the much-vaunted Nazi Luftwaffe? France, the largest of those nations and Germany's obvious main opponent initially, had suffered decades of political vacillation in regard to its military forces, particularly its air services. Even the prime role of its air force was undecided by 1939 : whether to be a tactical adjunct to the army and navy, or a separate strategic force of independent command – the same diversion of decision which had plagued most countries in determining the future of air power in the 1920s and

1930s. Politics had also created complete disorganisation of France's otherwise potentially healthy aircraft industry when its many individual firms came under the bureaucratic grip of nationalisation in 1936–37, resulting in a lack of co-ordinated production until 1940 – too late to stem disaster. The conflict in actual design requirements for operational aircraft, caused in large part by the wavering aims mooted for the French air forces, resulted in a proliferation of multi-role aircraft, intended ostensibly for reconnaissance, bombing and fighting in one 'package', a multiplicity of tasks in none of which the particular aircraft could be expected to excel.

At the end of August 1939 the French Air Force had on charge a total of some 3,600 aircraft of all types, excluding instructional and 'colonial' machines, plus some 350 maritime aircraft in France's naval air arm *Aeronautique Navale*. On paper such a quantity might have seemed reasonably formidable, but at least a third of these aeroplanes were obsolescent, if not already obsolete, and roughly 1,200 were ostensibly 'modern' designs. The total actually in firstline availability was 1,364, of which nearly two-thirds could not be classified as modern; the most updated section being almost 500 reasonably new fighters. Of the 390 bombers included in that operational line-up, 95 per cent were patently obsolete for any modern warfare, a state of affairs which had been noted by the French Chief of Air Staff, General Vuillemin as early as the autumn of 1938. Indeed, in August 1938, at the express invitation of Hermann Göring, Joseph Vuillemin had officially visited Germany to see the latest Luftwaffe aircraft, and had been so impressed by the clever bluff of Luftwaffe chiefs Milch and Udet as to their 'latest operational' designs that upon his return to France he had told the French Prime Minister, M. Daladier, 'If war breaks out, I'll apply to be relieved from my post and would go and die in a bomber over Berlin.'

To fill the gaps in modern aircraft equipment, due to the as-yet unproductive French aviation industry up until late 1939, foreign aircraft were purchased, particularly American designs such as the Curtiss Hawk 75 fighter and Martin Maryland and Douglas DB–7 bombers; but of the latter only the Curtiss Hawks had been delivered by September 1939 – a total of 176 aircraft which immediately re-equipped two French *Escadres*. The Douglas and Martin bombers only began to trickle to France in early 1940, too late to have any effect whatsoever on the air operations then. The *Armée de l'Air*'s principal fighters in late 1939 were the Morane-Saulnier 406, Dewoitine 510 and, by November, Bloch 151; all monoplanes with mixed cannon and machine gun armament, but none capable of exceeding 300 mph with full war load. The much superior, promised Dewoitine 520 fighter did not begin to reach firstline unit use until May 1940, and even then equipped just one *groupe*. In the bomber field, no design could be confidently expected to survive any intensive daylight operations against Luftwaffe opposition. Thus, the French air crews, well-trained by contemporary standards and in no way lacking in courage or determination, were ill-served for equipment. In cold summary, the French air force in September 1939 was ill-fitted to join battle with the Luftwaffe with even an equal chance of survival. The years of neglect and vacillation among French political circles in relation to the country's air power were to bear bitter fruit within less than a year of war.

Of the other European countries soon to feel the iron fist of massive Luftwaffe might, Poland – the first to offer armed opposition to Hitler's grandiose ambitions – possessed a weak and ill-equipped air force in 1939. First created as a single, unified command in December 1918, the Polish Air Force was born in strife. Its parent country, partitioned between Russia, Germany and Austria–Hungary for more than a century, emerged as an independent state in the autumn of 1918, but spent the next two years fighting a succession of campaigns against armed Russian occupation. This war ended in October 1920, and the existing air units were completely reorganised into 13 'new' squadrons, freshly numbered, as the basis for the future national air force. Its progress and expansion during the following fifteen years were rapid and of high quality. By early 1926 the PAF could count some 350 frontline operational aircraft, split between 32 squadrons; 12 of the latter were fighter units, and overall it became the second largest air arm (after the French) on the European continent. That same year saw a new regime come to power in Poland and command of the PAF passed into the capable hands of Colonel (then) Ludomil Rayski, who was to remain as the PAF supremo until his resignation early in 1939.

In common with most countries during the between-wars' era, Poland's government showed little real interest in its air arm in the context of provision of adequate funding for expansion and modernisation. Rayski, therefore, adopted Hugh Trenchard's ploy with the RAF when faced with lack of finance in the immediate post-1918 period – he decided to establish at least a sound foundation for the Polish Air Force onto which could, later, be added any possible expansion : funding training programmes, new airfields, maintenance facilities, and by no means least by placing development aircraft contracts for Polish-designed aircraft for the future PAF. Of the latter, perhaps the most significant Polish designs to emerge were the P.Z.L.P.–fighter, which entered squadron service from 1935–39, and the P.Z.L.P.–37 *Los* twin-engined medium bomber which went into service in 1938.

The assumption of power in Germany by Hitler in the early 1930s, combined with hasty re-armament programmes by most other European powers as a direct consequence, saw the Polish Air Force remain static numerically and qualitatively. Utterly inadequate finance – even the Polish Army's cavalry was allotted twice as much money as the air force – enforced a general slowing down of replacement equipment. In October 1936, however, came a PAF expansion plan which envisaged an air strength of some 1,300 aircraft – though this figure *included* 100 per cent reserves – by early 1942. The plan was destined never to reach anything approximating to fruition. Governmental indifference to the PAF, expressed in lack of proper financial backing, and even ordered cuts in production of the latest designs of bomber, all added to the rundown of the PAF to its weakest state by 1939. Attempts to purchase foreign aircraft from Britain and France totalling 100 bombers (Fairey Battles) and 175 fighters (Morane-Saulnier 406, Hawker Hurricanes and a lone Spitfire) were put in hand, but none of these was to reach Poland in time to help stem the Nazi invasion of Poland in 1939. On 1 September 1939, as the first waves of Luftwaffe bombers nosed over the Polish borders, the PAF could only muster a total of 396 combat aircraft plus a handful of unarmed light aeroplanes for communications. Of these, the firstline defenders were 156 fighters, mainly the gull-winged P.Z.L.P.– design monoplanes.

Any student of military aviation history as applicable to the locust years 1918–39 in the European context cannot fail to be struck by the similarity in circumstances in which each of the major countries facing the rapid rise of Nazidom in Germany neglected their air arms. Unheeding of the clear pointers to the future of air power part-exemplified in the closing stages of the 'Great War' of 1914–18, all such governments had ignored expert advice and counsel, allotted miserly financing, even argued at length as to need for any 'independent' air force – and then continued wallowing complacently in a fairyland euphoria of 'peace' and idealistic hopes of international disarmament. The consequent level of weakness in both defensive and offensive air power in each such country created near-panic when Hitler's 'secret', modern and (apparently) all-powerful Luftwaffe was finally acknowledged openly by the Nazi hierarchy.

Attempting to redress the overt neglect of almost two decades, subsequent expansion programmes for each air service were, to say the least, hasty – and in the event virtually too late to prevent the tragedy of another world war only twenty-one years after the cessation of the 'war to end all wars'. Indeed, it is ironic that governments who had spent years denying the potency of air power were now to expend vast sums and huge priority on their air services because of the latent threat of air power. . . .

The looming cataclysm of war was almost triggered off in late 1938 when Hitler set in motion plans for an armed invasion of Czechoslovakia, to commence at dawn on 1 October. Only the desperate political appeasement of the Munich Agreement prevented embroilment of the rest of Europe in a bloody conflict for which none was prepared or – at that moment – capable of sustaining. Nevertheless, Munich became the watershed – from that moment on few Europeans were in any doubt that war must come sooner or later. That war did not erupt for a further eleven months was fortunate for the countries which eventually opposed Germany – it was a breathing space which permitted a degree of last-minute rearmament, albeit still far short of a desirable level of strength.

At 1830 hours on 25 August 1939, the Luftwaffe supremo, Göring, flashed the codeword '*Ostmarkflug* 26, August, 0430 hours' to his two eastern *Luftflotten* based a few miles from the Polish border – the 'solution of the Polish question by violence' was about to be put into action. Then, nearly four hours after, an order direct from Hitler cancelled this, but the cancellation order failed to reach the waiting German army commanders until midnight. At precisely 0430 hours on 26 August, therefore, one army assault group which had yet to receive its orders to halt moved across the Polish border, engaged local Polish troops in a gun battle and was virtually destroyed. Despite Britain's announcement of a mutual aid pact with Poland on 25 August, Hitler decided to proceed with his 'Polish solution', and at 1240 hours on 31 August 'War Directive No 1' was issued. At 0445 hours the following morning the Second World War began.

The actual strength of the Luftwaffe on the first day of the war has been mooted in many post–1945 military histories as being as high as 7,000 firstline machines. According to figures published by the Freiburg military records office, a total of 4,093 front-line aircraft were actually available at the outbreak of war, of which perhaps ninety per cent were considered to be ready for immediate action. Of this gross total Göring detached a force of two *Luftflotten* for the Polish assault – a combined strength of 1,302 aircraft, with perhaps a further 600 aircraft in support for indirect operational duties. These represented almost two-thirds of the entire Luftwaffe's *effective* strength on 1 September 1939. The committal of such a high proportion of an entire air force to what – in objective view – might be regarded as a relatively easy, almost minor air campaign was nevertheless entirely in accord with the Luftwaffe's terms of reference : a 'shock wave' of intensive air power to be applied as a forward assault formation to clear the way ahead for the army on the ground. It was a practical application of *tactical* air power entirely. In September 1939 the Luftwaffe was neither structured or even capable of conducting any form of *strategic* air power beyond its immediate neighbouring countries, and certainly incapable of sustaining any air campaign against Britain. Its air staffs were perfectly aware of all this; as General Speidel, then *Luftflotte* 1's chief of staff, wrote, 'Our weaknesses in training, equipment and operational readiness were only too well known, and were again and again dutifully reported to higher authority'.

Hitler's adamant decision to proceed with the conquest of Poland merely dismayed his army and air force hierarchy. They were now committed to a global war and were in no way prepared for such a commitment. The myth of Luftwaffe invincibility, so carefully and deviously built up by the Nazi propaganda machinery over the previous five years, was now to be put to the ultimate acid testing.

CHAPTER TWO

Before the Holocaust

The bland promise of the British government in August 1939 to provide Poland with '. . . all support in our power' was in essence a hollow gesture. Far from being geared to despatch any form of effective fighting force to Poland, the British armed services at that time were still engaged in urgent expansion to meet the pressing requirements of purely metropolitan defence, and to fulfil pre-arranged commitments for physical military aid to France. Both British and French military authorities recognised the inevitability of an invasion of Poland by Germany – and possibly Russia – but concluded that any injection of British or French troops or air formations would be pointless waste. The 'invincible Luftwaffe' myth so carefully exploited by German propagandists over the years was still, at least in part, accepted by Allied leaders. An extension of that half-belief was the firm contemporary belief – in France and in Britain – that full war would be heralded by a devastating air assault by Luftwaffe bombers; an awesome 'knockout blow' aimed at capital cities and seats of government. On the other hand RAF Bomber Command from the outset was restricted – by mainly political decree – to future attacks on 'miiltary objectives' only, and was forbidden to initiate air attacks against the enemy civil population. Confusing this naive statement of intent was the lack of any precise definition of what exactly comprised a 'military objective' – could it include, for merely one obvious example, the vast armament industrial complex of the Ruhr?

It was essentially a policy of 'containment' – a waiting game in which the Allies' staffs apparently preferred to allow the Luftwaffe to strike the first blow. Indeed, the consensus of French military authority at that period heavily favoured an entirely defensive stance in the event of German assaults by land or air. This Gallic attitude was itself part-based on two homegrown myths: the 'invincibility' of the French Army when fighting on French soil, and the 'inviolability' of the Maginot Line. The sheer weakness and obsolescence of the French air force were acknowledged, if only in private, by French military chiefs, and accordingly agreements were made prior to the war for extensive direct support in aerial operations from RAF Bomber Command. In practical terms this policy was translated by the RAF making arrangements for the immediate transfer to France on the outbreak of war of a complete bomber Group, No 1, comprised of ten squadrons of Fairey Battles, backed by a further ten Blenheim squadrons – partly based in France or Britain – with a few fighter and army co-operation squadrons for overall support. The Air Staff in London was not entirely happy with this arrangement, but regarded it as an obligation. Nevertheless, it was made plain to the French that such RAF formations would remain under RAF control and were not intended merely to supplement the French air service in support of French army operations. The *raison d'être* of the RAF bombers based in France would be to carry out separate raids across the German borders once the 'balloon went up' – a semi-strategic, yet semi-tactical objective in purpose.

The undeclared state of war between Germany and Poland was officially commenced at 0445 hours on 1 September 1939, though in fact three Junkers Ju 87bs of *Stuka Geschwader* 1 anticipated this designated zero hour by some fifteen minutes by bombing known demolition points close to a bridge over the Vistula at Dirschau. The Luftwaffe's prime objective was complete air supremacy over Poland, a neecssary pre-requisite to successful land operations propounded by General Giulio Douhet in his book *Air Power* in 1921. It was a priority in aerial warfare adhered to by the Luftwaffe, in essence, throughout World War Two. Thus the first main targets for the German bombers were the Polish Air Force's airfields and bases. These latter were attacked on the first day of the onslaught by succeeding waves of Heinkels, Dorniers and Ju 87 *Stukas,* creating vast material damage to the buildings, installations and runways of the known PAF bases. The subsequent Command report claimed, '. . . air sovereignty over the entire Polish combat zone'.

The report was highly premature, however, because in the twenty-four hours preceding the Luftwaffe's initial attack, all PAF operational units had been moved from their normal peacetime airfields to dispersed, secret air strips. The only aircraft remaining were a motley bag of obsolete or unserviceable PAF machines, 28 of which were destroyed by bombing. At the secret airfields the alerted PAF firstline fighters took off and crossed the returning flight path of some Ju 87s which had just bombed Craców airfield. The brief engagement saw the Polish squadron commander killed by a Ju 87 gunner.

Another Polish pilot, Wladyslaw Gnys, flying a P.11c, destroyed a Do 17 – the first German aircraft to be shot down in aerial combat in World War Two.

The subsequent campaign in Poland was, inevitably, brief. Despite fierce and continuous opposition by the Polish fighters and bombers, the sheer weight of Luftwaffe numbers prevailed, and after reaching its peak of aerial activity on 16 and 17 September, the bulk of PAF fighters were withdrawn from the battle and some 300 Polish aircraft of all types were ordered to evacuate to Rumania. This seeming retreat resulted directly from the sudden 'stab in the back' invasion of eastern Poland by Soviet Russia on 17 September – a move pre-agreed in a secret pact between Russia and Germany which aimed at a partition of Polish territory between the aggressors. Further Polish resistance on the ground was finally ended by 5 October, while the city of Warsaw was systematically bombarded by land and from the air from 4 September until its eventual capitulation on 27 September – the first capital city to suffer terrifying air assault upon its civil population in the war.

Several legends have since been perpetuated by latter-day historians about the air war over Poland during those fateful weeks in the autumn of 1939. Perhaps the most-repeated assertion, based mainly on optimistic contemporary German reports, was the claim that the Polish Air Force was rendered effectively useless within the first forty-eight hours by the Luftwaffe's bombing attacks. In fact, no first-line RAF aircraft was even damaged by bombing during those two days, due to their dispersal to secret and well camouflaged alternative operational airstrips on 31 August.

Another inaccurate impression created by some postwar accounts was of the 'light' opposition offered by the PAF's admittedly obsolescent and outdated aircraft to the Luftwaffe. Nothing could be further from the truth. Knowing well the inferior performances and armament of their machines, PAF fighter and bomber crews put up a magnificent aerial confrontation whenever the opportunities presented themselves. Dogged by lack of central control, communications, and back-up organisation, PAF fighters were *officially* credited with totals of 126 confirmed aerial victories and 24 more German aircraft probably destroyed or at least seriously damaged. This tally was, in truth, an *under*estimation, as witnessed by official German reports and statistics from the office of the Luftwaffe's Quarter-Master General of the period.

Even as the Polish invasion gained its initial momentum, the RAF made its first moves to implement the Anglo-French mutual aid agreement. On 2 Septmber 1939 – the day *before* Britain's official declaration of war with Germany – the full complement of No 1 Group, Bomber Command made its way by air across the Channel to pre-designated French airfields in the Rheims area : a total of 160 Fairey Battles, one of which ditched in the sea en route, though its crew was safely retrieved. These ten squadrons were originally intended as the first of two echelons to be sent to France, but in the event – due largely to the lack of the expected Luftwaffe assault against France – the proposed second formation from No 2 Group, Bomber Command was postponed, then in December cancelled. The Battles comprised the Advanced Air Striking Force (AASF) and were simply intended as a semi-deterrent bombing force capable of reaching German targets should Germany attack France. As fighter protection for the obsolete Battles, the AASF was allotted just two units, Nos 1 and 73 Squadrons, flying Hurricanes. No 1 Squadron flew to France on 8 September, and was joined shortly after by its sister unit; yet initially these fighters were used merely to patrol the Channel ports; leaving the Battles to operate separately. The tragic lessons of 1917–18, that unescorted daylight bombing sorties were foredoomed to disastrous casualty rates, had yet to be re-learned by the RAF hierarchy . . .

Also despatched to France on the outbreak of war was a separate air formation, the Air Component of the British Expeditionary Force (BEF), comprised of five squadrons of Lysander army co-operation machines, four squadrons of Blenheim bombers, and two (later increased to four) Hurricane squadrons. This Air Component's terms of reference were equally simple : to provide immediate tactical air support for the BEF troops and armour on the ground. In December 1939 the AASF was further strengthened by the arrival from England of two Blenheim squadrons; while from 15 January 1940 both the AASF and the Air Component were brought together administratively under a single overall command titled British Air Forces in France (BAFF), commanded by Air Marshal Arthur 'Ugly' Barratt. Backing the bombing effort of BAFF, should Germany invade the Low Countries, or France, were seven Blenheim and two Whitley squadrons of Bomber Command, all based in England. At least, these were included in the original planning for the RAF's effort in support of the BEF and its French allies; yet it might be noted that while Barratt could exercise personal autocracy in respect of decisions for bombing sorties by the units under his command in France, he could still only 'request' the England-based bomber squadrons' aid if ever required.

The actual employment of any bombing force was, and for several months continued to be, a contentious question among the British and French commanders and politicians. Over-riding the whole debate was the distinct fear of the French that any form of air attack against Germany would inevitably provoke a savage retaliation in kind by the Luftwaffe against French cities and industry. The result of such trepidation was a stubborn reluctance by French leaders to be associated with any such 'precipitate' provocation. RAF bomber commanders, however, were also restricted in radius of action by their orders not to initiate all-out bombing offensives against the German homeland; but in any case they were not wholly convinced of the efficacy of the relatively meagre bomber forces available for any such offensive. The 'prize' target for any strategic bomber attack was, quite obviously, the vast Ruhr industrial complex; in area greater than the environs of London, and representing roughly sixty per cent of Germany's vital war industry.

Such a long-term view of the effect of bombing held no attraction for the French, who argued that while any such assault might well achieve its objective eventually, it would and could not prevent any immediate invasion of French soil by the German forces. It was a blinkered view which ignored the obvious fact that in the event of any German advance aerial warfare would automatically be greatly extended anyway. It was not until late April 1940 before the French generals reluctantly agreed that the RAF could initiate air attacks against Germany's industry should the Germans invade Holland or Belgium, though this agreement on paper was to dissolve quickly in the following month when that anticipated invasion actually occurred.

Against such a backdrop of indecision and disagreement, the AASF Battle squadrons quickly settled in to their respective French bases, adapting with good humour and plentiful confidence to the near-primitive conditions of operations and general maintenance literally 'in the field'. The opportunity to attack German forces along the Western Front while such a high proportion of German strength was fully occupied in the Polish campaign was patently obvious – yet was not taken. Instead the Battle squadrons prepared to carry out straightforward daylight reconnaissance flights over the immediate German border. On 20 September three Battles, unescorted by fighters, took off from 88 Squadron's base at Mourmelon le Grand for such a recce, and were bounced by a gaggle of Messerschmitt Bf 109Es and immediately lost two Battles to the fighters. The third Battle was left to fight for its life against the wheeling Bf 109s, but its rear gunner Sergeant F.

Letchford remained cool and destroyed at least one Messerschmitt with his hand-manipulated Vickers gun – the first air kill of the war by the RAF. Despite this blatant warning of the hazards of attempting unescorted daylight recces, only ten days later five Battles from 150 Squadron set out from Ecury-sur-Coole and were promptly jumped by 15 Messerschmitts, losing three bombers in the first pass by the fighters. Of the remaining pair, one was severely damaged and force-landed, wrecking itself in the process, while the other was also forced to land, completely riddled. Such attrition gave pause to further daylight sorties for a while, but the onset of winter – the coldest winter for decades in Europe – obviated all flying. The poor performance of the Battle in action led to a spate of local modifications, such as armour plate protection for the crews and attempts to include a belly gun for under-protection, but such additions merely dampened an already mediocre performance range. On 1 December the AASF's overall strength was reduced when Nos 15 and 40 Squadrons returned to England for re-equipment with Blenheims; a depletion which made little difference at the time due to the enforced inactivity generally among the AASF units due to near-Arctic weather conditions prevailing all over the combat zones.

This period of spasmodic activity by the air units, in what was already being dubbed by the popular press as the 'Phoney War', saw both the AASF's Hurricane squadrons open their scoreboards. On the last day of October Pilot Officer 'Boy' Mould of 1 Squadron shot down a Dornier bomber, and on 8 November Flying Officer Edgar 'Cobber' Kain of 73 Squadron destroyed another Dornier – the first of his eventually claimed 17 combat victims over the coming months. To a man the fighter pilots were eager for combat with the much-vaunted Messerschmitts of the Luftwaffe, and despite the contemporary lack of general air activity their morale and self-confidence were high. It was a mood and attitude reflected throughout every rank level in the BAFF during the winter of 1939–40.

In Britain the RAF, which had been fully mobilised since late August 1939, prepared for its second war against Germany in twenty-one years. At 1101 hours on 3 September 1939 – just sixty seconds after war began – Flying Officer Andrew McPherson of 139 Squadron was ordered to carry out a reconnaissance of Wilhelmshaven and north-west Germany areas; a task he had been standing by to accomplish for the past forty-eight hours. Leaving Wyton airfield at noon in Blenheim IV, N6215, McPherson plodded through icy mists to the Schillig

Roads, noted several German ships, but was unable to radio this intelligence to base due to a frozen wireless set. Continuing the sortie, his crew obtained seventy-five photos of 'military objectives' and eventually landed back at Wyton at 1650 hours.

In the early evening of that first day of war, three other bomber units despatched their first war sorties. At 1815 hours nine Hampdens, each loaded with 2,000 lb of bombs, left Scampton – six aircraft from 83 Squadron and three from 49 Squadron – with orders to seek out the German Fleet in the Schillig Roads. The third unit, 44 Squardon also sent off nine Hampdens, similarly armed, from Waddington, also heading for the Schillig Roads on what was termed an 'armed reconnaissance'. None succeeded in reaching their objective, all returned safely albeit with some skippers jettisoning their bomb loads in the North Sea en route to base, and all were back at their airfields by midnight.

The combination of the 'containment' policy of forbidding raids against civilian property or – curiously – dockyards, with the preoccupation with priority consideration of German naval objectives, had little bearing on any overall strategic plans for the future use of air power. The first night of the war, 3/4 September, had seen Whitleys of 51 and 58 Squadrons carry out the first night penetration of German territory when a total of ten Whitleys released six million (13 tons) of propaganda leaflets over Hamburg, Bremen and the Ruhr areas – a form of 'raiding' code-named 'Nickel' by the RAF. Of these, two Whitleys were forced to land in France and a third crashlanded without injury to the crew. As a sop to British morale such a 'raid' had some merit, but as an example of the potential of British aerial power it proved nothing. Not that RAF Bomber Command in 1939 was in any position to pursue any form of pure strategic air attacks against Germany. Of its official order of battle on the declaration of war, comprised of 53 squadrons of all states of war fitness, only 33 were able to be rightly called 'operational', and ten of those squadrons had already left England for France as the bomber element of the AASF, with four more units about to fly to France with the BEF's Air Component. Thus the strength of RAF Bomber Command at UK bases was already reduced to less than 20 operationally fit squadrons, plus approximately a one hundred per cent 'reserve' strength in squadrons then being hastily worked up to operational readiness; a factual strength of little more than 200 firstline bombers, plus reserves of slightly larger total.

The state of RAF Fighter Command on the eve of war offered

little consolation in the context of defence of the United Kingdom against any Luftwaffe 'knockout' attack. Having long been promised a minimum of 53 firstline fighter squadrons for such defence by his superiors, Hugh Dowding, commander of Fighter Command, could count only some seventy per cent of this supposed minimal strength by 1 September 1939, and then immediately 'lost' four experienced Hurricane squadrons to the AASF and BEF's Air Component in France, with further instructions to bring another six squadrons to a mobile state in readiness for possible additional despatch to France in the near future.

Apart from actual squadrons detached from the metropolitan air defence, Dowding was also required to ensure a steady flow of replacement aircraft and pilots for the units in France, as normal attrition by accidents or combat reduced the frontline strength of such squadrons. To Dowding, whose over-riding priority for his command was purely the aerial defence of Britain, the loss of such highly trained units to what he regarded as a secondary priority was serious – a prospective drain on his slim resources which, if unchecked, might easily bleed the UK air defences to a point of complete ineffectiveness.

As the first days of the war lengthened into weeks of non-appearance of the expected Luftwaffe bombers over London, Fighter Command remained on the *qui vive* but urgently continued to build its strength as fast as possible. Both aircraft and trained pilots were needed in quantity, and while the machines' production figures appeared to promise healthy numbers in the very near future, the prospect of sufficient pilots fully trained to operational status was not so encouraging. Even by the reduced training standards of wartime exigency, such pilots would never be available in adequate numbers until well in 1940 at the earliest. The bulk of Fighter Command's strength therefore lay with its existing pre-war trained regular-service crews for the first year of operations, supplemented by the equally well-experienced crews of the pre-1939 Auxiliary Air Force squadrons, all of whom had been called to the colours by late August 1939 'for the duration of the war'.

It fell to an AAF Spitfire unit, 602 Squadron based at Drem in Scotland, to parry the first venture over United Kingdom coastal waters by the Luftwaffe. On 16 October 1939 a Junkers Ju 88 from KG30, based at Sylt, was reported over the naval anchorage at the Firth of Forth, and three 602 Squadron Spitfires scrambled and attacked the lone Junkers, though without visible result. Later the same day 602 Squadron's Spitfires were joined in the air by a trio of Spitfires from 603 Squadron AAF in tackling a formation of nine

Ju 88s of 1/KG30 which had set out to bomb HMS *Hood* in the Firth of Forth. The brief subsequent clash saw Ju 88s brought down into the sea, one by each of the AAF units. Then, on 28 October, both AAF squadrons shared in shooting down a Heinkel He 111 on the Lammermuir Hills, the first German aircraft to be brought down on British soil during World War Two.

This was to be the pattern of operations for the UK-based RAF fighter squadrons throughout the first eight months of the war; individual probing reconnaissances or even attempted bombing raids on individual targets by tiny formations or even lone Luftwaffe aircraft which were promptly spotted by Britain's slim but expanding radar watchdogs, backed by the visual intelligence of the civil-manned Observer Corps. Each such German foray was immediately countered by at least a pair of fighter squadrons despatched from the nearest appropriate fighter base to the German incoming raid. It was a period of nervous tension in every facet of the UK defences, akin to the delicate gossamer web of the spider where each and any slightest touch against the web strands set the whole web shimmering in warning vibration, alerting the central figure. Mistakes inevitably occurred – tragic errors in identification by over-eager pilots itching to taste their first combat. Indeed, the *first* recorded victims for the slender Spitfires were two Hurricanes of 56 Squadron which were shot down, killing one pilot, by over-zealous pilots of 74 Squadron on 6 September 1939.

During those anxious months the UK defenders met only German bombers or reconnaissance aircraft – their true mettle against their counterpart Messerschmitt Bf 109 Luftwaffe fighters had yet to be tested. Such an encounter was foreseen by Hugh Dowding, whose private doubts about the French air force's ability to protect the Allied forces in France against any determined German invasion of French territory led logically to consideration of Britain's peril if the Luftwaffe ever gained operational bases along the northern French coastal areas. With only the English Channel dividing such forces, the Luftwaffe could not only mount heavy raids against London and southeastern England, but also provide fighter escort to the bombing formations, a ploy hardly envisaged in the Air Ministry's original plans for the UK's aerial defences.

If the fighter defenders were an immediate priority for Britain's sanctity, the less glamorous role of RAF Coastal Command was not a jot less vital. Recognition of Britain's utter dependency on imported raw materials and goods had been uppermost in British defence chiefs' minds for many decades, and until the 1914–18 war and the related

advent of the militarised aeroplane, protection of the United Kingdom's sea trading routes had been comfortably delegated to the Royal
Navy, Britain's centuries-old traditional shield. By 1939 such a priority
remained – necessarily and logically – primarily a naval matter. Now,
however, there was a new factor – air power. Aircraft could sink ships,
be they rusty cargo steamers or massive capital behemoths, a simple
fact clearly demonstrated during World War One and in the various
tests and trials in the post-1918 years. To the more enlightened naval
minds at the Admiralty the aeroplane was capable of a dual role;
either as aerial shepherd and guard-dog to merchant shipping convoys
or as a potent vehicle of destruction against both surface and underwater vessels – a combination of operational roles in a single weapon
of war. If slow to take root in the more conservatively-minded individuals among the naval hierarchy, recognition of the aeroplane's
potential in naval warfare could not be denied or ignored.

Britain's maritime air power in 1939, and indeed ever since, comprised two distinct formations, albeit inter-linked. The Royal Navy by
that time controlled its own Fleet Air Arm, a somewhat out-dated and
motley mixture of aircraft of many types based either aboard ships and
aircraft carriers, or on land at naval air stations in the UK. The main
formation, however, was the RAF's Coastal Command. Created as a
separate entity for maritime operations in mid-1936, Coastal Command was nevertheless low on the RAF's priority listing for re-equipment with suitable, modern aircraft and 'ironmongery' for its intended
roles. This was, perhaps, inevitable during the hasty expansion schemes
for the RAF during the late 1930s – ample money simply wasn't provided for *every* facet of the Service's up-dating and enlargement, and
the fighter and bomber arms held an over-riding importance.

Thus at the outbreak of war Coastal Command's overall aircraft
strength of, at best, 450 machines included a disturbingly high proportion of out-dated and obsolescent designs at squadron level. Moreover,
relatively little effort had been expended during the locust years of
'peace' in providing the command with the armament and weaponry
so necessary for its highly specialised role as an anti-shipping and, particularly, anti-submarine strike force. For example, the only explosive
stores available in 1939 were the standard RAF GP (General Purpose)
bombs which would have minimal effect on any armoured ship and
would be completely useless against any submerged submarine.

With the exception of a handful of the recently-introduced four-
engined Short Sunderland flying boats, Coastal Command's 1939 aircraft were simply incapable of supplying aerial cover for any shipping

convoys much beyond Britain's narrow coastal waters. Notwithstanding its myriad weaknesses, Coastal Command began its watch and ward role of shipping 'air umbrella' on 2 September 1939 – the day before Britain's entry into the war – and was to continue that grinding, monotonous, patient role *every* day and night until many months after the ultimate cessation of hostilities in Europe in 1945. Throughout the 1939–45 war, Coastal Command's war effort was concentrated in two major zones. In ever-increasing intensity the Battle of the Atlantic and its subsidiary zones of operations occupied the lion's share of the command's activities, but no less intensive, albeit much less publicised, was the command's continuing operation across the North Sea, above the English Channel, and along the Baltic coastlines. The command's official motto, 'Constant Endeavour' was possibly never better exemplified than by the unceasing offensive against the Axis maritime forces by Coastal crews above the merciless water of the North Sea.

From all the foregoing it should be clear that, in blunt terms, the Royal Air Force was a long way from being fully prepared for a major war by September 1939. Its air and ground crews were well-trained – probably to higher standards than any other contemporary air force in the world, including the new Luftwaffe, for all the latter's modernity in policy and outlook. Within its ranks, at most levels, were men with varying experience of aerial warfare or, at least, the effective use of air power, and among its more senior officers and commanders were a good proportion of men with vision of the potential use of air power in any global conflict. What it lacked generally was sheer quantitative muscle and a high enough percentage of strength in terms of truly modern aircraft designs. Only in Fighter Command were there designs actually in firstline squadron service capable of matching the latest German counterparts, i.e. the Hurricane and the Spitfire. Bomber Command was halfway through its transition from a short-range medium bomber force to a true 'heavy' strategic bomber formation. Coastal Command would only begin its trans-ocean responsibilities with aircraft and 'ironmongery' appropriate in in-shore coastal reconnaissance only. Yet – perhaps typical of the inherent British character – it is worth re-emphasising that little, if any, criticism could be directed at the crews who were expected to conduct today's war with yesterday's weapons. Morale on the eve of war was extraordinarily high, and never fell during the 'Phoney War' period. Once the 'real' war commenced in May 1940, that supreme confidence was to be fully justified.

If the RAF was admittedly unprepared and only partially equipped for a national war, the French air services were miserably unready for any such confrontation. With classic Gallic frankness, General Vuillemin, the Chief of Air Staff, in a report to his Air Minister dated 26 August 1939, stated in respect of the *Armée de l'Air*'s contemporary strength :

> The power of bombing units has remained unchanged since September 1938 and is as restricted now as it was then. The poor performance of our bombers will necessitate very prudent operations during the first months of the war . . . the renovation of our offensive air power will come to effectiveness only within four or five months.

His forecast of a few months before full efficiency was to prove over-optimistic; the French nationalised aviation industry did not produce the 'goods' in any worthwhile quantity before nemesis struck in mid-1940, though it is fair to add that by then production figures were rising rapidly and – given a further four or five months of 'Phoney War' relaxation in operational effort – might well have justified Vuillemin's forecast. Vuillemin's gloomy, but accurate, assessment of his outdated bomber force applied equally to his fighter and reconnaissance aircraft. All were patently inferior to their equivalents in the Luftwaffe and, to a great extent, even the RAF.

Stark evidence of the unsuitability of existing firstline French aircraft designs came within the opening weeks of desultory air activity over the Western Front, when an unacceptable casualty rate swiftly mounted among the French reconnaissance aircraft sent by day over German territory. Accordingly, some sixty per cent of the bomber units were withdrawn from the battle zone in mid-September 1939 and were moved to southern France where it was hoped they might eventually be re-equipped and retrained on 'modern' aircraft designs before being put back on frontline operations. Thus, the remaining thirty-odd per cent of France's bomber units were left on actual operations, flying Farman 221s and 222s and the incredibly out-moded, lumbering Amiot 143 *'Multiplace de Combat'* on leaflet-dropping and general recce sorties. General modernisation plans for virtually every arm of the French air services continued to be mooted as late as December 1939; all aimed at a complete conversion to modern aircraft by at least April 1940, or by mid-May at the latest. Considering the previous years of misguided policies, inadequate funding and sheer disorganisation of the nationalised aviation industry, it was a highly optimistic thought to expect 100 per cent conversion of a weary and ill-equipped national air force to a modern, efficient, trained and combat-ready force within mere months.

By April 1940 the French aviation industry was expected to have produced about 540 'modern' bombers: 250 LeO 451s, 210 Breguet 691s and 693s, and some 80 Amiot 351s and 354s. In addition the USA was supposed to have delivered the 215 Martin 167s and 105 Douglas DB-7s already ordered. To update the fighter units, more heavily armed versions of the existing Curtiss Hawk 75s and Morane-Saulnier 406s were gradually phased into service, and by January 1940 the neat Bloch 151 and 152 had entered *escadrille* strengths. France's finest fighter of the period, the Dewoitine 520, was urgently requested in quantity for the firstline units, but by 10 May 1940 only one *groupe* was actually equipped with the type.

In the event the industry failed to produce the anticipated quota of modern bombers or fighters before May 1940; and the USA orders failed to reach France in any significant numbers by that month. Analysis of the various official statistics relating to the French air force's actual strength on 10 May 1940, omitting aircraft in non-operational units, shows an overall tally of some 1,145 machines, of which at least thirty per cent were acknowledged as already obsolete, and the remainder hardly worthy of the description 'modern' with few exceptions. Having failed to pay the piper in the context of adequate finance and support for its air power, the French nation was about to concede to the Luftwaffe the privilege of calling the tune . . .

As the BEF and French army settled in to their slit trenches and Maginot Line fortifications during the closing months of 1939, an air of supreme confidence prevailed among the Allies. It all resembled closely the war of 1914–18 – static armies crouching in a line of mud and concrete channels in the earth, stretching along the eastern borders of France, waiting for the call to action. Complacency among British politicians and Service chiefs was rife, while the Allied servicemen in France had little to do except make themselves as comfortable as possible to combat the icy weather as winter began to take a frozen grip of Europe.

In England, RAF Bomber Command, which had commenced its war from the first hour of declared hostilities, despatched a sporadic series of sorties against German naval objectives. The first of these took place on 4 September 1939, when a total of 15 Blenheims – five each from Nos 107, 110 and 139 Squadrons – took off from their bases at Wyton and Wattisham, intent on bombing reported German warships at Wilhelmshaven and the Schillig Roads. Despite heavy clouds, the Blenheims of 107 and 110 Squadrons found their target and attacked; 139's five aircraft failed to find their objective and returned to base. Of the ten aircraft which actually attacked the *Admiral Scheer*, five were shot down by anti-aircraft fire, while many of the bombs dropped failed to explode. A simultaneous attack by Wellingtons from Nos 9 and 149 Squadrons against shipping at Brunsbüttel proved equally ineffective; two bombers were lost, one by the wall of anti-aircraft fire and a second falling victim to a Messerschmitt Bf 109 piloted by Sergeant Alfred Held of II/JG77 – the first British bomber to be shot down by a Luftwaffe fighter.

Both sorties had been undertaken by unescorted bombers in broad daylight, exemplifying a contemporary train of thought in higher RAF circles that armed bombers could defend themselves in combat conditions; this was an inherited myth from the 1918 experiences of the Independent Force, RAF which contended that a tight formation of bombers, with its barrage of defensive guns, could survive any fighter attacks. Persistence with this totally misguided policy over the ensuing months was to cost the RAF bomber crews tragic losses before the lesson was really learned. On 29 September 1939 eleven Hampdens of 144 Squadrons set out for Hemswell for an 'armed reconnaissance' – a euphemistic term for a bombing sortie then much in vogue – of the Heligoland Bight. One formation of six Hampdens located two German naval destroyers and attempted an attack from 300 feet, then returned to base safely. The other formation of five bombers, led by the squadron commander, was never seen again. On 18 December a total of 24 Wellingtons from Nos 9, 37 and 149 Squadrons left their bases and joined up for another armed recce of the Wilhelmshaven area. Near their objective, at 18,000 feet in perfectly clear summer skies, the precision formation of bombers was swamped by a succession of Luftwaffe fighters. Within minutes 12 Wellingtons had been lost, and a further three were wrecked on reaching England. All surviving aircraft suffered extensive damage.

Losses on such a proportional scale were clearly prohibitive and with some reluctance the RAF concluded that henceforth any significant attempts at bombing must be conducted under the cloak of night. Fighter escorts for any bombing force could not be made available – the operational range of Spitfires and Hurricanes was barely sufficient to reach even the nearest German targets, even if such fighters could be spared from Dowding's slender home defence force. The switch to night operations, which came only slowly in the early months of 1940, presented fresh problems for RAF commanders; the most frustrating was the ostensibly simple necessity of accurate navigation to any selected target, with a secondary problem of the RAF's contemporary capability of mounting any worthwhile raid in terms of aircraft numbers participating and, hence, the total tonnage of bombs which could be delivered to the objective. The thorny matter of imperfect navigation was to continue to nullify much of Bomber Command's raiding efforts against Germany for several years to come.

If the RAF and French air forces were restricted heavily during the first six months of war by the containment policy for avoiding provocation in selection of bombing targets, the Luftwaffe was no less frustrated by similar directives from the German Führer, Hitler, who clung for many months to the fond hope that England might yet sue for peace rather than face the might of Germany's armed forces exemplified in the lightning defeat of Poland. Bombing forays by the Luftwaffe against British targets were severely restricted to purely naval targets, and even these were not to be attacked if ships were actually tied up in harbour or dock; a parallel directive to Air Ministry orders for RAF Bomber Command. British bombers, nevertheless, pierced the night skies over Germany on many occasions during the winter of 1939–40, but their 'lethal' loads were merely propaganda leaflets. If such paper raids had any value at all it was the opportunity to practise long-range navigation by night over enemy territory, apart from the rather doubtful boost to British civilian morale knowing that the RAF was 'over Germany'.

Notwithstanding his personal 'instinct' that Britain would eventually back down from any frontal confrontation with Germany, Hitler's plans for the conquest of Europe continued to be issued. With the defeat of Poland accomplished by early October 1939, he calmly initiated a Führer Directive to his generals on 9 October ordering immediate preparations for

an attack operation on the northern flank of the western front, through the areas of Luxembourg, Belgium and Holland. This attack to be carried out with as much strength and at as early a date as possible.

Despite protests by the army and Luftwaffe commanders that the services needed recuperation and replenishment before undertaking

any such hazardous enterprise, Hitler next issued a confirming order
for such an operation, code-named *Fall Gelb* ('Case Yellow') and
authorised the date 12 November for the opening thrust. Only the
appalling winter weather forced a slight postponement of this date
until 17 January 1940; but before that day circumstances nullified
the proposed invasion of the neutral countries when, on 10 January, a
German light aircraft carrying two Luftwaffe staff officers on a mission
to Cologne got lost and crashlanded in Belgian territory. In the brief-
case of one officer were documents giving an outline of the proposed
German offensive, including a timetable and even details of airborne
landing objectives *et al*. The officer was only partly successful in his
attempts to destroy the documents, and Belgian authorities were immediately alerted and the information passed quickly to British and
French intelligence.

Hitler, on hearing of this incident, immediately revised his whole
plan; then he presented *Fall Gelb* in its final form to his senior staff
officers, with its ultimate date of initiation – 10 May 1940.

Preliminaries to the intended *Blitzkrieg* to the west occurred in early
April 1940, when German naval, land and air forces invaded and
occupied Denmark and Norway, campaigns that proved highly
successful in swiftness and execution. Key to that success was again the
efficient and powerful use of the Luftwaffe to secure complete domination of the air over the land forces' objectives in order that occupation
troops could complete their initial phases unheeded and virtually blood-
lessly. And it was in these campaigns that Germany showed yet another
trump card : its paratroop weapon.

The way was now clear for Hitler to pursue his ambitions in the
west. The core of Hitler's intention for his drive to the Atlantic seaboard was essentially a knockout punch through the middle of the
Western Front, thereby dividing the Allied armies immediately. Nevertheless, the German generals considered it vital that the northern flank
in Holland and Belgium must first be secured; hence their approval of
the preliminary assault through those neutral countries. The Luftwaffe's part in all these plans was an extension of the successful campaigns in Poland, Denmark and Norway; spearhead attacks on 'enemy'
airfields to achieve complete air supremacy, transportation of airborne
troops to key assault positions ahead of the land army formations, and
widespread tactical support for the infantry and tanks during the main
attacks.

For *Fall Gelb* the Luftwaffe could assemble approximately 4,000
aircraft of all types; of this tally some 1,300 were 'long range' bombers

and a further 380 dive-bombers which would act as flying artillery. In support were roughly 1,200 fighters of varying types, though the bulk were the tried and tested Messerschmitt Bf 109E and Bf 110.

Blitzkrieg

As the blackness of night eased to pre-dawn grey on 10 May 1940, at 0230 hours the first trio of a force totalling 42 Junkers Ju 52 transport aircraft commenced their straining take-off runs from the Butzweiler-hof and Ostheim airfields close to Cologne. Each had in tow a DFS 230 glider containing a handful of fully-armed paratroopers of the *Sturmabteilung Koch*, a tough, superbly trained shock-assault force which had by then spent six months on intensive preparation for their task on this cold, clear morning – 'taking out' the Belgian Fort Eben Emael which lay at the junction of the River Maas and the Albert Canal. Some three hours later the Dutch defences on Waalhaven air-field, near Rotterdam, and two other key air bases at Amsterdam-Schiphol and Ypenburg, near the Hague, were bombed with high precision by a formation of Heinkel He 111s from KG4, followed almost immediately by the 'special purpose' III/KG zb VI's Junkers Ju 52s which smothered the skies over Waalhaven with a profusion of paratroopers from III Battalion of Paratroop Regiment 1, whose aim was to secure the airfield for later heavy reinforcement. In the event some 475 Ju 52s were to be used to convey paratroops and other air-borne infantry into Holland, including some 1,200 airborne troops onto Waalhaven airfield alone by the early afternoon.

As these two hammer-blows began to take effect in Belgium and Holland, the Luftwaffe thrust westwards over the 'invincible' Maginot Line and attacked a series of French airfields, on which both French and RAF units were based, and extended its attentions to vital French rail centres further west. It was the third facet of a brilliantly planned triple punch by the Wehrmacht : the first two assaults against neutral countries were insurance against being outflanked by the Allies while the main attack into French territory was underway. Thus Hitler had finally committed the Third Reich to an all-out international war which could only be halted now by utter defeat or ultimate victory for the German nation. The hitherto velvet-glove confrontation, so lightly termed the 'Phoney War', had dissolved savagely into a massive, bloody struggle between mighty armies. It was, too, the real beginning

of the European aerial war – a fluctuating contest in pure air power which was destined to last, day and night, for five long years. During those years the past prophets of the deadly potential of aerial power were to see their gloomy presages practised and expanded a hundredfold.

The fates of Belgium and Holland were destined to be yet further tragic examples of ill-prepared and poorly armed forces, fighting desperately courageous yet foredoomed campaigns against vastly superior air and land opponents. Each was a victim of esoteric nationalism relying too much on isolated neutrality. Aid from France and Britain, even had this been available in adequate quantity and quality, could never arrive in time to stem the lightning thrusts of the Luftwaffe and its associated spearhead assault forces. The Belgian Air Force, mainly equipped with less-than-modern aircraft, possessed three *Regiments d'Aeronautique*; an operationally ready force of far less than 200 aircraft of all types – the only monoplanes were a handful of Hawker Hurricanes and Fairey Battles. The first Luftwaffe attacks against Belgian airfields on 10–11 May promptly destroyed 110 of this meagre force, including the Hurricanes of the 2nd *Escadrille* lined neatly as on parade alongside the tarmac at Schaffen-Diest airfield at first light on 10 May. Those few Belgian pilots still able to find serviceable aircraft fought the Luftwaffe with near-suicidal ferocity, but their cause was hopeless from the start, and most survivors eventually flew to French territory to continue the fight later.

In Holland the situation was little better in May 1940. With some 130 available aircraft actually in service (all either obsolescent designs or, at best, still inferior in performance by a large margin to their German counterparts); the initial air strafing of Dutch air bases on the morning of 10 May almost nullified Dutch resistance in the air within hours. From Waalhaven eight Fokker G1as, the most modern fighters in Dutch service then, managed to take off to tackle the incoming Luftwaffe, and their pilots claimed 14 German victims. That same evening, however, only one Fokker was still serviceable for combat. Dutch bombers – those that escaped destruction on the ground – attempted near-heroic sorties against the invading German armies, but were shot out of the skies by cannon-armed Messerschmitts. Within five days all effective Dutch resistance both on land and in the air had to all significant intent ceased.

On 14 May a force of 100 Heinkel He 111 bombers of KG54 set out to destroy the fierce defences entrenched in the city of Rotterdam unbeknowing that urgent surrender negotiations for the city were already underway. Recall signals failed to reach the bombers en route, and it was only the sight of some red Very Lights being fired near the target area by just one leading pilot that prevented 43 Heinkels from actually bombing. The other formation of 57 He 111s unloaded 97 tons of high explosive into the designated target area, initiating fires which were extended by prevailing winds into the old sections of Rotterdam and spread destruction across the ancient city. A total of 814 people were killed by this raid,* and nearly 80,000 were deprived of their homes. Within less than twenty-four hours the Dutch accepted surrender terms.

At the close of the third day of the *Blitzkrieg* against Belgium and Holland, the Luftwaffe's supremecy in the air was almost total, and the following day General von Rundstedt launched the prime attack westwards into France, knowing his northern flanks were safe from possible Allied attack. The cost to the Luftwaffe over Belgium and Holland had not been small. While air opposition had taken a relatively modest toll, the Junkers Ju 52 transports had suffered appalling casualties. Of the 430 Ju 52s launched against Holland alone, two-thirds were either destroyed by anti-aircraft fire or opposing aircraft, or damaged to the point of write-off severity by a combination of Dutch resistance fire. Many of the Junkers' air crews had been experienced instructors temporarily detached from Luftwaffe training establishments – a loss almost impossible to replace for many months, even years to come, and which would have long-term consequences on future Luftwaffe operational efficiency.

The failure of Göring, as the Luftwaffe supremo, and his Chief of Staff in 1940, Hans Jeschonnek, to grasp the importance of creating a separately equipped transport command to handle the airborne aspects of aerial warfare meant an inevitable denuding of the Luftwaffe's training command, thereby imperilling future depth and strength in crew replacement. This failure was wholly prompted by a general euphoria prevalent in the German military higher command – particularly in the minds of Hitler and Göring – that the European war would be of short duration, obviating any need for long-term planning in the contexts of training build-up, new fighter or bomber development, or indeed increase in pure aircraft production targets by the aviation industry. These omissions in strategic planning by the Luftwaffe's leaders in 1938–40 were to be some of the seeds of the Luftwaffe's ultimate defeat and destruction.

* Allied propaganda at the time claimed casualty figures of some 25,000 killed, mainly civilians, and used this figure to condemn the German air force's '. . . evil war against the unarmed civilian population of Holland'.

On the morning of 10 May 1940, however, the possibility of the Luftwaffe's ever being defeated was unthinkable in all German – and no few Allied – minds. Flushed with the palpable successes in Poland, Denmark and Norway, the German air arm, from its supreme commander to its lowest mechanic, felt indomitable. It was the period later referred to in Luftwaffe circles as the 'Happy Time'. In such a frame of mind, utterly confident and eager to exploit continuing triumph, the Luftwaffe crews set out to crush the French air force and the allied RAF formations based on French soil. As in all preceding campaigns, the initial plan was to attain immediate air supremacy by saturation destruction of the opposing air services, translated in action by first attempting to destroy all enemy aircraft on their own airfields. Thereafter the German crews would spearhead the army's advance by close tactical support, blasting a path forward with pinpoint dive-bombing and strafing sorties. Speed was the essence of the *Blitzkrieg* style of war, backed by overwhelming weight in numbers. It had worked well against the weak neutral countries, and there seemed to be no reason for it to fail against France. The only query in any German mind was how the Luftwaffe might fare against the RAF, though few Germans doubted the eventual outcome.

For the opening assault on 10 May, *Luftflotten* 2 and 3 had a total firstline aircraft strength of 2,750 aircraft: 1,444 bombers, 1,264 fighters, and motley reconnaissance machines. In addition were a host of transport and general communications aircraft. Allowing for the employment of some Air Corps for the initial attacks against Belgium and Holland, which would later join the formations supporting the assault against France, the Luftwaffe could theoretically count on perhaps 3,500 aircraft for their overall campaigns against the Anglo-French and allied opponents – almost 75–80 per cent of the entire Luftwaffe then existing. Based in France on that date were seven RAF fighter squadrons (supplemented by a further three squadrons on 11 May); while RAF bomber and army co-operation squadrons amounted to at best 250 aircraft based on French airfields for immediate retaliation. Further RAF support could be expected from units based in south-east England, though this would be necessarily somewhat limited in sheer numbers. Of the French air services based within striking distance of the Maginot Line, it is doubtful if more than some 700 aircraft of all types could be immediately available for operations, none of which could hope to match any German counterpart.

The RAF's fighter force – eight Hurricane and two Gladiator squadrons by 11 May – was primarily a *defensive* force for escort and protection of the bombers and recce aircraft of BAFF. The bomber squadrons – a total of 135 Battles and Blenheims on 10 May – were, in the main, intended for retaliatory raids against German targets in the *offensive* role. The latter striking force was under the RAF direction of Air Marshal Barratt, but he in turn was directly under the command of the French Generalissimo Gamelin, and – according to the chain of Allied command extant – needed Gamelin's permission to let loose the RAF bombers.

As the first surprise attacks on more than twenty French airfields by Luftwaffe aircraft arrived in the early dawn of 10 May, Barratt waited for Gamelin's formal permission to send off his Blenheims and Battles against the reported German army incursions – but waited in vain. Still reluctant to 'provoke' German bombing assaults on French towns, Gamelin remained silent.

By noon Barratt could no longer curb his impatience and, on his own authority, ordered the RAF bombers into action. A first wave of Battles, drawn from various of the eight squadrons available, was despatched against German troop columns in the Luxembourg area, and lost three to fierce anti-aircraft fire. A second wave later repeated the low-level attack, and by the end of the day, of the 32 Battles used for these unescorted sorties, 13 had been shot down and the rest damaged in varying degree. It was an omen of the imminent fate of virtually all the RAF's Fairey Battle crews in France.

The initial Luftwaffe attacks on French airfields, though accurate in location and carried out with almost a hundred per cent advantage of surprise, failed to destroy even a significant proportion of the Anglo-French air strength. The French air force suffered the loss of less than 60 aircraft actually destroyed, with roughly a similar total damaged; while the RAF squadrons bore little loss. On the morning of 11 May, however, Dorniers of KG2 caught 114 Squadron RAF napping at its Condré Vraux base, and virtually wiped out the unit's entire strength of Blenheims. At dawn on 12 May, nine Blenheims of 139 Squadron set out to strafe a troop column near Maastricht and ran into a swarm of Messerschmitt fighters. Only two Blenheims returned. Thus, within twenty-four hours, the RAF's Blenheim 'retaliatory' force was to all intents nullified, and the onus of remaining bombing operations fell upon the Battle squadrons. Extra support from Bomber Command squadrons based in England was also forthcoming. By night Wellingtons and Blenheims carried out raids against the German-occupied Belgian and Dutch airfields, while by day Blenheims joined in attacks against advancing German troops. Most of the latter managed to return to their English bases but almost all had been scathed severely by high density ground-fire.

The pace and severity of the air operations during May 1940 over eastern France can be measured in high degree by the saga of the eight RAF Fairey Battle squadrons which existed on 10 May. From the outset of the *Blitzkrieg* key objectives had been the many bridges crossing the Maas (Meuse) and the Albert Canal, and German capture of several of these was accomplished in the early hours of the offensive. French and British attempts to dislodge the – at first – thin German defences at these bridges failed against the violent reaction of both ground and air opposition. By 12 May the ground defences had been greatly increased, while strong Luftwaffe aerial defence was given to such priority keypoints. On that date five of six volunteer crews from 12 (Battle) Squadron set out to destroy the bridges at Vroenhoven and Veldwezelt across the Albert Canal, and Hurricanes from 1 Squadron were detailed to clear the way of any German fighter opposition. Before the Hurricanes even reached the target zone they were swamped by some 50 Messerschmitts and proceeded to fight for their lives. The five Battles – in two formations, one for each bridge – were met by a veritable wall of 88mm flak. Four of the Battles were shot down, and the fifth barely managed to crash-land in French territory. In the leading Battle of one sub-formation Flying Officer Donald Garland and his observer, Sergeant Thomas Gray, perished, but were both later awarded posthumous Victoria Crosses.

Elsewhere that day Bomber Command Blenheims were valiantly attempting to break bridges over the Meuse. No significant damage was achieved and ten of the 24 raiding Blenheims failed to return to base. Meanwhile the Battle crews' casualty rate was rising rapidly. On 11 May seven out of eight Battles sent to the Luxembourg area were shot down, and on the 12th fifteen Battles despatched to bomb targets near Bouillon lost six of their number to marauding Messerschmitts and anti-aircraft fire. The loss rate for 10–11–12 May was frightening : 40 per cent, 100 per cent, and 62 per cent of despatched formations respectively. Of almost 140 bombers serviceably available on the morning of 10 May, the AASF was reduced to 72 by dusk on 12 May.

To conserve strength, only one Battle raid took place on 13 May, a road-blocking operation by aircraft of 226 Squadron near Breda, but 14 May brought disastrous results. Both French and British operations that day were focused on the ground battle for the Sedan bridgehead; the French air service tried first, only to be so severely mauled that it

flew no further operations during the rest of the day. In the late afternoon came the RAF's turn, and the entire AASF bomber strength was
flung against the bridgehead – a total of 71 Blenheims and (mainly)
Battles from Nos 12, 105, 139, 150 and 218 Squadrons. Intercepted
by swarms of wheeling Messerschmitts the bombers were virtually
massacred, losing 40 bombers in all. Of the 62 Battles participating,
35 failed to return, including 10 of the 11 Battles sent by 218 Squadron. It was the highest loss *rate* ever suffered by the RAF.

The shattered Battle force – Nos 105 and 218 Squadrons now possessed merely two aircraft apiece and were thus 'disbanded' and ab-
sorbed into other units – undertook no daylight operations on 15 May,
and next day was withdrawn to the Troyes area for regrouping and,
it was hoped, replenishment of crews and machines. For the next two
weeks isolated night sorties and occasional day raids against the relentlessly advancing German armies were undertaken with relatively small
losses, but on 3 June the six remaining squadrons were forced to retire
further back to the Le Mans area. The swan song of the Battles came
on 13 June. Ten well-patched aircraft first attacked German troops on
the banks of the Seine, while later two formations totalling 38 aircraft lost six crews to 88mm flak during raids against German positions
by the Marne.

Within forty-eight hours the utterly hopeless situation in France
was so evident that an order was given to all surviving bombers to fly
to England. A pitiful procession of scarred Battles with exhausted crews
wended its way across the English Channel to the nearest available
airfields. Between 10 May and 15 June the AASF had lost 115 aircraft
and almost as many crews, virtually the equivalent strength available
on the opening day of the *Blitzkrieg*. Evidence for the incredible valour
of the bomber crews lay in a hundred charred and wrecked aircraft
strewn among the forests and valleys of France, alongside smouldering
pyres of the English-based bombers sent to bolster a campaign doomed
from the outset.

What of the fighters? If the tragic bomber casualties caused dismay
in London, the plight of the fighter squadrons swiftly became a nightmare for Fighter Command's leader Hugh Dowding, who had emphasised constantly that the real battle for survival would be over England,
not France. His visionary forecast, largely ignored by the Whitehall
politicians, was to be starkly confirmed. The French-based RAF fighter
squadrons were in constant action from the very beginning of the
German onslaught, with individual pilots flying five, six or even seven
sorties each day. Facing overwhelmingly superior numerical odds on

virtually every sortie, the fighter pilots fought to the point of exhaustion, ever-determined to oppose any swastika-marked aircraft within their range. By 24 May No 1 Squadron alone had lost a total of 38 Hurricanes, but the original pilots, who were withdrawn to England on that date and replaced by fresh men, had claimed nearly 100 victims in air combat. The other squadrons could claim an equally courageous record of fighting. No 87 Squadron, from 10–20 May, claimed at least 80 victories for the loss of 10 pilots killed; 85 Squadron, from 10–22 May, claimed no fewer than 90 German aircraft destroyed, but mourned the loss of 17 pilots killed, wounded or 'missing', and returned to England on 22 May with just 3 Hurricanes intact. The record showed equally determined tallies in the other fighter squadrons : claims of 9 or 10 Luftwaffe victims for every RAF pilot killed or incapacitated.

On the German side many hitherto unpublicised Luftwaffe pilots rose rapidly to fame and glory during the brief French campaign. Wilhelm Balthasar of JG *'Richthofen'* who claimed 22 victims from 10 May to 22 May, including the astonishing record (then) of 9 in a single day's combat; Werner Mölders, already credited with 14 victories with the Spanish 'Condor Legion', who claimed a further 25 victims over France; Adolf Galland, later to command all Luftwaffe fighters, whose tally for the French campaign totalled 17; Helmuth Wick, destined to claim 56 victories before his death in late 1940 : all these and many other young eagles of the black cross founded deserved reputations during the early summer months in French skies. Their weapon of destruction was the Messerschmitt Bf 109E, a fighter with very few equals in 1940, and a vehicle well tailored for its deadly role. With rare exception, only the British Hawker Hurricane had given the Bf 109 pilots any real cause for concern in combat, an adversary which if admittedly slower in speed was still capable of handling and despatching any Bf 109 if piloted by a determined 'driver'.

The main disadvantage for the RAF fighter pilots was primarily the huge disparity in pure numbers of aircraft available in any combat with the Luftwaffe, but also lay in the useless pre-1939 peacetime types of tactical formations initially employed by the Hurricane crews. Experience soon taught the vital need for much flexibility in air combat tactics, a lesson already assimilated by the Luftwaffe's fighter arm during its invaluable testing time over Spain.

The almost unbelievable speed and efficiency of the German advance into France left the French air force bewildered, and French air resistance varied sharply from near-fanatical opposition from certain individual pilots and crews, including veterans of the Polish air force and others who had fled to France to continue their particular vendettas against Germany, and near-apathy among no few other French *escadrilles* and *groupes*. Those who did not hesitate to challenge this latest invasion from Germany took a relatively heavy toll of German opponents before the chaos and lack of efficiency by ground support facilities forced their withdrawal; many such men eventually escaped to England where they joined the RAF to continue the fight against Nazism.

Meanwhile, on the ground, the triumphant German infantry in the wake of their forward *Panzer* units, and aided constantly by the notorious Ju 87 *Stuka* * dive-bombers which petrified any stumbling blocks of Allied resistance en route, swept through northwards and westwards, and by 24 May Guderian's tanks had invested Boulogne, some twenty miles from a little-known coastal town titled Dunkerque (Dunkirk). Four days later the Belgian Army formally surrendered, leaving nine divisions of the British BEF and ten divisions of the French 1st Army cramped into a corridor to the sea barely fifty miles long and fifteen miles wide. The scene was thus set for the final *pièce de résistance* of German tactical planning: a crushing pincer movement by the German army groups south and north of the corridor which might engulf some half a million Allied men and cripple all further opposition.

At that exact high point of the German military achievement Hitler intervened personally by issuing a personal order for Guderian's *Panzers* to halt their advance. This extraordinary decision – partly based on misgivings about the vastly stretched supply lines of the forward *Panzer* elements, but in no small part by Göring's insistence that his Luftwaffe alone could now eliminate the remaining Allied forces heading towards Dunkirk – was to give a brief breathing space of three days to the besieged BEF and French armies during which the first shiploads of evacuated soldiers were taken off the Dunkirk beaches.

Operation Dynamo, the Allied code-name for the evacuation of the trapped British and French divisions filtering to Dunkirk, commenced on 26 May, masterminded by the Royal Navy. Aerial protection for this mass exodus – patently a priority target for the Luftwaffe – became the prime responsibility of RAF Fighter Command in south-east England, in particular No 11 Group, commanded by the brilliant

---

* A mnemonic for *Sturzkampfflugzeug* applied generally to all German dive-bombers, but mostly applied by common usage to the Junkers Ju 87.

New Zealander Keith Park. At that time Park had at his disposal, at most, 200 fighters spread thinly over 16 squadrons, all based within fighting distance of the beleaguered port. His only possible reserves were the other fighter squadrons allotted to defence of the Midlands and northern Britain, squadrons which his superior, Dowding, was not prepared immediately to throw into an already wasteful campaign in France. The Admiralty, conscious of the extreme vulnerability of its ships and the army at Dunkirk to air attack, duly requested forcibly continuous air cover from Fighter Command, a demand simply beyond Park's capability to provide in any such form. Instead Park chose to despatch single or pairs of squadrons on a type of patrol rotation above and inland from the Dunkirk area, primarily to prevent the Luftwaffe reaching the beachline in any concentrated strength. Clearly, the Luftwaffe's numerical superiority and huge tactical advantages would mean that a percentage of German bombers would get to Dunkirk, but Park's resources were too slender to prevent them achieving some success.

A lingering accusation against the RAF by many soldiers who survived the hell of Dunkirk has been a bitterly scathing complaint of the 'lack of air cover' above the beaches. It is a calumny undeserved by the fighter pilots who flew daily to their limits, seeking out the German bombers beyond Dunkirk and exacting a heavy toll of these potential raiders. On 27 May, for merely one example, 23 German aircraft were lost along with 64 German air crew killed, and, as Major Werner Kreipe of III/KG2 reported : 'The enemy fighters pounced on our tightly knit formations with the fury of maniacs.'

It was during the days immediately prior to the official evacuation commencing that the Luftwaffe first encountered the RAF's Spitfires in strength, and indeed provided the opportunity for many Spitfire pilots to experience their first taste of combat with large formations of German aircraft. Men who were soon to become internationally recognised fighting leaders, such as the legless Douglas Bader, 'Sailor' Malan and Robert Tuck, all claimed the first of their eventual large tallies of combat victims in the skies above or near Dunkirk in May and early June 1940. A measure of the achievement of the RAF fighters over Dunkirk is the simple fact that from 26 May to 4 June when Dynamo officially ceased, the Luftwaffe was only able seriously to intervene in the BEF evacuation on two and a half of the nine days; while a third of a million Allied troops were retrieved from the beaches and taken to England. Some 40,000 troops, mainly French, remained to be taken prisoner, and it was their continuing resistance to the encircling German army which may be regarded as the prime factor in the bulk of Allied troops' escape to Britain from the scarred beaches of Dunkirk.

When Operation Dynamo was completed on 4 June, Hugh Dowding took stock of his command's immediate strength. From 10 May until 4 June a total of 432 Hurricanes (mainly), Spitfires and other fighters had been lost in action – a rough equivalent of 20 firstline squadrons – apart from the almost irreplaceable pilots in so many of these. By 18 June, when the last remnants of the RAF units in France finally returned to England, the whole *Blitzkrieg* had cost the RAF the frightening total loss of 959 aircraft. Of this tally 477 were fighters of all types. Added to the 32 fighters lost in the ill-fated Norwegian campaign, the RAF had sacrificed the near-equivalent of 40 complete operational squadrons.

The *Blitzkrieg* had also cost the Luftwaffe dear. At least 1,300 aircraft were lost in combat, mainly to the RAF opposition, while an equivalent total was considered to be either in need of extensive repair or replacement if they were to be brought back to operational fitness. Such losses were considered tragic but bearable in view of the amazing successes of the whole campaign. In England, however, Hugh Dowding, now faced with the situation he had foretold – a triumphant Luftwaffe now based less than 100 miles from London – apart from German air bases in Norway *et al*, could only count a total of 446 fighters in his command, of which only 331 were Hurricanes or Spitfires. With this puny force, had Göring immediately extended his Luftwaffe's assaults against British mainland targets, Dowding was expected to defend the United Kingdom.

Once the Dunkirk operation was completed, more thoughtful Luftwaffe senior officers realised that here had been the German air force's first real setback. Despite Göring's vainglorious boasts that his Luftwaffe alone would destroy the BEF in Dunkirk, his bombers had failed to accomplish anything like a crushing defeat. Indeed, the bulk of Allied troops had been retrieved to fight again in the future, and under the very noses of the Luftwaffe. The continuing invasion of France was a foregone conclusion, with the Luftwaffe mainly engaged in destroying the disorganised remaining French air service. One such air operation, *Operation Paula*, used some 300 Stukas and other bombers, well escorted by fighters, to attack airfields and aircraft factories around Paris, and lost about 30 aircraft to groundfire. It was the only true *strategic* air operation mounted by the Luftwaffe throughout the *Blitzkrieg* campaign, taking place on 3 and 4 June, and accounted for more than 100 French aircraft destroyed in the air and many more on the ground. Less than three weeks later the formal surrender of France was ratified by signature in the Forest of Compiègne : the *Blitzkrieg* was over.

With the signing of the truce, Hitler's ambitions reached a personal peak, while the German armed forces had achieved their greatest level of triumph, a pinnacle they were destined never to reach again throughout the succeeding war years. In the context of the Luftwaffe's contribution there was cause for celebration and misgiving. No one could deny the vital ingredient for success supplied by the air arm in every facet of the 1940 campaigns in every country defeated by Germany. Its swift establishment of overt aerial supremacy from the outset of each onslaught had paved the pathways to ultimate victory in each case, and the propaganda-originated legend of Luftwaffe 'invincibility' fostered in pre-1939 days had apparently been totally justified. Actual air losses in men and machines had been admittedly alarmingly high in toto, but the end had justified the means, and such casualties were accepted as inevitable, if regrettable.

On the darker face of the overall victory, however, were several omens of future problems for any continuance of the air war against the sole remaining Allied nation yet to be overcome : Britain. The much-vaunted two-seat, twin-engined Messerschmitt Bf 110 *Zerstörer* – intended as a long-range escort fighter for the Luftwaffe's bombers – had already been shown to be ineffective against determined fighter opposition. Even the much-feared Junkers Ju 87 *Stuka* was patently incapable of carrying out its specific role without ample fighter escort, or at least complete Luftwaffe aerial supremacy in the areas intended for *Stuka* operations. And as some Luftwaffe generals turned their thoughts to the possibilities of attacks against England in the near future, the air force's complete lack of a truly long-range heavy bomber obviously placed cramping restrictions on the scope of any such air assault.

Any such doubts about the future were, nevertheless, swept aside for the moment as Hitler and his hierarchy revelled in the heady atmosphere of the complete victory over France. A flood of celebratory promotions and glittering awards and honours was liberally showered upon the armed services; no less than twelve generals receiving promotion to field marshal, with accompanying waves of elevations in rank in descending order throughout each service department. For Hermann Göring, now being loudly proclaimed as the 'creator of the

Luftwaffe', came especial honours. For his Luftwaffe supremo, Hitler created an entirely new rank, that of *Reichsmarschall des Grossdeutschen Reiches* – Marshal of the Greater German Reich – and also awarded him the Grand Cross of the Iron Cross, the sole example of this medal to be awarded throughout the whole war. On the firstline fighter and bomber *Geschwader* too a liberal sprinkling of medals and promotions descended as the crews began to settle into their latest bases along the northern French coastal areas and the Baltic coast. Recuperation, refurbishment and replacements of war-scathed equipment were the order of the day, and operations were reduced accordingly as an air of relaxation pervaded the armed services generally.

Such relaxation did not mean any cessation entirely of the German war machinery. The priority objective now had to be the subjugation of Britain if Germany was to feel in total command of western Europe, and Hitler, after a few weeks of hesitation hoping faintly for Britain to sue for peaceful termination to the conflict, issued his approval on 2 July for the start of preparations for a possible 'landing operation against England'. Two weeks later, on 16 July, in the continued absence of any peace overtures from the British government now headed by Winston Churchill, Hitler confirmed his intention to invade England and issued Operational Directive No 16, . . . to eliminate the English homeland as a base for the carrying on of the war against Germany, and, if it should become necessary, to occupy it completely'.

Such preparations were more easily propounded than actually made at the time. The Luftwaffe had yet to recover fully from the rigours of an exhausting, continuing campaign lasting for two months without let-up, and necessary resettlement in fresh bases, establishment of new supply and communication arteries, replacement aircraft, spares and crews, were far from ready for any renewed aerial conflict. Whatever the state of the army or navy, the Luftwaffe was necessarily the spearhead for any such invasion attempt across the Channel. Without firm air supremacy over southern England, no German landing force could hope to succeed, while no naval operation across the Channel could be guaranteed to be safe. The onus for attaining the vital pre-requisite of air control was firmly on the preening Göring's flabby shoulders. In typical Göring-fashion, the bulky *Reichsmarschall* boasted to a gathering of his Luftwaffe commanders that the RAF's fighter forces would be destroyed on the ground and in the air '. . . within two or three days'.

It was from the start a forlorn prophecy. Apart from its baseless underestimation of the RAF's potential fighting strength and ability,

Göring's statement failed utterly to recognise the limitations in strike power inherent in his Luftwaffe. By its nature and establishment the German air arm was never equipped for any form of long-range strategic air war. It possessed only twin-engined, medium range bombers – a result of the pre-war cancellation of any four-engined bomber development programme – and was entirely shaped for short-range tactical use against neighbouring countries in Europe. To expect such a force to undertake a form of strategic operation for which it had neither training or equipment was pure folly. The available strength on 20 July of the three *Luftflotten* detailed to overwhelm the RAF, was 1,610 bombers and 1,155 fighters, though of these totals only 944 bombers and 824 fighters were actually fit for immediate operations on that date. Against such an array the RAF, on the same day, could muster little more than 600 fighters, some of which, like the Boulton Paul Defiant and 'converted' Blenheims, were obviously outmatched by Göring's Messerschmitts.

If grave doubts about the capability of the Luftwaffe to fulfil Göring's boasts lingered among some Luftwaffe generals, the mood of the operational crews was buoyant and confident. Though sporadic sorties were undertaken throughout June and July across the *Kanal* (Channel), the pace of operational activity during those high summer weeks, in contrast to the previous weeks, was hardly taxing. Indeed, many fighter pilots expressed mildly irritated frustration at not receiving any orders to carry the war into English skies.

Across that same strip of water, the RAF's fighter pilots too were impatient to get to grips with the Luftwaffe, fully confident in their ability to defend their homeland. The scene was set for an aerial battle which would prove a significant turning point in the conduct of the whole war — pure air power was to be entrusted with a responsibility never before granted to its advocates.

CHAPTER FOUR

Clash of Eagles

The preliminary air struggle to Hitler's intended invasion of the United Kingdom, now permanently titled the Battle of Britain, was to be a watershed in the progression of the war in various ways. Primarily, it was a battle solely decided by air power – the first in human history – and set patterns for the use of that power in succeeding years. It was also the first major defeat for Göring's Luftwaffe and shattered the crystal-thin outward shell of German aerial might so readily believed by most European countries. That facade of Luftwaffe 'invincibility' had been seriously cracked during the Polish and French campaigns, though not in any way obvious to spectators. The Battle of Britain confirmed without doubt the vulnerability and potential weaknesses of Göring's vaunted air arm. It also exploded the myth of Göring's personal grasp and understanding of the correct use of air power in modern contexts. After the Battle Hermann Göring's star began to wane rapidly in Germany and he lost forever any faith in his abilities as an air force commander hitherto held by any of his subordinates. In any other country such a defeat would almost certainly have resulted in his removal from office, yet Hitler's private loyalty to one of his earliest supporters in the rise of Nazism kept Göring firmly in the Luftwaffe supremo's seat until the final days of the war, an act of misplaced personal loyalty for which the Allied air commanders were to be grateful, if only in retrospect.

Unlike any classic land battle in history, however, the Battle of Britain did not commence at a specific 'zero hour' on a designated date; though British officialdom later gave bureaucratic time parameters for the struggle as commencing at 0001 hours on 10 July 1940 and ceasing at 2359 hours on 31 October 1940. Such an arbitrary selection of dates takes no account of many significant factors affecting the eventual victory by the RAF. It ignores the importance of air operations which occurred between the end of Operation Dynamo and the official beginning of the battle; it fails to emphasise the unceasing efforts of Bomber Command crews throughout the period May to

64

December 1940 – the *only* form of *offensive* air power then available to Britain for striking at the heart of Germany and the German preparations for invasion of England; it fails to highlight the unceasing endeavours of many thousands of unpublicised civilians and servicemen and women who provided a background foundation of loyal service and labour in order to give the RAF its weapons and fighting facilities. Indeed, those official parameters can only be regarded as a convenient basis for Whitehall administrators in deciding who should be awarded the eventual 'Battle of Britain Star' gilt rosette to be worn on the otherwise mundane 1939–42 Star medal ribbon.

The preceding weeks of June and early July 1940 are often described as a period of virtual 'pause' in aerial activity in both the Luftwaffe and the RAF, whereas in fact no day or night went by without some form of operations. RAF Bomber Command had made its first attacks on the mainland of Germany on the night of 10–11 May 1940 and continued nightly attacks on German communications behind the invading forces investing Holland and France; but its first true strategic raid came on the night of 15–16 May when ninety-nine bombers set out from English bases to attack targets in the Ruhr. The entry of Italy into the war on 10 June, as a partner to Germany, saw 36 bombers set out to attack Turin on 11–12 June, though 23 of these returned early due to severe weather conditions over the Alps. By mid-July 1940 Bomber Command began concentrating much of its efforts against enemy ships and barges being accumulated in various Channel ports, patently part of the intended sea-invasion force which would sail against England in the near future. This 'battle of the barges' was to continue with little let-up until well into October.

The first phase of the German air campaign began in July with attacks against the many Allied merchant shipping convoys plodding through the English Channel towards east England ports – a minor form of attempted aerial 'blockade' hoping to cut off vital resupply of war materials from the neutral west nations. At the same time a number of fairly unco-ordinated and isolated bombing attacks against British mainland targets were undertaken from French and Norwegian airfields. None was in any large numbers and they were in the nature of probing sorties to test British defences, while Hitler remained hopeful that Britain might yet sue for peace rather than fight on alone. The clashes of RAF fighters and the Luftwaffe over the Channel convoys in the first nine days of July were usually brief but fiercely fought, and in that period the RAF claimed at least 56 German aircraft shot down, but lost a total of 28 fighters, with 23 of their pilots killed or wounded.

Ironically, none of the pilots mentioned was considered eligible for the later award of the 'Battle of Britain Star' . . .

Though this initial phase of the Luftwaffe offensive ended by 24 July, it was an integral part of what turned out to be a five-phase conduct of the battle. The second 'phase' was a deliberate attempt by German fighters to draw RAF fighters into a battle of fighter attrition in the air and lasted until about 7 August. It was a vain attempt – Hugh Dowding's Fighter Command had been patiently built up as a *defence* force to protect Britain from aerial attack; fighter-versus-fighter combat was, in Dowding's eyes, purely a peripheral priority and merely wasteful of men and machines. The prime targets for RAF fighters were the German bombers, a policy emphasised by Dowding to all his subordinates and one which he resolutely adhered to throughout the coming months.

The Luftwaffe's ability to conduct any such battle of attrition was severely restricted. Its standard Messerschmitt Bf 109E fighter, even when based along the northern French coast, could only count on an operational fighting radius of barely 120 miles, hardly sufficient to reach London's outskirts and leaving the German pilots with little more than a twenty-minute overlap period for actual combat. In the words of one of Germany's greatest fighting leaders, Adolf Galland, 'The German fighters found themselves in a similar predicament to a dog on a chain which wants to attack the foe, but cannot harm him because of his limited orbit.'

It was, in varying degrees, the crux of the inherent problem for the whole Luftwaffe in 1940. No German operational aircraft then had been designed for long-range, deep penetration, sustainable bombing sorties, or for extended fighter escort and combat capability so far from base facilities. To expect such an air force to provide any significant aerial 'blanket' over Britain was simply a pipedream, a phantasy of Göring's fertile imagination.

This fighter-versus-fighter phase was notable for the tenor of its intensity of attitude and effort by the opposing fighter pilots. On the German side high morale and an eagerness to come to grips with the RAF Spitfires and Hurricanes were prevalent throughout the *Jagdgeschwader*. Refreshed and recuperated from the previous months of hard campaigning, the Luftwaffe crews were more than ready for their appointed task of eliminating RAF fighter defenders over Britain, and flew to battle with high heart. Among the RAF fighter squadrons morale was equally high but was underlined with a thin veil of grim determination to 'revenge' the many losses of France and elsewhere.

Added to this mood was the knowledge that they would be fighting over their own land, a shield to ward off almost certain invasion of Britain. This sober realisation gave many RAF crews an extra 'edge' to their traditional stubborn refusal to quit any field of combat.

Such a responsibility, nevertheless, sat lightly on the shoulders of a large proportion of the younger RAF fighter pilots at first; deeper issues of strategy and the like were no part of the 'average' pilot's outlook – to be able to fly and fight from the cockpit of a Spitfire against a well-matched opponent was sufficient unto the day. Aerial combat, to those many young RAF pilots who had yet to experience it, still retained an almost sporting charisma – even a faint air of the chivalrous man-to-man pitting of strength and guile of yesteryear. Such quixotic notions were swiftly and cruelly shattered once combat was joined and the first sweat of naked fear penetrated a pilot's consciousness; adolescent views of the 'glory' and 'glamour' of air fighting dissolved like spilt mercury when he found himself facing death from the searing flames of a shell-ruptured petrol tank, or juggled frantically with unresponsive, bullet-riven controls as a Messerschmitt bore in to administer a *coup de grâce*.

One other huge advantage to the RAF fighter defences was its pre-intelligence radar system. By July 1940 a chain of 51 radar posts were operational along the southern and eastern coasts of England, each linked with Fighter Command Headquarters at Bentley Priory, Stanmore; while in visual vigilance in more than a thousand 'listening posts' were some 30,000 unpaid volunteer civilian members of the Observer Corps. This combination provided detection of any Luftwaffe formation setting out for England, even as some formed into battle array over their northern France bases. On receipt of any such pre-warning, RAF fighters could be sent up in available strength at fairly short notice to intercept the incoming German bombers or fighters. This capability for appearing in the right place at the right time confused many German crews during the early forays against Britain, and even later, when they realised that the RAF had such a system, tended to increase apprehension even before actual engagement. To every Luftwaffe fighter pilot, already very conscious of the limited range and 'combat time' available to him on every sortie, the knowledge that his opponents already knew where and when he would arrive over the main combat area of southern England robbed him of the first essential of all successful fighting tactics: surprise. In English skies he felt naked and unprotected every minute he was airborne. His one distinct advantage over any RAF opposition was in numerical strength, flying in formations which, almost always, far outnumbered any RAF fighters sent against them. Theoretically, such high odds *should* eventually prevail, and the RAF's defences would be whittled down to a point of nullification.

While the attacks on Channel convoys continued in July, the first Luftwaffe bombing raids against England became a daily occurrence, duly escorted by Messerschmitt Bf 110s and Bf 109s. Initially such sorties were in no great strength, compared to those made in the following months, yet were sufficient to test Britain's defence web and gain response from RAF fighters. As early as 10 July, however, clashes with 'escort' Bf 110s emphasised the unsuitability of the design for its ostensible role when formations of the twin-engined *Zerstörer*, on being attacked, promptly formed self-protection defensive circles, thereby deserting their bomber 'charges'. These daytime forays were usually supplemented by night attacks against a number of English towns and centres, though not as part of any particularly systematic night offensive. In the main the night bombers suffered few losses, and these mainly to anti-aircraft fire or accidents rather than nightfighters. The RAF in mid-1940 was not equipped with any succinct night-fighting force as a separate form of aerial defence; it relied on day fighter aircraft with few if any night aids, apart from a relative handful of 'converted' aircraft fitted with the early, and unreliable, radar equipment then available. This gap in the RAF's home defence equipment was but one more result of the peacetime sloth and neglect of the air arm by the decision-makers and keepers of the national purse-strings in government circles.

In the period 10 July to 31 July inclusive, the RAF flew a total of approximately 12,000 individual fighter sorties against the Luftwaffe and shot down some 270 for the loss of 145 British fighters. The British losses in aircraft caused little concern to Hugh Dowding, inasmuch as aircraft production from the many factories could replace these within a week. The loss of 51 pilots killed and 18 others wounded or injured was far more serious. These could not be replaced so easily. Dowding's policy of concentrating his main efforts towards defeat of the German bombers meant a deliberate tendency to withhold fighter opposition to mainly fighter formations, although the Spitfire and Hurricane interceptors seldom had much choice but to fight their way *through* the German fighter escorts in order to tackle the Heinkels, Dorniers and Junkers below. In Dowding's assessment of the situation – a correct one in the event – the bulk of the Luftwaffe's July sorties were testing probes of Fighter Command's resources and weaknesses, albeit flown in some strength on occasion. With this in mind, therefore, Dowding refused to commit all his fighter squadrons to the south-eastern England combat sectors, but continued to retain a fair proportion of his force based further north or westwards as a standby reserve. This defence in depth not only kept the reserve squadrons fresh and combat-ready, but provided an immediate interception force to throw against any 'flanking' air attacks either side of the main thrust over Kent, Sussex and Surrey etc. As the pace of fighting intensified during August and September, Dowding was able to modify this disposition of his squadrons to act as a rotation system for withdrawing exhausted first line units from the vital combat zone and replacing them with rested squadrons.

This ability to apparently produce 'fresh' Hurricanes and Spitfires throughout the battle, particularly during the peak months of August and September, baffled many of the Luftwaffe crews. Their intelligence constantly assured them that the RAF was being steadily drained to a level of ineffectiveness – yet every sortie continued to be met by savage opposition and in – it seemed – increasing strength. Faulty Luftwaffe intelligence assessments of RAF daily strength and disposition – to some degree unconsciously bolstered by a too-ready acceptance of exaggerated claims by many German crews for combat victories * – merely added to the general misdirection of the various facets and phases of the battle by the over-optimistic Göring and his nearest cronies. With no qualifications or experience of up-to-date aerial strategy or tactics, Göring continued to view the aerial struggle in terms of 1918 tactics, ignoring the advice and views of the men who were expected to pursue such outmoded forms of warfare. It must be emphasised, however, that relatively few of Göring's subordinate commanders shared his views on the conduct of the battle; nevertheless, being professional soldiers in the traditional German mould, they obeyed orders.

The Luftwaffe's attempts to suck RAF fighters into a battle of attrition in the air continued until 8 August, on which date the German bombing offensive was increased significantly. That day waves of Junkers Ju 87s were flung against a large convoy, CW9, code-named 'Peewit', in the Channel and it was heavily attacked resulting in the losses of 34 German and 19 RAF aircraft. Meanwhile the first deliber-

---

* Throughout the Battle, both RAF and Luftwaffe claims for aerial 'victories' were exaggerated by a factor of at least three – claims perfectly comprehensible in the white heat of a combat zone so deep and wide, and all made in good faith. To rely on such figures for progressive conduct of the fighting was, nevertheless, a folly.

ate attacks were being made on RAF fighter airfields. These were the preliminaries to Göring's promised *Adler Tag* – 'Eagle Day' – which in four days (according to Göring) the RAF fighter force would be eliminated, and was due to commence on 13 August. The increase in intensity of combat was evident during that second week of August, with losses on both sides steadily escalating. It was the beginning of Fighter Command's 'finest hour' – the ultimate testing of its fortitude and determination.

In the hours before dawn on 13 August – the intended 'zero hour' for the launching of *Adlerangriff* – 74 Dorniers of KG2 based in north-east France completed preparations for an assault on the Isle of Sheppey, and minutes after 0500 hours set out for their objective. Their earmarked escort of Messerschmitt Bf 110s of ZG26, 60 in total, duly rendezvoused at the French coast – then promptly vanished! Baffled by this apparent desertion, the Dornier crews decided to carry on and complete their task alone. Reaching Eastchurch airfield they bombed, creating widespread damage and then fought their way back despite the attentions of three RAF fighter squadrons who shot down five bombers. Only on arrival at base did the Dornier commander learn the reason for his lack of fighter protection : Göring had person-ally ordered a postponement of the initial air assault until the after-noon, but the order had not reached the bombers' bases in time. In the mid-afternoon *Adlerangriff* finally gained momentum, with mass attacks against Portland, Southampton and targets stretching across Kent to the Thames Estuary. Preceded by a spearhead wave of Bf 109s, the bomber formations made two main thrusts, westwards and north-east, flanking the hitherto main combat zone over Kent, Sussex and Surrey. The outcome was a bag of mixed fortunes for the Luft-waffe.

Of an overall total of some 200 Junkers Ju 88s and Ju 87s, with roughly 90 Messerschmitt Bf 109 and 110 escorts, 80 Ju 88s forced their way through heavy RAF fighter opposition and bombed South-ampton, inflicting heavy damage to the port and its docks. Elsewhere, however, many bombers failed to locate designated targets and bombed at random. One gaggle of Ju 87s from II/SG2 intending to bomb Middle Wallop airfield were caught in a perfect fighter 'bounce' by Spitfires of 609 Squadron and lost nine within minutes. Further east 40 Ju 87s dive-bombed Detling airfield, creating havoc in physical damage to buildings, destroying 22 aircraft on the ground, and killing 67 people including the station commander. By the evening the Luft-waffe had flown a tally of 1,485 sorties and claimed the destruction of

88 aircraft, apart from ground casualties. The RAF fighters, in 700 sorties, claimed to have shot down 64 German aircraft. The true loss statistics were 46 German and 13 RAF fighters lost in actual combat, a reasonably normal example of the constant over-claiming by both air forces. On the RAF side three pilots had been killed and five wounded, a relatively minor casualty rate compared to the damage inflicted upon the Luftwaffe that day.

The pace of combat was maintained the following day, though the main German attacks were more thinly and widely spread this time – doubtless in view of the high losses of 13 August – and therefore presented scattered targets for RAF interception. Airfields at Manston, Middle Wallop and Sealand were bombed to some effect, and Southampton again suffered heavy damage, but at the end of the day the Luftwaffe had lost 19 aircraft and crews against the RAF's loss of 8 fighters with 13 pilots killed.

August 15 saw the Luftwaffe make its greatest bid for victory to date. In a series of deliberately widespread attacks along south and south-east England, German bomber formations attempted to erase RAF fighter bases; while a bombing force was also launched against north-east England from German airfields in Norway, partly in the hope of forcing Dowding to withdraw fighters from the southern zones, and partly in the belief that RAF defences were necessarily weak north of London – a misconception created by the faulty German intelligence assessments of the period. For all these attacks Göring provided virtually the entire fighter strength of the Luftwaffe, and almost half its existing bomber availability. The optimistic flanking attack from Norway against north-east England, though in comparative strength of some 160 bombers and fighters, was surprised to find several RAF fighter squadrons already airborne and awaiting their arrival near the coastline – RAF radar had given an hour's pre-warning of the incoming attacks. The resulting engagements saw the German bombers do little damage and lose 16 aircraft to the defenders, apart from 7 of their escort fighters – almost twenty per cent casualty losses for this single sortie.

The main efforts of the day in the south saw several RAF stations attacked in varying degrees of success, with Manston, Lympne, Martlesham, Croydon and Worthy Down all receiving attention of German bombers. Additional raids were made against the Short Brothers aircraft factory at Rochester, Southampton and Portland naval base. Yet apart from the forward landing grounds at Manston and Lympne, none of these objectives had any significant relevance to Fighter Command

– yet another outcome of poor intelligence within the Luftwaffe staff environs. By evening the Luftwaffe had flown well over 2,000 individual sorties and claimed 101 combat victories; RAF fighters had flown 974 sorties and claimed 182 victims. Again, such exaggerated claims, though heartening to the morale of both antagonists, were wildly optimistic. True figures for the day show a German loss figure of 75 aircraft, while the RAF fighters lost 34 aircraft, with 16 pilots wounded and a further 17 killed. The day had been the greatest test to date of Dowding's defence command, and Fighter Command had triumphed. It was to prove a vital turning point in the conduct of the battle by Göring.

The heavy losses of 15 August caused the day to become referred to thereafter within Luftwaffe ranks as 'Black Thursday'; while the significance of events that day caused Göring to revise his orders for future employment of various aircraft types. His prime concern was for his bombers, especially the highly vulnerable Ju 87, and accordingly he issued a directive that in future German fighters must stay with the bombers at all times. This order – a clear indication of Göring's ignorance of modern aerial strategy or tactics – immediately had the effect of severely hampering the Messerschmitt pilots' freedom to entice the RAF into all-out combat, and relegated them to the role of mere shepherd dogs to the flock of unwieldy bombers, unable to exploit the full potential of either their aircraft or the specialised training they had received.

Göring next emphasised that the main objectives would continue to be RAF fighter bases and the British aviation industrial plants, but then continued with the astonishing statement that, 'It is doubtful whether there is any point in continuing the attacks on radar sites . . .' Considering the vital importance of the RAF's radar chain for direction and pre-warning, such a decision can only be regarded as one of the major errors of the many tactical mistakes initiated by the obese *Reichsmarschall* during the summer of 1940.

Compounding the stupidity of the Luftwaffe supremo was the latest highly fictional assessment of existing RAF fighter strength by Luftwaffe Intelligence. In its summary of 16 August, the latter confidently claimed the destruction of a total of 572 RAF fighters during the period 1 July to 15 August, 1940, and then calmly asserted that RAF Fighter Command now possessed a mere 300 aircraft available for operations at best. Against such 'weak defences' the Luftwaffe could, at that date, muster a gross total of more than 3,000 fighters, bombers and reconnaissance aircraft, of which at least two-thirds could be regarded as immediately available for operations. In fact, during the period studied – July to 15 August – the RAF had lost 300 fighter aircraft, while on 15 August it had a firstline strength of 749 operationally-fit fighters, with an immediate standby reserve of a further 290 in 'storage' i.e. ready for issue to squadrons. Moreover, German calculations failed to give sufficient importance to the potential of Britain's aviation production and repair facilities which at that period were performing prodigious feats in surpassing given target-figures in making fighters available.

Nevertheless, RAF Fighter Command's healthy state in the context of aircraft did not reflect entirely its operational punch in the high-key and continuing pressure of circumstances in August 1940. Two main factors still remained, both, if anything, much more important to the possible outcome than mere totting up of airframes available. One was the vital need to protect the truly important Fighter Command airfields in the south and south-east corners of England. Should these be destroyed or rendered useless for long periods, the forward landing grounds such as Manston – already part-razed – would not provide the requisite facilities for refurbishment and control of the fighters.

Even more serious was the steady bleeding of Fighter Command's pilots by mid-August. On 17 August Fighter Command had a total of 1,379 pilots on the operational strength, at least 200 less than its formal needs to bring each existing squadron up to operational establishment. To achieve even this number of firstline pilots, Fighter Command had been forced to scour all other RAF commands and even Fleet Air Arm units to fill the cockpits. A number of such newcomers had never flown a fighter, and had to be content with less than two weeks' hastily-arranged conversion instruction before being thrown in at the deep end.

The main potential source for trained pilots was, obviously, Bomber Command, but the bomber chiefs were understandably reluctant to release too many such men; should the still-expected German invasion erupt, Bomber Command would become a prime striking force. Already heavily committed to its night-bombing role in attempting to destroy German build-up of barges and other vessels being brought together in the Channel ports – with the inevitable losses in men and machines inherent with such enterprise – Bomber Command simply could not afford to deplete its strength except in marginal numbers. Thus a majority of the converted fighter pilots being transferred to Dowding came from Training Command, Coastal Command, and communications units.

If the RAF's effectiveness against the all-out efforts of 15 August gave pause to many Luftwaffe commanders, it did not prevent the German airmen from returning in massive weight next day. Targets were primarily presumed-fighter airfields, and in a series of well-planned tactical sorties the stations at West Malling, Farnborough, Lee-on-Solent, Gosport, Brize Norton and Tangmere. The latter objective, the only true fighter field, was badly hit, with widespread destruction of hangars and runways; while a particularly audacious sortie by just two Junkers Ju 88s against Brize Norton resulted in the destruction of a hangar housing more than 50 training aircraft, and damaging another hangar which held a dozen Hurricanes of the resident Maintenance Unit. An attack by Ju 87s against the Ventnor CH radar post put this link in the defence chain out of action for a week. In all the Luftwaffe flew a gross total of 1,715 sorties on the 16th, losing 45 aircraft, while the RAF had 22 aircraft shot down and 8 pilots killed. In contrast, 17 August provided little activity, with Fighter Command mounting only 288 sorties against, mainly, reconnaissance probes by the Luftwaffe.

August 18 brought renewed desperate action as the Luftwaffe again pressed its offensive against the fighter bases. It was also the day which finally buried the myth of the dreaded Junkers Ju 87 *Stuka* dive-bomber. The initial raids aimed at Biggin Hill, Kenley and Croydon, causing near-devastation at Kenley but relatively minor damage at the other airfields. Clashes between RAF fighters over their own bases claimed several victims from the leading Dornier formations, but also gave the marauding Messerschmitt Bf 109 escorts a number of 'kills'.

Second waves of German bombers then attacked the air stations at Ford, Gosport and Thorney Island, while a force of Ju 87s lined up the Poling CH radar post, near Littlehampton, as their target. Though heavily escorted by the Bf 109s of the crack JG27, the Junkers were caught by Hurricanes as they commenced their dives – and were massacred. In all, 16 Ju 87s were shot down, 4 others seriously damaged, while 2 more crashed on return to base. The Messerschmitts fared little better, losing 8 of their number and claiming only 6 RAF fighters. Notwithstanding such successes by the defenders, Poling was damaged sufficiently to render it non-operational for a week. In the late afternoon further attacks were carried out against Croydon and Manston; on the latter by a dozen Bf 109s which streaked in at ultra-low level under the radar web. By evening the results of this latest day of bitter fighting showed a loss to the Luftwaffe of 71 aircraft shot down, and 27 RAF fighters destroyed, with 10 pilots killed.

For the remainder of August and the first days of September the assault on Fighter Command's airfields was maintained. Nerve-centre stations like Biggin Hill, Hornchurch, Kenley and Tangmere were relentlessly bombed and virtually razed to the ground, yet the fighters still rose to meet the next Luftwaffe formations. The bombers, owing to Göring's restrictive order, were now invariably heavily escorted by Messerschmitts, thereby presenting RAF pilots with a constant problem of trying to pierce the escort umbrella in order to get at their prime targets, the bombers. The pace of combat by late August was achieving the Luftwaffe's aim in essence : RAF fighter squadrons were reaching exhaustion point quicker, needing replacement after, perhaps, only days of frontline action. The reserve units ostensibly resting further north were thus being returned to battle before they had fully recuperated. Aircraft losses – on both sides – continued to be high, but, as always, aircraft were not Dowding's premier worry because these were being replaced with ease daily by the aviation factories and maintenance units. The tragic toll in pilots was an entirely different matter; such combat-blooded young men could not be replaced overnight. During the period 24 August to 6 September the RAF lost more than 100 pilots killed, and a further 128 were seriously wounded or injured. Such figures represented roughly twenty-five per cent of all available RAF fighter pilots at any given date of the battle.

As the fighting potential of Fighter Command ground inexorably less, the Luftwaffe – virtually within sight of ultimate victory in their prolonged offensive – was given fresh tactical directives from Göring. Starting on 7 September the main effort was now to be directed at the English capital city, London. Though 'justified' by Göring as a switch in targets which would force the RAF to fling in its last reserves to defend the city, thereby still being part of the overall aim of bringing the RAF fighters into an aerial battle of attrition, in fact this decision to change the objective came from Hitler himself. Infuriated by RAF Bomber Command's raids against Berlin on four nights, the Führer abandoned his former reluctance (and specific orders not) to bomb London. 'Since they attack our cities, we shall wipe out theirs.'

It was, to a great extent, Dowding's salvation. As the first heavy daylight attacks on London developed into a pattern, Fighter Command could now rationalise its major efforts to a single, relatively uncomplicated tactic : pure defence of a single target. The overall logistics remained a serious problem – Dowding's pilot strength was still far short of any safe minimum figure – but such strength as existed could now be marshalled and concentrated in defence. The crass ignorance of both Hitler and Göring of aerial strategy had once more robbed their air force of any real hope of final triumph.

This new phase – usually titled the Battle of London – quickly became a round-the-clock offensive, with night bombers taking over from the daytime raiders and being guided to their target by the fire and explosions resulting from the daylight sorties. It was an ordeal for London which was to last until the spring of 1941, with little let-up. To Dowding and his brilliant 11 Group commander, Keith Park, the immediate concern was prevention of the massive daytime attacks. Whereas much of the previous weeks of the battle had seen Park despatching his 11 Group defenders up in one or two-squadron strength in successive waves, it was now possible to supplement any such tactics by calling on 12 Group, based north-east of London, to provide four and five-squadron 'Wings' in massed formation. The efficacy of this 'double-blow' strength was epitomised on 15 September, a day of fighting which was to prove the final blow to any lingering German hopes of a 1940 invasion of England, and the date selected to commemorate the Battle of Britain annually ever since.

For several days prior to 15 September Fighter Command had seen less exhaustive action than before, thereby permitting a modicum of rest and recovery among the squadrons. It was merely relative relaxation, because fighting continued daily and losses were sustained. Nevertheless, Park's pilots were in better physical state by 15 September than had been the case throughout the late August battles. Aircraft serviceability and replacements had been brought to almost full operational fitness, and on that day Dowding could count 1,500 pilots in the frontline squadrons, still well below desired establishment, but generally in finer fettle than had been possible previously. Among the Luftwaffe crews by then an increasing disillusionment with the tactical direction by Göring of the air offensive had begun to disaffect some crews. Reassurances by higher authority that the RAF was now 'down to its last 50 Spitfires' were blatantly ridiculous to the men who flew daily over Kent and Sussex, although the days leading up to 15 September had indeed seen an apparent reduction in RAF fighter opposition. Some bomber crews were even returning virtually unmolested from bombing sorties.

The fateful Sunday opened quietly enough; a handful of individual German reconnaissance sorties over south-east England which were virtually ignored by Park, except to bring several of his squadrons on the ground to full 'Readiness' state from 0700 hours onwards. The first main bomber waves, some 70 Dorniers from KG2 and KG3, heavily escorted by Messerschmitts, began wheeling into pre-formation over Calais and Boulogne shortly before 1100 hours. Pre-warned by the radar chain, Park waited until this force was reported as moving across the Channel, then sent up eleven squadrons at brief spacings, while 12 Group further north-west, despatched its five-squadron 'Wing' based at Duxford, led by the legless Douglas Bader. All the signs pointed towards London as being the target, and Park accordingly arranged a 'staircase carpet' of interception all along the incoming route of the Dorniers. Shortly after 1130 the bombers crossed the Kent coast near Dungeness, where 20 Spitfires from 72 and 92 Squadrons attacked in one ferocious line-abreast, head-on pass; the first of five pairs of squadrons planned by Park to harry the Dorniers along their flightpath. For the next thirty minutes the German crews ran the gauntlet of Hurricanes and Spitfires in succeeding waves, but continued their intention of reaching London. Each attack cost the Germans some losses – individual aircraft which reeled drunkenly out of cohort with bullet damage or smashed engines – but by noon the bulk of the bombers reached their objective.

Immediately they were set upon by the Duxford 'Balbo'; a fresh force of some 60 fighters attacked in unison. It was a shock to the Luftwaffe crews, and each aircraft immediately sought its own salvation. Bomb loads were jettisoned haphazardly in many cases as Bader's 'Wing' slashed its way through the tiers of Dorniers and Messerschmitts, and those who survived the initial impact fled southwards at top speed. They found little respite over Kent as Park sent up four more squadrons to peck and maul the retreating bombers. By 1300 hours the RAF fighters were back on the ground, refuelling and re-arming after what Bader personally termed, '. . . the finest shambles I've ever been in.'

A second Luftwaffe wave of bombers had been intended to follow immediately, and had it done so it would have met little opposition while Park's fighters were on their airfields being replenished. As it happened, this second formation – some 150 Dorniers and Heinkels from KG2, KG53 and KG76, protected by the elite JG26 and JG54, led respectively by Galland and Trautloft – was still sliding into initial battle formation over France as the RAF defenders completed their turn-round. Thus, when the awesome array of Luftwaffe aircraft approached London shortly before 1400 hours, Park's men were either already airborne or about to take off.

Over Kent, before penetrating London's suburbs, the bombers were swamped by some 170 fighters and ensuing engagements with the veteran Messerschmitt pilots were vicious and close-fought. Shaking off this onslaught the bombers reached London – only to be jumped by the five-squadron Duxford 'Wing' and eight other squadrons from 10 and 11 Groups. The impact of nearly 300 RAF fighters battered all semblance of cohesion out of the Luftwaffe formation, and the bright blue skies over Westminster became a fantastic pattern of twisting contrails as a hundred individual combats occurred simultaneously. Above the city German and RAF aircraft careered in every possible direction and the hammering of machine guns and cannons was clearly audible to the fascinated civilian spectators below.

As the splintered German formations fled southwards, they continued to be savaged by yet more fighters from 10 and 11 Groups, in some cases until well out over the Channel. Even as the bullet-riven Heinkels and Dorniers sighted their haven of the French coast, three other smaller raids crossed into English air space, attacking Portland, southern Kent, and the Spitfire-producing Supermarine factory at Woolston, Southampton. None of these accomplished much damage. They were the final daylight raids of 15 September. On RAF dispersals a host of excited RAF fighter pilots exchanged experiences, and within hours the British nation heard over their radios the astonishing claim for 185 German aircraft destroyed. Later more detailed analysis has reduced this German loss figure to 60 at most, with at least an equal number so seriously battle-damaged as to be useless for further operations. The RAF had lost 26 fighters, but retrieved 13 of their pilots to fight again. In the broader view, the figures were relatively unimportant. What mattered was the effect and significance of the undisputed triumph of the RAF's fighters that day. Within the Luftwaffe it was blatantly obvious that, far from being down to its 'last 50 Spitfires', the RAF was if anything stronger than before. Clearly Göring's vain boast to Hitler and the generals that his Luftwaffe would eliminate all RAF fighters '. . . in four or five days' was yet another figment of imagination, pure phantasy.

Faced with such unpalatable but incontrovertible evidence of the Luftwaffe's failure to prepare the way for the German army and navy, Hitler issued a personal order on 17 September that Operation Sea-Lion – the planned invasion of Britain – was postponed 'until further notice'; and four days later the massive concentration of invasion barges *et al* was ordered to commence dispersal. Although the daylight battle was to continue until November, still fiercely fought and entailing heavy casualties on the part of the opposing air forces, 15 September must be recognised as the crucial turning point. The *effect* of that day's victory by Dowding's men upon German war planning and intention was clear-cut. Despite half-hearted proposals later for such an operation, the Wehrmacht was never again to be capable of mounting any significant threat of invasion of Britain; never again would the Luftwaffe come so close to defeating the RAF. The reasons for its failure were many, but could chiefly be blamed upon the gross misdirection of the German air offensive by Hermann Göring, and the historical background to the original build-up of the Luftwaffe as a purely tactical adjunct to the German army. The latter aspect produced an ostensibly efficient, modern fighting force which, in fact, was incapable of undertaking any sustained, long-range air offensive; a short-sighted policy emphasised by the lack of urgency accorded to aircraft production and development from 1938–40.

In human and material terms the Battle of Britain was grievous. Accepting the highly arbitrary parameters of the daylight struggle as from 10 July to 31 October inclusive, RAF Fighter Command had 481 pilots killed or listed as 'Missing', while a further 422 received wounds, burns or other serious injuries. Losses in aircraft destroyed or written-off due to battle damage amounted to 1,140. In 'balance' the RAF fighter pilots had destroyed at least 1,733 German aircraft and damaged nearly 650 others. In broad terms the RAF's fighter arm had lost almost one in three of the young pilots who fought during the battle, either killed or incapacitated in varying degrees. Of the survivors, a further 800 at least were destined to die in battle later in the war. The victory had not been won by any particular band of brilliant fighter aces – it had been the accumulative, unpublicised, dogged devotion to duty of the vast 'silent majority' which had ensured the freedom of a nation in the ever-blue skies of Britain during that fateful summer of 1940.

CHAPTER FIVE

Death by Night

If RAF Fighter Command's desperate defence of Britain in the high summer of 1940 tended to overshadow other events during the first year of the war – at least, in the layman's view via the contemporary media – equally grim determination in prosecution of the air war was being exemplified by the men of the bombers. RAF Bomber Command had begun its war within minutes of the opening of hostilities, albeit in driblet numbers and cramped in scope by its inherent weaknesses in many facets, apart from the inhibitions in action imposed by the political pundits of the day.

The Luftwaffe on the other hand was almost fully committed to the initial invasions of Poland *et al*. Even without such heavy responsibilities, it was in no position to launch anything resembling the much-feared 'knockout blow' which the British population had for years been led to expect from it on the outbreak of any war. It was again an example of an air force, apart from inability in practical context to mount any such massive onslaught, being hampered by direction from its political master, in this case Hitler himself. In his first War Directive, dated 31 August 1939, Hitler made it perfectly clear that only British naval targets might be attacked, if opportunities arose, and that raids against mainland objectives and cities were – for the moment – forbidden. Such restriction, unlike the British and French hesitation, was not motivated by any particular fear of 'provocation' or 'retaliation', but simply accorded with Hitler's personal wishful thinking that Britain might yet sue for peace once the Polish campaign had forcibly demonstrated German military might.

Thus the first German bombing sorties into British air space were against strictly naval targets, HMS *Hood* and some attendant cruisers and other vessels anchored in the Firth of Forth. Nine Junkers Ju 88s from KG30 undertook this raid on 16 October 1939 – and lost two Ju 88s to defending Spitfires of 602 and 603 Squadrons of the AAF, while a third Junkers barely returned to base with one engine shattered. It had been a daylight raid, unescorted by fighters, and was a tiny pointer to the future fate of any bomber formation operating by day without the vital umbrella of fighter protection, a lesson which all air forces failed to learn for many months. Such isolated sorties, in small numbers, became the pattern of German bombing efforts against Britain for the first nine months of the war – necessarily so in view of the Luftwaffe's huge participation in the various campaigns in Europe up until July 1940. All were aimed at classified 'naval' targets, which included the tactic of mine-laying across the approaches to ports and harbours or in recognised merchant shipping lines.

The first winter of the war also saw Bomber Command open its offensive on a 'soft pedal' tone. Sorties – usually in small numbers and unco-ordinated – were mainly by day, without fighter escort, and against 'naval objectives'. Though forbidden to drop bombs on German land targets, RAF bombers penetrated German skies for the first time on the night of 1–2 October 1939 when three Whitleys of 10 Squadron showered the city of Berlin with bundles of propaganda leaflets – 'Nickelling' as this form of paper-bombing was coded by the RAF. In the main, however, RAF bomber sorties were initially confined to armed reconnaissances, mine-laying, and very occasional forays against German naval targets. The relatively few night raids undertaken quickly demonstrated RAF bombers' lack of adequate navigational aids, while the physical need for such items as heating and ample oxygen supply for crews became apparent. The various daylight sorties also illustrated vividly a crucial need for such things as self-sealing fuel tanks, armour plate protection for engines and pilots, and immediate upgrading of defensive armament in the light of the early engagements with defending Luftwaffe fighters which produced high casualty rates among the unescorted RAF bombers.

Perhaps the most serious deficiency in all cases of night raiding was the lack of accurate navigation displayed by too many bomber crews. With little if any peacetime practice in the art of locating any distant target by night, and having to rely on the dead reckoning methods then in vogue, too many bombers simply failed to find even large objectives, while a high percentage claimed to have bombed primary targets when in fact they were over entirely different objectives or cities. It was to be a constant problem for RAF bomber crews during the first four years of the war.

The main hazards of Bomber Command's first seven months of operations were mainly attributable to the deadly cold weather conditions prevailing right across Europe. The bitterly icy conditions froze instruments, radios, hydraulics and gun turrets, and coated control surfaces with immovable coats of frozen vapour. Inside the unheated fuselages of the Whitleys and Wellingtons the crews suffered agonising hours of stultifying cold, not daring to remove any article of clothing in case an accidental touch on metal froze them to the object. Oxygen lines froze solid, leaving them to gulp the icy air, and internal communication between crew members became almost impossible. Psychologically, having to endure such conditions merely to drop leaflets over Germany was little incentive to ultimate efficiency; yet the early crews remained stoical and determined, and at least began to accumulate hard experience in the various facets of operating at long range by night. Until July 1940 RAF bombers over German territory were, in the main, untroubled by the very few German 'nightfighters' available – these being merely day fighters detailed for night operations without any specific modifications for such sorties – and any opposition came from the *Flak* * arm of the Luftwaffe, a ground force comprised then of some 450 heavy calibre anti-aircraft guns and slightly more than a hundred searchlight batteries, all spread thinly to cover the most important industrial centres or major cities. None of the flak units of the period had yet received any form of radar prediction or guidance aids and, like the contemporary British anti-aircraft defences, relied heavily upon sound location and similar fairly primitive devices for pinpointing aerial raiders.

By late July 1940, however, the situation began to change rapidly when, on orders direct from Göring, a nightfighter division was formed: *Nachtjagdgeschwader 1*, commanded by Major Wolfgang Falck and equipped with a variety of modified twin- and single-engined fighters, and supplemented by radar equipment and searchlight units. The overall night defence system became the responsibility of the energetic Oberst Josef Kammhuber, and by the late autumn of 1940 the first 'Kammhuber Line' of defences stretched athwart the main Allied bomber routes to Germany. Then, in the evening of 16 October, Ludwig Becker, a Dornier pilot of NJG1, shot down a Wellington over Holland – the first German radar-assisted interception kill. It was a tiny pointer to the future pattern of night combat over Hitler's Reich. One other major facet of Kammhuber's organisation was the inauguration of night intruders, whose role was to tackle British bombers above their own airfields; either attacking as the bombers prepared to set out for Germany, or, more commonly, to follow returning bombers to their bases and strafe them as they prepared to land. It was a form of nightfighting originated in 1918 by the RAF, though then ignored by the policy-makers of all air forces during the decades of peace. In material

* *Flak* – a common abbreviation for *Fliegerabwehrkanonen* ('Anti-aircraft guns').

terms those early intrusion sorties produced little result, but the effect on bomber crews' morale was not inconsiderable; the knowledge that they might be attacked at literally any stage of a sortie increased an already high and natural apprehension prior to all operations.

The introduction of Kammhuber's organisation virtually coincided with the increase in pure bombing offensive against Britain inherent with the Battle of Britain operations, and indeed by October, when the Luftwaffe turned from daytime operations to an 'all-out' night offensive against London and other major cities in the United Kingdom, the bombing phase became the final section of Göring's bid to subdue the RAF and the British population as the pre-requisite to, at first, the intended invasion. However, before this night assault had really begun in earnest Hitler had 'postponed' his projected Operation Sea-Lion. As early as July 1940 Hitler had taken the decision to 'lay Russia low in one swift campaign'; in his view it was a necessary safeguard against possible Soviet invasion on Germany's eastern front before he could truly concentrate all his efforts to conquering Britain. Thus by October 1940 Hitler's thoughts were mainly concerned with the planning of the *Blitzkrieg* offensive in the east; the pressure of aerial assault on the British was to be maintained until the eve of that Russian campaign but mainly for '. . . exerting political and military pressure on England' in keeping alive the threat of invasion. In essence, Hitler's intention was simply to interrupt the campaign against Britain in order to deal with the 'Red Menace' on his eastern border.

The blitz on Britain, during the final stages of the Battle of Britain and thence throughout the winter nights of 1940–41, was the world's first *sustained* effort by any air force to defeat, or at least subdue to the point of surrender, an enemy civil population by means of aerial bombing. Many precedents of brief, successful air assaults on individual cities existed, yet all had been isolated *tactical* objectives, adjuncts to existing land campaigns by opposing armies. Until mid-1940 no air force had attempted to conduct what was in essence a *strategical* air offensive which might alone achieve victory in some form, without the immediate presence of an invading army. That Göring's Luftwaffe should be the first to make such an attempt was ironic : strategic concepts had been no part of the construction programmes for the new German air force, while Göring himself had already illustrated his overt ignorance of tactical use of air power, and knew nothing of the deeper issues of aerial strategy. Those of his subordinates who had tried to introduce any form of strategical forward planning in the 1930s – for merely one example, the plans for development of four-

engined, long-range bomber designs – had been over-ruled, resulting
in a 1940 Luftwaffe bereft of the types of aircraft even capable of
pursuing any strategic air offensive over any long period. In Göring's
eyes such bombers were unnecessary; what his Luftwaffe might lack
in particular heavy bomber designs was far out-weighed by the sheer
numerical strength in medium bomber types.

On 7 September 1940 the Luftwaffe launched a series of heavy
raids against London and its environs in daylight, dropping more than
300 tons of high explosive bombs and thousands of incendiaries on and
around the city within some ninety minutes. It was officially the start
of a fresh phase of German operations in the Battle of Britain, intended
primarily to force Hugh Dowding to commit his remaining fighter
reserves to defence of the capital and thus into battle with much-
strengthened German fighters escorting the bomber formations. The
raid was designated as the inaugural attack of a series of bombing
attacks, by day and by night, against large cities and other areas of high
density civilian population.

On that date the principal Luftwaffe forces based in France were
Luftflotten 2 and 3, which between them counted gross totals of 1,258
Heinkel He 111s, Junkers Ju 88s and Dorniers for main bombing
efforts, apart from some 200 Junkers Ju 87s for 'side-show' raids.
Actual serviceability states, nevertheless, amounted to no more than
65 per cent shown to be immediately fit for operations. Such numbers
– well over 700 firstline bombers – may not have been a formidable
force for destruction in the immediate circumstances. Their effectiveness may be judged by the fact that by the end of September the
bombers of *Luftflotten* 2 and 3 delivered some 5,300 tons of high explosive bombs and uncounted thousands of incendiary stores on
London alone. The cost to the Luftwaffe of those three weeks of overall offensive was heavy; a total of 433 aircraft of every type employed,
including, of course, the heavy Messerschmitt fighter escorts.

While Fighter Command opposition throughout September accounted for the vast bulk of German casualties during the continuing
daylight struggle, the German night formations suffered relatively few
losses to British defences of the period. The RAF's night-fighting potential then was meagre, comprised of just eight squadrons so-designated
in role, and these all equipped with either converted Blenheim bombers
or the ill-starred Defiant turret fighter. None possessed any reliable
form of radar guidance for interception of night raiders. To supplement these aircraft, an Air Council instruction to Dowding ordered
him, despite his dissension, to allot at least three single-seat Hurricane

squadrons to night defence duties. Fragmentary support for the campaign against the night bomber included an element of several other single-seat fighter units tasked with providing Spitfires or Hurricanes when required. It was, at best, an unco-ordinated overall organisation, almost wholly equipped with aircraft either unsuited, ill-equipped, or plainly useless for locating and destroying night bombers. New designs of aircraft for the role were about to be introduced to RAF squadrons; the outstanding example was the bulky Beaufighter with its (eventual) devastating armament of four 20mm cannons and six machine guns. The first Beaufighter went to Tangmere's Fighter Interception Unit on 12 August 1940 and flew its first operational sortie on the night of 7–8 September. The first Beaufighter kill came on 25 October by a 219 Squadron crew, but the first *radar*-assisted Beau victory was not to occur until 19–20 November when the redoubtable nightfighter ace John Cunningham of 604 Squadron accounted for a Junkers Ju 88.

From 7 September until mid-November the aerial onslaught against London continued with only occasional relief due to weather conditions preventing concentration of attacks in significant weight of numbers. In the main it must be said that German objectives were chiefly specific : London's dock areas and associated targets were the prime objects of attack. Inevitably, nearby civilian communities suffered heavily in terms of human and material losses, but deliberate indiscriminate bombing was not yet included in the Luftwaffe crews' terms of reference for raiding Britain. Nevertheless, to expect precision bombing of pinpoint targets by *any* bomber crew at this early stage of the air offensive was, to say the least, highly optimistic.

Airborne radar aids were still in their infancy, and the nearest equivalent technical assistance to accurate bombing in use by German crews was the so-termed 'X-system' of radio-direction beams brought into operational use from November 1940. Emanating from a *Knickebein* transmitter on the French coast, a radio beam was directed precisely at an English objective, while two other crossing beams were also sent out from a source much further north-east in France. A bomber crew flew along the original beam, receiving radio dots and dashes to indicate any deviation in course, left or right of the true flightpath, until it reached the point of intersection of the 'advance' signal of the other 'X' beams. This indicated a point roughly twelve miles from target and the next six miles were clock-timed. On reaching the intersection of the third, 'main' signal, the final bomb-run was virtually automatically timed up to the actual bomb-release point.

On the night of 14 November two squadrons of Heinkel He 111H-3s from KG100, fitted with this 'X' apparatus, spearheaded a concentrated attack on the ancient cathedral city of Coventry. A total of 449 bombers released 530 tons of high explosive and incendiary bombs into the heart of that city and devastated the area, a raid that was thereafter regarded as supreme example of German terror-raiding against a civil population.

On 12 October Hitler finally cancelled the intended invasion of England, but ordered the Luftwaffe to continue its 'pressure' on Britain, partly to maintain the illusion of a possible invasion, but no less to mask the intensive preparations then beginning for the attack on Russia. The six months of day and (mainly) night raids from September 1940 to February 1941 showed a steady decline in effort by the Luftwaffe as more of its French-based units were gradually transferred to the eastern front. Gross tonnage of bombs dropped on Britain during those months reflect this decline :

September 1940	7044
October 1940	9113
November 1940	6510
December 1940	4323
January 1941	2424
February 1941	1127

During the same period German bomber crews had flown well in excess of 30,000 individual sorties, an overall mean of some 170 sorties every twenty-four hours. The strain on air and ground crews, apart from the continuing wear and tear of such operations' density, was barely supportable in view of the lack of adequate aircraft and crew replacements then available to the Luftwaffe. Moreover, such strain was increasingly placed upon the shoulders of fewer squadrons as the general transfer of firstline units from France to the east increased in early 1941.

To the populations of London, Coventry, Liverpool, Birmingham, Manchester, Plymouth and a dozen other cities, any such 'decline' was not readily apparent. As the victims of Göring's determination to prove that air power alone could win a war, they were enduring an unprecedented air assault with little pause, by day and by night, and with an almost regular monotony. Often bereft of homes, essential necessities, and suffering tragic losses of family, relatives and close friends, the British civilian populace seemed to gather an inner, community strength of will from the common peril, and a new fellowship between all social classes developed, allied to a stubborn determination to 'fight on' whatever the Luftwaffe might do. Though often claimed as a spirit inherent in the British national character when fighting high odds against survival, it was by no means unique to the British, as was to be epitomised in the years ahead when in its turn the German civil population was forced to endure an Allied bombing offensive far greater in scope and weight.

'Business as usual' became almost a national motto as each dawn revealed fresh devastation in the cities of Britain, and civilian workers threaded their way to their place of business through fire-racked, bomb-broken, glass- and brick-carpeted streets and alleys. The normal raven-black cloak of winter night sky now became an almost permanent red and pink ceiling over target towns, a veritable backdrop in celestial form for scenes reminiscent of Dante's Inferno.

Apart from the diminishing number of *Geschwader* tasked with *'pressurising'* Britain through the winter nights of 1940/41, the Luftwaffe's offensive suffered overall by a lack of cohesive direction and successful concentration in attack. The raid on Coventry on 14 November, for one example, caused damage on a fearful scale to the inner city, killed some 554 people and seriously injured nearly 900 more. Yet within forty-eight hours much of the huge industrial production of aircraft and vehicles *et al* based in and around the city was resumed at near full pace. Had Göring repeated the raid on succeeding nights, such recovery might well have proved impossible, yet the following night the Luftwaffe switched its attentions mainly to Birmingham and other targets, thereby permitting an early resumption of Coventry's contribution to the war effort. This almost piecemeal selection of targets and failure to profit from the results of each initial heavy assault negated the ultimate intention of Göring's bombing offensive. Such an omission also had an unforeseen – by Göring – effect on future RAF bombing policies. By November 1940 RAF Bomber Command had begun a series of so-termed 'area attacks' against German economic and industrial centres with a partial intention of demoralising the German population while striking at more 'legitimate' military objectives. The stoical bearing of the British civilians of London, Coventry and other cities under the German air attacks of the 1940/41 winter gave ample evidence to RAF policy-makers of the will to resist which could result from any such onslaught.

Opposition to the German night-raiders throughout the winter remained relatively ineffective as RAF Fighter Command continued its struggle to perfect radar devices which would enable the nightfighter crews to intercept incoming bombers, along with devising the necessary air and ground organisation which would provide workable techniques in using such equipment successfully. Under the operational control of the commanders of Fighter Command throughout the war were the anti-aircraft guns and searchlights of the army, as were the balloons of Balloon Command from 1941; but these together claimed relatively few victims from the Luftwaffe formations – relative, that is, to the enormous energy and expense of maintaining these latter defensive measures. Shortages of adequate numbers of modern guns capable of reaching high-flying bombers hampered the AA force to a great extent, while the prime necessity of actually locating aircraft remained, for the moment, something akin to intelligent guesswork rather than scientifically calculated precision. The true antidote lay clearly in radar-equipped nightfighters with an allied ground organisation capable of directing them onto any 'bandit' accurately and in good time.

On 25 November 1940 Hugh Dowding was replaced at the head of RAF Fighter Command by Air Marshal Sholto Douglas, who inherited a nightfighting strength of eleven full squadrons, plus several 'special' units, all of which still awaited updated aircraft for their particular role. Immediately, Sholto Douglas requested an increase to at least 20 squadrons for night defence, plus all the requisite facilities for fitting out appropriate aerodromes from which these could operate, stretched along a belt from Newcastle to Devonshire.

Fulfilling Douglas's request could not be accomplished with any urgency; air crews trained to reasonable standards were simply not available without denuding other equally vital RAF commands, while supply of suitable aircraft – ideally Beaufighters – was still too slow to equip so many fresh units. In the interim, the existing Blenheim and Defiant crews continued their highly frustrating task of seeking the enemy 'by guess and God' in the night skies, with negligible results to show for their many hours of exhausting labours. The gradual introduction of a handful of GCI (Ground Controlled Interception) sets in 1940 began to show encouraging signs of an ability to direct nightfighting crews onto incoming bombers by early 1941, though actual success in shooting these down remained relatively small; of the 90 Luftwaffe aircraft lost over England during the three months January to March 1941, slightly less than a third were claimed by RAF fighters. The German night offensive, already weakening due to withdrawals of units to the eastern front, and suffering heavy maintenance and replacement problems, was further diminished in December 1940 and the early weeks of 1941 by near-impossible weather conditions. Only occasionally could individual heavy raids be carried out, with London remaining the principal target, though other cities each received destructive visits.

The apparent waning of the Luftwaffe's attacks, coupled with a steadily increasing success rate in RAF interception, appeared to some as a sign that Britain's nightly ordeal would soon be over. In early May 1941, however, the remaining German bomber units in France mounted a fresh series of particularly heavy raids against key ports and cities across Britain, virtually a final fling prior to Hitler's imminent moves against Russia. In strengths varying from more than a hundred up to more than 500 bombers, the Luftwaffe pressed home concentrated attacks which gave London and other cities some of the most destructive onslaughts of the entire blitz period.

The final raid on London, for example, occurred on 10 May, when 541 sorties were despatched (some of these being double trips by certain crews) which unloaded 711 tons of high explosive and 2,393 incendiary canisters into the heart of the capital. For a loss of 14 German bombers to the defences, this raid alone killed 1,436 people and seriously injured nearly 2,000 others. Some 10,000 houses or other domestic buildings were destroyed or heavily damaged, and more than 2,000 separate fires started, consuming *in toto* some 700 acres of the city. Six days later, on 16 May, a total force of 111 bombers raided Birmingham in Britain's industrial 'heart', dropping 160 tons of high explosive and merely 58 incendiary canisters. It was to be the ultimate attack of the long winter blitz – indeed, the last attack in any strength against Britain for nearly two years.

The agony of the long months' air siege suffered by the British civil population is reflected to some extent by the cold statistics of casualties and general destruction created. Nearly 44,000 civilians had been killed during bombing raids between early August 1940 and mid-May 1941, while a further 103,000 had been injured in varying degrees. Roughly two-thirds of all such casualties had occurred within the Greater London area, but in terms of percentage of actual population, Liverpool, Birmingham, Swansea and several other cities had suffered almost equally. Such a grim catalogue of tragedy might well have been expected – indeed, *was* expected by both German and British authorities prior to the war – to have reduced civilian morale to a point of surrender. In fact the very opposite occurred. Throughout Britain was born a determination not only to bear whatever Hitler might throw against the island kingdom, but to retaliate whenever opportunity occurred and, even more significantly, to see the war through to the bitter end whatever the cost.

In the context of the air struggle between the RAF and the Luftwaffe by night, there can be little quibbling with the conclusion that the RAF measures available made little impact upon German raiders. This in no way implies any lack of effort or hazard by the RAF nightfighter crews of the period, merely a lack of preparation and thereby suitable equipment by the pre-1939 authorities for any such night assault against Britain by air. By May 1941 clear indications of rapidly increasing successful measures against the German bombers were evident in the mounting nightly toll claimed by RAF nightfighter crews – too late to balance the grave deficiencies all too prevalent in previous months.

The cessation of the Luftwaffe's blitz after 16 May 1941 led to a somewhat complacent statement later by Sholto Douglas, who said, 'We were confident that if the enemy had not chosen that moment to pull out, we should soon have been inflicting such casualties on his night-bombers that the continuance of his night-offensive on a similar scale would have been impossible.'

Such an hypothesis at that time was, at best, over-optimistic. German losses throughout the ten months' night offensive had barely reached three per cent level overall, a completely supportable casualty rate in any bombing operations' context. Moreover, the bulk of those losses were to anti-aircraft guns, balloon barrages, accidents and a host of other minor causes, few were directly attributable to RAF air-to-air actions. Nevertheless, the basis for an expanding and increasingly successful nightfighter force had been established by mid-1941, and in later years was to accrue enormous advantages over the Luftwaffe as the aerial war progressed. The patient determination of the 1940/41 crews and their back-up organisation in pursuing their struggle for defeat of the darkness was to pay huge dividends in the future.

One facet of the night battles seldom mentioned in the many published accounts of the blitz period was the clandestine 'intruder' operations flown by fighters of both the Luftwaffe and the RAF. First in this particular field of operations during World War Two was the Luftwaffe, which with the twin-engined Dornier Do 17 and Junkers Ju 88s of Germany's only long-range nightfighter unit, *Nachtjagdgeschwader* 2, commenced intruder sorties against RAF bomber airfields in England during mid-1940. Between 1 October 1940 and 31 March 1941 the crews of NJG2 made some fifty individual attacks on Bomber

Command aircraft, destroying seven and severely damaging a further twenty.

Parallel raids against German airfield installations in France had been carried out by Bomber and Coastal Command aircraft during the summer and autumn of 1940, but the first RAF fighter intruder sorties were those of six Blenheims of 23 Squadron on the night of 21 December 1940. These patrolled the Abbeville/Amiens/Poix areas but sighted no German aircraft. On 2 January, however, Flying Officer P. S. B. Ensor of 23 Squadron sighted a Heinkel He 111 near Caen, trailed it to Dreux, attacked and saw it fall away apparently out of control. From March 1941 the squadron's slow Blenheims began being replaced by converted Douglas Bostons – named Havocs by the RAF – and the squadron commenced Havoc intruder sorties on 7 April.

While the RAF continued to add to its night air arm, the Luftwaffe, paradoxically, reduced its equivalent force. NJG2, though initially intended to be built up to full *Geschwader* strength in aircraft and crews – in December 1940 Göring even gave his personal permission for Josef Kammhuber to form a total of three long-range *Nachtjäger Geschwader* – became a victim of Hitler's private disbelief in the effectiveness of long-range intruder sorties and was consequently refused authority to expand. Thus the German intruder force of 1940–41 never enlarged beyond *Gruppe* level. Indeed, in November 1940, I/NJG2 had only 15 aircraft at its disposal for operations, and by February was down to seven machines. This mere handful of intrepid crews not only caused direct losses among RAF bomber and night-training aircraft, but created far wider morale effects among RAF bomber crews than operating against German targets. To Hitler such success meant little; the nightfighters must shoot down RAF 'terror-raiders' (sic) over *Germany*, where the civil population could witness such victories. Accordingly, in October 1941, he forbade any further intruder operations over Britain, and the *Gruppe* was shortly after transferred to Sicily for more normal duties in the Mediterranean theatre of war.

At 0315 hours on Sunday, 22 June 1941, Hitler's long-dreamed of armed invasion of Russia, code-named Operation Barbarossa, commenced officially, though nearly thirty hand-picked veteran bomber crews were already airborne before that 'zero hour' en route to strafe selected Russian fighter airfields. At that moment the Luftwaffe had deployed 1,945 aircraft (sixty-one per cent of total strength) for the initial hammer-blow, of which total 1,280 were considered fully serviceable. Estimated strength of the Russian air force was at least double such a figure; one German intelligence report claimed Russian air opposition to be as high as 12,000 machines.

At first light the Luftwaffe struck in full strength at every known Russian airfield and achieved total surprise. By noon the Russians had lost more than 2,000 aircraft destroyed, nearly eighty per cent while still earthbound. The Luftwaffe's losses amounted to 35 aircraft. It was an incredible victory – almost certainly the greatest ever achieved by one air force against another in the annals of military aviation. Subsequent air operations in direct tactical support of the invading German armies produced equally startling mass victories in air combat as the Russian fighters and bombers were destroyed in droves by Luftwaffe fighters. The whole air plan was a repetition of the *Blitzkrieg* tactics of the 1939–40 German campaigns in Poland and France, only on a vaster geographical scale. The difference now was that, in spite of German optimism that the Russian invasion would prove victorious within some six weeks, the Luftwaffe had in the main been committed to a sustained, long-term war for which it was never designed. The Eastern Front – within less than a year to be regarded by all German forces as a dreaded posting – was to prove a bottomless pit, draining the life-blood of Germany's young manhood, including vast resources in men and machines and material for the Luftwaffe which would be needed desperately by the air defences of the German homeland from 1943 until the end of the war.

By concentrating the major percentage of total Luftwaffe strength along the eastern zones of operations in 1941, Göring inevitably left only a small proportion allocated for day and night defence of Germany and German-occupied Europe. By ceasing intruder and bomber offensive operations against England, he had also permitted the Allies near-complete freedom from interference to build their air strength in Britain as a fortress-base for future offensives against Germany from the west. Hitler's fatal move against Russia – thereby committing Germany to war on two major fighting fronts – was the beginning of the end for the Third Reich.

CHAPTER SIX

Seek and Destroy

With the ending of the 1940/41 blitz against Britain, and a coincidental final shift of main air strength to the Russian venture in the east, Luftwaffe units still based on French soil tasked with facing the RAF in defence of Germany and German-occupied territories were thin and widely dispersed. The RAF, gradually gathering momentum in its programmes of recovery from the disastrous losses of 1940, maintained a relatively small but constant pressure with night bombing raids against Germany itself; and Fighter Command, already much healthier in numerical terms than during the peak of the Battle of Britain, cautiously commenced a fresh policy advocated by the Air Staff in general and its new commander, Sholto Douglas, in particular, of 'leaning forward' into France and the Low Countries.

Apart from its value as a boost to RAF morale by going over to a true offensive after a year of desperate defensive operations, deliberate taunting of the Luftwaffe over its own territory was hoped to assist the Russian cause by forcing Göring to maintain reasonably strong air forces in the west, away from the new eastern front. The first such sorties by RAF fighters were despatched on 20 December 1940, when two Spitfires of 66 Squadron left their Biggin Hill base and strafed the German airfield at Le Touquet. A week later another Spitfire duo, from 92 Squadron, scoured the Abbeville area and had to be content with a low-level raking of a German vehicle convoy.

The new RAF policy for air offensive was put into practice in two main forms. Fighter Command's independent roving operations, code-named Rhubarbs, sought direct Luftwaffe fighter opposition, and continued through most of 1941 as a straightforward fighter offensive, with the added 'spice' of ground-strafing attacks for variation. The second form, coded Circus, was more complex and involved both Fighter and Bomber Commands. Medium-range (at first) bombers were briefed for daylight attacks on French targets, but were heavily escorted by whole wings of Spitfires and Hurricanes. The theory was simple : the bombers were to be live bait to tempt the Luftwaffe up into a battle of attrition with the RAF fighters. In practice, the bomber crews soon became disenchanted with being cast in a mere carrot-on-a-stick role, while German fighter opposition, though violent on occasion, tended to be spasmodic and only offered when the crews of the *Jagdgeschwader* considered the prevailing conditions to be shaded in their favour. Indeed, most circumstances were essentially in the Luftwaffe's favour in such daylight sorties – plentiful pre-warning of incoming RAF 'sweeps' from coastal radar listening posts, a choice of actual battle engagement area if needed, and the only possibilities for surprise tactics in the capable hands of the German fighter leaders. Had German fighter strength in the west been significantly larger in 1941, such RAF sorties might well have proved as disastrously unprofitable as the German forays into English skies in the previous year.

The whole air scene over France was, in essence, an exact reversal of the operations over England during the Battle of Britain. Despite the overall intention of a fighter attrition struggle, the Spitfires and Hurricanes were virtually leashed to slower, cumbersome bomber formations and thereby prevented from exploiting to the full the initiative and flexibility so necessary for any fighter pilot if he is to fulfil the succinct role for which he had been solely trained. Only the pure fighter Rhubarbs gave him such elbow room for freedom of action, yet these type of sorties were despatched infrequently and in relatively mild strength only. By the late summer of 1941 the value of Circus operations was being seriously questioned by RAF higher authorities. Casualties were high during the initial weeks, due mainly to the RAF's inexperience in planning and mounting such operations, and subsequent losses remained disturbingly high as the organisational complexities became even more of a problem. On the face of it, the Circus type of offensive *appeared* to be achieving its over-riding purpose i.e. wearing down the Luftwaffe in the west. Claims by RAF fighter pilots for the six weeks of June–July 1941 for 322 enemy aircraft destroyed seemed to balance the loss of 123 RAF fighter pilots in 46 such operations. In fact, the RAF claims' total was highly exaggerated and represented a higher figure than the entire German fighter strength in the west at that period. Indeed, claims by RAF fighter pilots for the whole period from 14 June 1941 until the end of the year amounted to 731 German aircraft (mainly fighters) destroyed, whereas actual Luftwaffe losses for the same period were 103 destroyed by daytime RAF sorties, 11 others 'missing' from operations over England, and a further 51 written-off due to non-related causes.

In balance the RAF lost 426 fighter pilots killed, missing or known to be prisoners of war. Such a grim figure was bad enough, but was doubly tragic in that many of the pilots actually killed or taken prisoner were veterans of the French campaign and the Battle of Britain, men who by 1941 were flight or squadron commanders providing the hard-core 'spine' of irreplaceable experience needed to nurture and educate the growing influx of fresh young pilots now reaching the frontline squadrons. This ratio of success in the Luftwaffe's favour – almost four to one – was all the more remarkable when it is remembered that German fighter strength in France then was at its lowest numerical level since the beginning of the war. Those few *Geschwader* facing the RAF in the west were, however, led by well-experienced veterans – men like Adolf Galland of JG26 who had fought through the Spanish Civil War and every subsequent campaign, and who registered his 70th confirmed combat victory on 21 June 1941, his third *Luftsieg* of that particular day. With such seasoned fighting leaders, the Luftwaffe fighter units displayed guile and skill in their daily clashes with numerically superior formations, helped to a great extent by the receipt of improved and new designs of aircraft. By mid-1941 the Messer-schmitt Bf 109F variant was well in service, and by August an entirely new fighter type, the radial-engined Focke Wulf Fw 109 entered the lists.

Opposing these fighters the RAF had introduced the Spitfire Mk V and Hurricane Mk II. The latter was clearly out-classed by the latest German designs and was accordingly relegated mainly to low-level fighter-bomber operations; but the Fw 190 immediately outflew and outfought the contemporary Spitfires at all levels, giving the Luftwaffe a decided edge in technical superiority for many months to come. The only fresh RAF fighter-design brought into operations by the close of 1941 were both armed with batteries of four 20mm cannons: the twin-engined Westland Whirlwind, introduced in December 1940 but which equipped only two squadrons for low-level escort duties, and the brutish-looking Hawker Typhoon, which entered RAF firstline service slowly from September 1941 but was fated to undergo pro-longed teething troubles for another year or more before becoming truly effective on any wide scale.

A third facet of the RAF's offensive outlook in 1941 involved the concerted efforts of Fighter, Bomber and Coastal Commands to pre-vent enemy shipping traffic using the English Channel and other Euro-pean coastal waters – in simple terms, added muscle to the Royal Navy's continuing attempts to impose a sea blockade of all imports to Germany and her conquered territories. Such merchant shipping life-lines were vital to the German war effort, and were invariably heavily escorted by air cover and flanking, heavily-armed flak-ships. Code-named Roadstead by the RAF, a campaign of anti-shipping sorties was intensified throughout 1941. Light and medium bombers under-took bombing or torpedo attacks at zero height against the armoured, well-alerted flak-ships and merchant vessels, flying head-on into a lattice-work of murderous tracers and cannon shells to press home a pointblank attack. Spearheading the bombers were the escorting fighters, warding off Luftwaffe fighter interference and attempting to smother the deadly flak-gunners' defiance in order to let the bombers complete their near-suicidal tasks.

Roadstead casualties were high, but the heaviest toll was to be suffered by the doughty crews of No 2 Group's Blenheims who bore appalling losses. During August 1941 alone, of 77 aircraft of 2 Group attacking German ships, 23 were lost – a casualty rate of some 30 per cent; of 480 individual sorties flown that month by this Group, 36 aircraft failed to return. Such insupportable loss rates forced the with-drawal of 2 Group from Roadstead sorties by late October 1941, though the Fighter and Coastal Command effort continued. Postwar research reveals that the overall Roadstead offensive achieved com-paratively little material loss to enemy shipping; totals of 29 ships sunk and a further 21 seriously damaged – less than a third of the contem-porary, cautious claims by the British Air Ministry and Admiralty.

If the overall picture of the RAF's offensive from mid-1941 ap-peared gloomy in the contexts of casualties and results achieved, it was nevertheless a year of invaluable testing and training for both Fighter and Bomber Command. Had the operations gained nothing else, they remained a period of intensive and varied activity for the air crews, their commanders and planners. Moreover, it was a period in which many thousands of newly-operational pilots and crews accumulated their first hard taste of fighting experience, lessons learned in a way that not even the finest instructional syllabus could provide. Whether groping through the midnight blackness seeking an elusive enemy bomber, plunging through a hail of flak shells to attack a ship, weaving through the probing beams of searchlights and racing red necklaces of anti-aircraft fire above the Ruhr, or grappling in the azure blue of a sunlit sky with a flock of yellow-nosed Messerschmitts wheel-ing to kill, each air crew member faced death for the first time with apprehension, and then swiftly adapted mentally and physically to the constant repetition of the hazards of aerial warfare.

The actual battle zones of that summer and autumn were relatively small in area. The limit of operational penetration into France by 1941

RAF fighters was little more than seventy miles, thus giving the Luftwaffe counterparts a slim coastal strip to protect. Bomber sorties flying any deeper into enemy-occupied country had to accept the overt risk of completing their tasks bereft of any fighter escort beyond that coastal battle area. In daylight this form of 'press-on' attitude simply invited disaster for the bomber crews, only the shield of darkness offered any real protection to bombing crews of the time.

Notwithstanding a sobering crop of casualties in men and aircraft throughout the various forms of offensive operations of 1941, the RAF had little alternative but to continue such 'forward' sorties. Despite outstanding efforts by the aircraft production industries, the RAF had yet to attain anything like sufficient strength to contemplate any form of real strategic air warfare; moreover its main striking arm, Bomber Command, was not only under-strength but still relying on obsolescent aircraft for attacking Germany.

The eagerly-awaited advent of the promised four-engined heavy bombers came very slowly to operational squadrons. First of the new giants was the mammoth Short Stirling, the first example for unit use going to 7 Squadron as early as 7 August 1940 as a conversion trainer for crews. By the end of the year, however, 7 Squadron had only six Stirlings on strength, all non-operational as yet, and each giving myriad headaches to both air and ground crews because of technical defects. In the air a loaded Stirling was remarkably manoeuvrable but crews soon realised that the aircraft lacked safe ceiling altitude for bombing sorties. The bomber's first operations were flown by three of 7 Squadron's trainers on 10 February 1941, against Rotterdam, but continuing unserviceability problems restricted Stirling operations for many weeks thereafter. On 9 April three more Stirlings set out, rather ambitiously, to bomb Berlin. One aborted at the Dutch coast with propeller trouble, a second aborted the sortie with engine trouble, while the third (N6011) was shot down near Lingen by Feldwebel Scherling of 7/NJG1.

Anxious to strengthen the Circus daylight offensive, the Air Ministry pressed for use of the Stirling on such sorties, and Stirlings were first used by day from 27 April. Three days later a second Stirling-equipped unit, 15 Squadron, commenced operations by night, sending a total of nine Stirlings to Berlin. One crashed on return, while several others bombed alternative objectives. Engine and other defects continued to restrict Stirling operations, while those few managing to lift a bomb-load as far as Germany found the aircraft's dangerously low operating ceiling forced them to run a constant gauntlet of flak and nightfighters. In the early hours of 11 May, N3654 of 15 Squadron became another victim of poor performance when it was attacked eight times by a Messerschmitt Bf 110 of NJG/1, piloted by Prinz zur Lippe-Weissenfeld. The crew, including the squadron commander, Wing Commander Dale, were forced to bale out over Holland when the Stirling erupted in flames. Mainly night operations continued spasmodically until 5 July, on which date the Stirling was first used on a Circus operation. Within less than three weeks Stirlings were taken off Circus sorties – losses and poor weather had created – in a 15 Squaddon report's words – '. . . a colossal waste of effort, fuel and bombs'; though normal daylight operations continued thereafter.

The second 'heavy' to enter RAF squadron service was the chunky Handley Page Halifax; the first example was collected on 13 November 1940 for delivery to the recently-reformed 35 Squadron at Boscombe Down. Subsequent equipment and training progress by 35 Squadron paralleled the Stirling saga; slow production of aircraft for the unit and a seemingly endless tale of technical woes. On 10 March 1941, however, seven of 35 Squadron's Halifaxes were sent off to bomb Le Havre as the initial 'Hallie' operational venture. One aborted on take-off with hydraulic failure, one bombed an alternative target, a third jettisoned its bombload in the Channel, while a fourth (L9489/F) was shot down by a *British* nightfighter over Surrey, killing all but two of its crew.

For the next three months only isolated sorties were possible, due mainly to technical faults, but operations were renewed by 35 Squadron from 11 June when nine Halifaxes were despatched to Duisburg with modest success. Meantime a second Halifax unit, 76 Squadron, commenced reforming in April 1941 and, based at Middleton St George, began its Halifax operations on 12 June.

A third 'heavy' intended to give added 'beef' to the long arm of Bomber Command was the twin-engined Avro Manchester. On 1 November 1940 No 207 Squadron was reformed for the specific purpose of introducing the Manchester to operational service, and the unit's first example was duly delivered to Waddington on 10 November. By 14 February the following year, 1941, the squadron could muster a total of 18 aircraft; on this date six of the unit's Manchesters were sent on their initial sorties, a hastily-arranged raid against a reported *Hipper*-class cruiser in Brest harbour. All six managed to return but one crashed on landing due to faulty hydraulics, the beginning of a lengthy, dismal saga of similar defects which were to dog the Manchester throughout the following sixteen months of firstline ser-

1. PZL P.11s of No 122 ('Paper Horse' insigne) Squadron, Polish Air Force in September 1939.

2. The notorious Junkers Ju 87 *Stuka* dive-bomber.

3. A *Rotte* ('Pair' or 'Cell') of Messerschmitt Bf 109Bs - the basic fighting unit of the Luftwaffe's fighter tactics.

4. Amiot 143 bombers of the *Armèe de L'Air* in early 1940.

5. Morane-Saulnier MS 406 fighters of a French *escadrille*, early 1940.

6. Hawker Hurricanes of *2-eme Escadrille*, Belgian Air Force, at Schaffen-Diest airfield. This was the scene which greeted German bombers on 10 May 1940 as they strafed the airfield from the direction of the woods in the far background.

7. Fairey Battle L5540, JN-C, of 150 Squadron RAF which was one of the first to be shot down on 10 May 1940.

8. Messerschmitt Bf 110 of II/ZG 76 '*Haifische*' ('Shark') group, flying along the English south coast in the summer of 1940.

9. Spitfire of 602 Squadron, Auxiliary Air Force in 1940, being re-armed and prepared for further combat.

10. Air Chief Marshal Sir (later, Lord) Hugh Dowding, commander of RAF Fighter Command from 1936 to 1940 - the architect of the RAF's victory in 1940.

11. Third of Bomber Command's doughty designs in the early war years was the Vickers Wellington - or 'Wimpy' as it was dubbed by its crews. This example, T2835, AA-C, belonged to No 75 (New Zealand) Squadron in 1940.

12. Scoreboard. Pilots of No 85 Squadron RAF, early 1941 with a propeller blade from a German victim acting as the unit victory tally. From left: Hemingway, Howett, Marshall, Carnaby. Kneeling is the unit commander Sqn Ldr Peter Townsend, DFC with the unit Alsatian mascot 'Kim'.

13. North American B-25C 'Mitchell' (FV985) of 98 Squadron RAF.

14. Short Stirling – the first of the RAF's four-engined heavy bombers to enter operational service.

15. Second RAF 'heavy' to join operational squadrons was the angular Handley Page Halifax; in this view, during a daylight raid on a synthetic oil plant at Wanne-Eickel.

16. Precursor of the Avro Lancaster was its stable-mate the twin-engined Manchester, which saw operational service 1941-42. This machine is L7515 of No 207 Squadron, based at Waddington in 1941.

17. Avro Lancaster NG347, QB-P, 'Princess Pat' of No 424 Squadron RCAF with H2S scanner under fuselage.

18. Air Chief Marshal (later, MRAF) Sir Arthur Harris, KCB, OBE, AFC, known affectionately to his crews as 'Butch', who commanded RAF Bomber Command from 1942-45.

19. A Lancaster of a main bomber stream over Germany gets a direct hit by flak – seven men have just died. Photo taken on 19 February 1945.

20. How some came back. Lancaster C-Charlie of No 101 Squadron RAF which crash-landed at Ludford Magna airfield on return from a sortie. The pipe-lines evident were part of the airfield's FIDO (fog dispersal) petrol installation.

21. Focke Wulf Fw 190A-4 of II/JG2 at dispersal.

22. Lieutenant Joseph 'Sepp' Wurmheller, *Staffelkapitän* of 9/JG2 and his Focke Wulf Fw 190, with 18 *Luftsieg* (victories) marked on the fighter's rudder, surmounted by his full score (then) of 60, and a Knight's Cross emblem.

23. Adolf Galland (in white jacket) with other *Luftwaffe Experten* fighter pilots.

24. Boeing B-17G Fortress of the 524th BS, 379th BG, 1st Air Division USAAF, based at Kimbolton in 1944. This aircraft has the later 'Cheyenne' tail gun turret fitted.

25. Consolidated B-24J-145-CO Liberator of the 565th BS, 389th BG, 2nd Air Division, USAAF, based at Hethell in late 1943-early 1944.

26. 'Little Friend'. Republic P-47C-5 Thunderbolt at Kingscliffe in March 1943. The white bands on tail and nose were ETO (European Theater of Operations) markings to distinguish the early P-47s from Focke Wulf Fw 190s in the heat of combat.

27. North American P-51D (nearest) and P-51Bs of the 359th FG at East Wretham, late 1944 – the magnificent Mustangs.

28. Box bombing. B-17Fs of the 390th BG – the 569th BS – from Framlingham commence a bombing pattern over Germany, circa late 1943.

29. Precision bombing. B-17s of the 390th Bomb Group over the Focke Wulf aircraft assembly plant at Marienburg on 9 October 1943 – part of a 350 – aircraft attack which cost 28 bombers shot down.

30. Victim. B-24H Liberator, 'Little Warrior', of the 493rd BG gets flak in its fuel tanks over Quakenbrück on 29 June 1944.

31. Battle souvenir. A cheerful Bf 109G-5 pilot with a 'souvenir' from one of his USAAF bomber victims.

32. Two 'Ton-Up' Lancasters, ED860, QR-N of 61 Sqn, and ED588, VN-G, of 50 Squadron, which eventually completed 118 and 116 sorties respectively.

33. An Ammunition depot north of Falaise receives the attention of Halifaxes and Lancasters, late 1944.

34. Loaded for game. Beaufighters of 236 Squadron, RAF Coastal Command in October 1944, with full complements of 3-inch rockets prior to an anti-shipping strike sortie.

35. *Nachtjäger* – Messerschmitt Bf 110G-4b/R3 with revised SN-2 radar array for the G-4d/R3, and belly cannon-tray.

36. Nightfighters. *Hauptmann* zur Lippe-Weissenfeld, Major Lent, Major Herrmann and *Hauptmann* Meurer, four noted German nightfighter *Kanonen* with the *Luftwaffe* commander-in-chief Hermann Göring, September 1943.

37. Dornier Do 217J-2 nightfighter of 4/NJG3, based at Svlt, in October 1943.

38. Air Chief Marshal Sir Arthur Tedder, supreme air commander of the Allied air forces which participated in the invasion of Normandy in 1944.

39. Loading a Typhoon of No 247 Squadron RAF with 3-inch rockets, France, July 1944.

40.(Bottom left) The scene at Pforzheim on the night of 23/24 February 1945. The Master Bomber for this raid, Captain Edwin Swales, SAAF of No 582 Squadron, PFF, was killed and later awarded a posthumous Victoria Cross.

41. The notorious target of the Dortmund-Ems canal, a constant objective for the RAF from 1940, seen utterly destroyed by 1945.

42. Some of the USAAF's highest-scoring fighter aces, 56th FG, 1944. Standing foreground, from left: FS Gabreski, R. Johnson, Walker, M. Mahurin, R. B. Landry. Seated on wing: W. A. Cook and D. C. Schilling.

43. 'Black Nan', a B-24L Liberator of the 779th BS, 464th BG of the USAAF's 15th Air Force receives a direct hit from 88mm flak over northern Italy on 9 April 1945. The shock turned the bomber onto its back, throwing clear Lieutenant E. F. Walsh, radar bombardier, the only crew survivor.

44. Messerschmitt Me 262A-1a '*Schwalbe*' ('Swallow') twin-jet fighter.

45. Messerschmitt Me 163 '*Komet*' was a rocket propelled fighter designed to intercept the Allied bomber formations. It had only sufficient fuel for seven minutes powered flying time and had to make a glided landing. Any unused fuel left in the tanks could cause an explosion upon landing.

46. Heinkel He 162 '*Volksjäger*' ('People's Fighter') twin-jet fighter. In the last few months of the war 116 were produced, but they saw only a few weeks of action.

47. Accuracy. Heligoland Bight under bombardment by a Lancaster force on 18 April 1945, viewed from 19,000 feet. Photo taken by Flying Officer Johns in Lancaster 'O-Orange' of No 153 Squadron RAF.

48. The strike Wings of RAF Coastal Command maintained their long-range anti-shipping offensive until the end of hostilities; exemplified here by Mosquito 'A-Apple' of No 143 Squadron strafing targets at Sandefiord, Norway on 2 April 1945.

49. Mercy bomber. B-17G of 569th BS, 390th BG, Eighth Air Force dropping food supplies to Dutch civilian May 1945.

vice. As its crews were to discover quickly, the Manchester suffered from being designed to take twin Rolls-Royce Vulture engines, untried, almost experimental powerplants which were to be a constant source of troubles. In simplest terms, the Vultures were unreliable, and almost always failed to produce sufficient 'urge' to give the bomber a respectable performance. Maximum altitude obtainable in a bomb-loaded Manchester was often no higher than 7,000 feet, a height which left Manchester crews completely at the mercy of the flak and nightfighters over Germany. Supplemented by such items as leaking hydraulics, defective engine feathering controls, and even complete fins' fabric calmly shedding in flight, and the prospect of flying operations in Manchesters was understandably disconcerting . . .

Notwithstanding its evil reputation among Bomber Command crews, the Manchester – without its Vulture engines – was a fine aircraft design basically, a fact recognised from the start of its career, and thereby encouraging its designers to continue its potential development. Doubts about the Vulture powerplants were felt by the parent company even before the first Manchester had been manufactured, and several alternatives were considered by 1939, including an expanded-wing variant, originally titled 'Manchester III', with four Rolls Royce Merlin engines. From this latter train of thought was to evolve the Avro Lancaster, the RAF's finest bomber of World War Two. Nevertheless, the Lancaster was not to reach its first operational squadron until December 1941 leaving Bomber Command with three newly-introduced heavy bomber designs none of which showed any particular promise as war winners, and the existing, rapidly wearing mixture of Wellingtons, Hampdens, and sundry lesser types with which to prosecute the war. To discontinue employing any of these aircraft – 'warts and all' – would have seriously crippled Bomber Command's gradual mounting assault on Germany in 1941; hence the bomber commanders had no option but to persevere with ironing out the snags in the latest designs, and extend the working lives of the remaining obsolescent aircraft at the sharp end of the air offensive.

Before the year was out, 1941 saw the arrival on firstline strength of Bomber Command of the initial examples of two new types of bomber which were to be highly significant in the near future. On 15 November the first DH Mosquito light bomber version (W4064) was delivered to 105 Squadron at Swanton Morley, Norfolk; and on 24 December three Avro Lancasters (L7530, L7537 and L7538) arrived at Waddington, Lincoln, where they joined the prototype Lancaster (BT308) on the strength of 44 Squadron for conversion and working-up training of future Lancaster crews. Within a year both types of bomber were to represent a major factor in Bomber Command's efforts to mount a telling air offensive against Germany, but in early 1942 the command was as yet far from ready for any such all-out assault. As the new year commenced Bomber Command had a gross total of 58 squadrons, though seven of these were non-operational for various reasons, and others were often under-strength. In all the command could only call on little more than 600 serviceable, operationally-fit aircraft on any given night, and less than 100 of these were four-engined heavy bombers.

Such was the situation inherited by Air Vice-Marshal Arthur Harris on 23 February 1942 when he became the command's fourth Air Officer Commanding-in-Chief (AOC-in-C) within a year. Harris, who was to remain AOC-in-C. Bomber Command for the remaining years of the war, soon found that shortage of aircraft was by no means his only problem in his latest task.

Apart from the pressure of increasing demands by Coastal Command and the Admiralty for bomber squadrons to be diverted to the vital anti-submarine war in the Atlantic, Harris's command in the two and a half years' operations up until his appointment had produced relatively little success to show for the unquestioned courage and determination of its crews. Despite many claims made all in good faith by the crews to have attacked various key objectives and created vast damage, reconnaissance photographs clearly indicated that too high a proportion of the bombs dropped over Germany had not hit designated targets; indeed, few were even within ten miles of specified aiming points. The main failure was navigational accuracy. Using standard pre-1939 methods of astro-navigation and 'Dead Reckoning', the crews had no way of locating or bombing targets during anything but perfect weather conditions. To expect crews to attack precise targets in such circumstances was, to say the least, optimistic. Thus, the area bombing policy initiated in late 1940 by Bomber Command was in reality a tacit admittance of the command's overall inability to do anything else. Only by day could bomber crews even hope to destroy pinpointed objectives, and the appalling casualties imposed on daylight sorties during the first year of the war had clearly indicated the folly of such a form of air offensive by the RAF. Yet operations by night continued to produce little significant result. As merely one example, during eight raids against Essen from 8 March to 12 April 1942, almost ninety per cent of all bombers despatched had dropped their bombs from five to 100 miles away from the actual designated target area.

The glaring need for accurate navigation aids had been recognised much earlier by both the Luftwaffe and the RAF. In 1940 German bombing raids had occasionally been preceded by crews from *Kampfgruppe* 100, a specially formed 'pathfinder-marking' force, which had its Heinkels fitted with the radio direction-beam apparatus code-named 'X'. Co-ordinated with a second *Knickebein* transmitter beam, the 'X' apparatus enabled spot-on location of bomb-release point over precise targets, as exemplified in the 'terror' raid against Coventry. It was to be August 1941 before the RAF bombers were to commence use of a similar aid – Gee – which was not only accurate within its range limits but was independent of weather conditions. Gee-aircraft first fixed the bombing point, and were then backed up by a small force of 'illuminators', bombers which showered the 'fix' with incendiary loads as a visual marker for the following main force of raiders. Though the Gee-crews were delighted with the new device – among other things, it helped enormously in the return journey to base – it had distinct limitations; the most significant was that it could be jammed by enemy radio. RAF authorities estimated that within six months Gee would be useless for operations because of German jamming, and pressed ahead with development of Oboe, a ground-controlled blind-bombing device which was to prove remarkably accurate when used in conjuction with several new Target Indicator (TI) pyrotechnic 'bombs' then being produced for target-marking and illumination. The first Oboe operations did not take place until 20/21 December 1942, however, and in the interim several important factors affected the future of Harris's command.

Primarily, Harris was concerned with not only enlarging and improving his force, but actually preserving it intact as an offensive strike force. The mounting clamour from army, navy and political circles for dispersal of Bomber Command into a variety of purely tactical adjunct formations with other services and commands threatened the very existence of Bomber Command as a separate entity. Harris accordingly decided upon a series of three highly concentrated bombing attacks against German cities as a demonstration of the bombers' potential. Each was to be undertaken by a force of '1,000 bombers' – a figure unheard of in bomber annals, and one calculated to achieve maximum publicity for Bomber Command. The first such 'thousand-bomber raid' was designated to attack the cathedral city of Cologne on the night of 30/31 May 1942, followed by Essen on 1/2 June and Bremen on 25/26 June. For the Cologne 'opener', Harris's staff scraped the barrel of Bomber Command strength to produce the magic figure of 1,000 aircraft and crews. It meant combing the Operational Training Units (OTUs) as well as a 'maximum effort' by all operational squadrons, and in the event a total force of 1,046 bombers, plus 88 intruders, was despatched to Cologne.

In three very concentrated waves, the bulk of this force devastated Cologne. Over 21,000 homes were destroyed or seriously damaged, 2,000 commercial and industrial premises wrecked, 36 major factories destroyed and 300 others severely damaged, 469 people killed and nearly 5,000 more injured. The RAF lost 44 aircraft en route and a further seven which crashed on return to England. In less than two hours the RAF had created higher casualties and damage than the gross figures for more than 100 previous raids on the same target.

The propaganda effect of this massive blow nullified all further attempts to dismember Bomber Command, thereby achieving Harris's prime motive for what in effect was a confidence trick. Had the raid failed to inflict serious destruction, or RAF casualties been appreciably higher, such raids could never have been mounted again for years. Moreover, it is a moot point whether Bomber Command would have retained its individual identity as a whole striking force. Harris's enormous gamble had paid off. The second and third 'Thousand-Plan' raids achieved no such success, due mainly to weather conditions, but this mattered little in the long view : the *apparent* ability of the RAF to despatch such heavy forces gave chilling warning to the German military and civil hierarchy of possible repetition on an escalating scale in the future. The Luftwaffe could take little comfort from its claims of thirty-seven of the Cologne raiders shot down by flak or nightfighters; the *Nachtjäger* force under Kammhuber was still far short of even adequate strength to attempt significant defence of Germany against bombing assault, by day or by night. Hitler – and therefore the toadying Göring – still refused to recognise any urgency for a build-up of aerial defence of the Reich; hence Kammhuber's constant requests for more and better equipment, personnel *et al* were in the main refused or diluted by higher command.

The achievements of German nightfighters, in view of the various restrictions placed upon them, were not inconsiderable during the first years of the war. Night victories had leapt from 42 during the year 1940 to a total of 421 in 1941 and further rose to 687 in the year 1942. However, compared directly with the escalation in the RAF's bombing effort against the German homeland during 1941–42, such figures actually reflected a decline in success rate in the context of the increased number of RAF bombers despatched during 1942.

At that stage of the air war, with the RAF still well below requisite numerical strength for any sustained all-out air offensive, and the American air potential still eighteen months away from even beginning to have any telling effect in Europe, Germany could have invested in a night defence force which would have imposed intolerable cost on any aerial incursions over German territory. That the German high command chose not to do this at that period was partly based on the illusion that the war against Russia would quickly prove victorious, thereby releasing vast material and personnel resources for any defence of Germany's western 'front'. It was no less in accord with the belief by certain German senior commanders that a purely defensive air war against superior odds in numbers could never succeed – despite RAF Fighter Command's overt demonstration of the opposite conclusion during the summer of 1940.

The 1,000-bomber raids of May–June 1943 marked the real beginning of the new-wave RAF bombing offensive against Germany, which under the blunt direction of 'Butch' Harris was aimed at the total subjugation of German morale and the will to resist, apart from hoped-for crippling of German industrial capacity to continue the war. By mid-1942 RAF Bomber Command was receiving increasing numbers of Lancasters, Halifaxes, Mosquitos in its firstline squadrons, aircraft of greater lifting capacity for the heavier bombs and radar aids entering service and possessing wider range of operation.

In addition, in August 1942, a fresh formation was created within the command tasked with solving the many problems of accuracy in target location and marking for main force bombers. This was the Path Finder Force (PFF), commanded by a 32-years old Australian-born navigational expert, Don Bennett. Initially comprised of four squadrons, the PFF was to grow in strength and expertise over the following years, and spearheaded the bulk of major raids throughout the remaining war years with mounting success. Creation of the PFF originally had been accomplished against Harris's expressed objections to having any form of elite sub-formation within his command, but his views were over-ruled by the Air Staff.

The year 1942 also heralded a completely new threat to Germany : the arrival of the first elements of the American Eighth Air Force in England. Even before America's entry into the war against the Axis powers, plans had been initiated for eventual USA participation in the European war. Intended partly as a proving ground for the USAAF's doctrine of high-altitude *daylight* precision bombing, but also as a necessary pre-requisite for a possible land invasion of Hitler's Europe by mid-1943 at the earliest, an ultimate force of some 3,500 American bombers and fighters was planned to be available based in the United Kingdom by mid-1943. Preceded by various batches of administrative personnel, the first USAAF bombers began arriving in England in July 1942. On 17 August a total of 12 Boeing B-17Es, with heavy fighter escort, made the Eighth Air Force's first bombing mission against the Rouen-Sotteville marshalling yards in France, and all returned safely to base. The American eagle had been 'blooded'.

In view of the later heavy commitment of the USAAF's heavy bombers to the Allied strategic air offensive against Germany, it should be emphasised that in 1942 the object of basing USAAF air power in Britain was still as a preliminary strike force to prepare the way for an invasion of Europe, and was *not*, at that stage, envisaged as simply slotting in to any form of strategic aerial war alone. The overall stubborn determination by USAAF commanders to prove the efficacy of *daytime* precision bombing was looked at askance by experienced RAF bomber personnel – memories of the tragic toll of similar daylight sorties in 1939–41 still lingered clearly – but co-operation between the RAF and USAAF at every level and in all facets of training, intelligence, organisation, equipment *et al* was virtually 100 per cent from the beginning. The USAAF air crews had much to learn in even routine matters of wartime aerial operations, and willingly adopted various RAF methods during the initial months. Whatever the American airmen might have lacked in sheer experience was, however, more than compensated by a general impatience, even eagerness to 'get into the war', an attitude thoroughly approved by otherwise slightly sceptical RAF bomber veterans of the time.

Though the 'American invasion' of England started in earnest in 1942, it is often forgotten that among the multi-nationals threaded throughout RAF air crews during the period 1939–42 were no small numbers of American citizens. Ostensibly neutral until the USA entry into the war in December 1941, such men had found their way into the ranks of the RAF by many paths. A high proportion had slipped across the Canadian border to enlist in the RCAF and then came to England thinly disguised as 'Canucks', while others had joined an eventual total of three fighter squadrons – Nos 71, 121 and 133 – known collectively as the 'Eagle Squadrons' by 1942. The latter trio of combat-tested veteran units were legally transferred to the aegis of the USAAF on 12 September 1942, but many individual Americans among the RAF's operational bomber and fighter crews simply refused to be tempted by the higher pay, promotion prospects, smooth uniforms and other advantages of joining their national air service, preferring to remain with the RAF.

The early months of USAAF bomber operations over France and Germany, attempting to vindicate the daylight precision theory, proved relatively costly to the Fortress crews. The greatest enemy was European weather conditions, so different to the sunny climes of southern USA where the crews had first tested such tactics; but inexperience was an inevitable factor. The heavy defensive armament of the B-17 'Flying Fortress', so loudly acclaimed in the popular press, relied too much on hand-swivelled machine guns instead of power-operated gun turrets. Undue optimism was also engendered by the many wildly exaggerated claims for combat victories in clashes with the Luftwaffe by USAAF air gunners – claims perfectly understandable when made by tyro combat crews on their first operational missions, and especially among the tightly-formated 'boxes' of Fortresses which the Eighth Air Force favoured for interdependent self-defence.

Like RAF bombers employed on daylight raids in earlier years, the USAAF bombers were severely restricted in choice of really important targets deep into enemy-occupied territory by the lack of long-range fighter escort. Once beyond roughly seventy miles into German-held air, the bombers were on their own, and the meagre Luftwaffe day-fighter force quickly learned to defer attacks against the 'mad Americans' (*sic*) until the raiders were beyond RAF fighter range. Adopting a variety of tactics, including heart-stopping 600 mph closing-speed head-on charges, the veteran Luftwaffe fighter pilots steadily got the measure of the gun-bristling Fortress box-formations, picking off any stragglers almost at will and forcing the main formations to run a gauntlet of cannon-shells and flak each time they penetrated German skies.

The feasibility and overall value of the USAAF's daytime bombing was still very much in question by the close of 1942, and at the Casablanca joint conference in January 1943, British leaders expressed the view that the American bomber effort would be better used to supplement RAF night bombing raids. The outcome, however, was a policy of compromise, whereby from mid-1943 the two air services would combine in a form of round-the-clock air offensive; the RAF would continue its night assault, with the USAAF persisting in its daylight precision attacks. Meanwhile, the obvious need for much longer-range fighter performance was being treated as a matter of operational urgency; without such protection deep penetration into the German heartland could only become more prohibitive in bomber losses. Nor

was such fighter protection confined to day raids. The still-mounting
night raids by RAF Bomber Command were meeting increasingly determined Luftwaffe opposition. Hitler's misguided decision to halt the
German nightfighter intruder attacks against RAF bomber bases had
given RAF crews a long and welcome respite from such an additional
hazard; but increasing improvement in the Kammhuber defence
system, particularly in the matters of airborne radar in nightfighters,
ground controlling techniques, and not least the accumulating experience of the relatively few German nightfighter crews, lessened the
chances of survival over Germany for RAF bomber crews. In the year
1942 the RAF night raiders employed purely on bombing sorties had
lost 1,291 aircraft and their crews – the rough equivalent of 50 complete bomber squadrons. More than half of these had been victims of
Luftwaffe nightfighters, and this total does not account for at least
another thousand RAF bombers which returned to base in semi-
shattered condition and/or bearing dead and wounded air crew members.

CHAPTER SEVEN

Around the Clock

On 20 January 1943 General Ira Eaker, commander of the USAAF's Eighth Air Force, handed Winston Churchill a single page of succinct reasons for allowing his Fortress and Liberator crews to continue their struggle to perfect daylight precision bombing policy. One sentence therein captured Churchill's well-practised sense of the dramatic: 'By bombing the devils around the clock, we can prevent the German defences from getting any rest'.

The punchy phrasing delighted Churchill, who until that moment had intended to press for the USAAF's bombing offensive to be added to the RAF's nightly onslaught, and the next day's Allied Leaders' conference at Casablanca endorsed Eaker's arguments, defining future Allied bombing policy for both air forces, by day and by night. In a document titled the Casablanca Directive, top priority targets were listed as U-boat construction yards, aircraft manufacturing works, oil installations and other industrial objectives; while the overall intention of this fresh policy was described as: 'Your primary object will be the progressive destruction and dislocation of the German military, industrial and economic systems, and the undermining of the morale of the German people to a point where their capacity for armed resistance is fatally weakened.'

To the layman such a clarion call for an all-out bombing offensive against Germany may have sounded purposeful and impressive in intent; to commanders like Harris and Eaker its implementation was far from simple at that time. The concept that a civilian population could be intimidated to a point of surrender merely by unceasing bombing had been demonstrably ill-advised during the Luftwaffe's attempts to do just that in 1940–41. As for the actual offensive, both the Eighth Air Force and Bomber Command were well understrength for any such co-ordinated succession of operational effort. Admittedly, by the end of 1942 RAF bomber strength was improving in quality as obsolete aircraft types were phased out in favour of Halifaxes, Lancasters and Mosquitos, but numerically it had gained little during the year. Much of its projected increases in men and machines had been diverted or transferred to the vital anti-submarine war being waged by Coastal Command, or to the North African battle zones. The introduction of any large numbers of new, four-engined bombers automatically reduced operational effort while crews were converted or even freshly trained to master the more complicated aircraft, and meant usually taking squadrons off the nightly battle order for several weeks before such re-equipped and retrained units could be safely put back at the sharp end. In addition, each new bomber delivered from the factories or storage depots inevitably required an average of 400 man-hours' labour by the ground maintenance crews merely to bring the machine to the latest modification state for operations. The main saving grace of the 1942 year of transition to heavier bombers was an increase of forty-four per cent – compared to 1941 – in the gross tonnage of explosive stores dropped on targets. Each of the new bombers could lift two, three or even four times the weight of bombs carried by its twin-engined predecessor.

Eaker had similar problems in fighting higher authority for sufficient bombers to equip his Eighth Air Force in order finally to prove the daylight precision principle. The USA's war against Japan in the Pacific gave the US Navy hierarchy ample ammunition for demanding top priorities for long-range bombers and fighters, apart from American participation in the Battle of the Atlantic against Germany's U-boat wolf-packs preying on Allied merchant shipping lifelines. Eaker's barrage of pleas for more men, aircraft and equipment to his supreme commander 'Hap' Arnold in Washington, USA eventually bore fruit. On 4 May 1943 the US Joint Chiefs of Staff approved an Anglo-American joint directive, titled *Pointblank*, which was issued formally on 10 June. Part of its commitment was to supply Eaker with an additional 944 heavy bombers by 1 July 1943, and almost twice that number before the year was out. It meant that Eaker's Eighth would, at least on paper, be brought to parity with Harris's Bomber Command, and in preparation for such an expansion the RAF promptly handed over a large number of UK airfields to the USAAF. This latter move accordingly reduced the number of new suitable airfields for use by the RAF's four-engined 'heavies' then arriving on squadrons, a situation already exacerbated by the need to lengthen existing airfield runways, perimeter tracking and dispersal accommodation for Lancasters and Halifaxes.

The six months' operations flown by the Eighth Air Force from November 1942 to May 1943 illustrated Eaker's urgent need for reinforcements. Throughout those pioneering missions Eaker had to rely almost wholly on just four B-17 Fortress Groups – a total of perhaps 140 bombers – plus a handful of B-24 Liberators which were entering service slowly. It was, as Eaker expressed his dilemma to 'Hap' Arnold, '. . . a piddling little force' with which to be expected to vindicate the USAAF's faith in daylight aerial bombing. Losses during those early missions, though usually in single figures, reflected a high *percentage* rate of loss of the total aircraft despatched on each occasion, and as the new year 1943 began the crews of the Eighth suffered their greatest defeat to date.

On 3 January a force of 85 bombers set out to raid St Nazaire, and at altitudes varying from 20,000 to 22,000 feet, and in the teeth of a howling gale during the final bombing run-up, these ran into a vicious barrage of predicted flak and close-in attacks from a succession of Focke Wulf Fw 190s and Messerschmitts. Seven bombers were shot down, two more crashed on return, and 47 others returned to England bearing horrifying scars of battle damage, an overall loss of nearly 100 air crew men killed or wounded.

As a proportion of the raiding force, such losses were insupportable over even a brief period of operational flying, but the fighting spirit of the surviving crews never flagged, and a boost to morale came on 27 January when the Eighth Air Force flew its first missions to Germany itself. Led by the senior 306th Bombardment Group (BG), 64 Fortresses were despatched to destroy the U-boat yards at Vegesack. Yet again cloud conditions along the German coast forced the B-17s to divert to their secondary objective, Wilhelmshaven where at least 58 bombers dropped their loads into the docks area. Opposition from an estimated 50–75 Luftwaffe fighters along the return leg of the mission accounted for a single B-17, while Fortress gunners were later credited with 22 combat victories. Although postwar research reveals that actual German losses amounted to only seven fighters, it remained a clear victory for the Eighth's crews.

The increasingly accurate predicted flak and, at times, almost overwhelming Luftwaffe opposition encountered on each mission by the Fortresses and Liberator crews were, paradoxically, the lesser hazards of the Eighth Air Force's early months. The European winter of 1942–43 produced conditions entirely new to the Americans and they were relatively ill-equipped to combat such discomforts. Following faithfully the USAAF policy of high altitude bombing, the crews found a common, constant enemy in below-zero temperatures. Fur-lined clothing and boots etc failed to nullify the stifling cold, and frostbite became almost a routine risk to feet and hands. Oxygen equipment, so vital at such heights above 15,000 feet, simply froze solid and suffocated the unwary; while control surfaces, oil and hydraulic pipe-lines refused to function. Guns and bombs failed to operate due to the crippling cold, and engines laboured in the ultra-thin air. Even normal physical movement became a nightmare for crews, particularly when under attack from the ever-present Focke Wulfs and Messerschmitts.

Even after reaching objectives dense cloud conditions too often caused the bombers to divert to alternative targets; while general weather conditions over England caused more postponements or cancellations of pre-briefed missions than actual operations flown. If anything such 'scrubs' were responsible for a greater lowering of morale than most other causes. Yet another worrying aspect of the initial operations was the realisation that the much-publicised 'impregnability' of a B-17 'Flying Fortress' due to its heavy defensive armament was something of a myth. Hand-held and operated machine guns were by no means as effective against the cannons of Luftwaffe fighters as had been imagined, while such German tactics as head-on assault clearly demonstrated serious blind-spots in the bombers' defensive systems. Local modifications introduced additional gun positions in the noses and beam locations, but these remained hand-swivelled guns only.

If the bulk of the Eighth Air Force's operational problems could readily be ascribed to sheer inexperience of aerial warfare, no such criterion could properly be applied to RAF Bomber Command crews of the same period. With the hard-won lessons of three years under its operational belt, Bomber Command by early 1943 should, logically, have been in a position to deliver an increasingly heavy programme of destruction upon Germany. In plain fact, it still had some way to go before reaching any such capability. Navigation accuracy by night, allied to target location, remained the major bugbears, and while the Gee apparatus already used had proved helpful within its limitations, its imminent jamming by German radio was expected, leaving the bomber crews to rely on pure mathematics or, in a very few cases, to the recently-tested Oboe beam 'black box' installations, still very much under operational trial. Trained air crews emerging from the vast Empire Training Schemes promised plentiful replacements for casualties and tour-expired veterans, while the gradual conversion of the command to an all-heavy, strategic force of bombers continued apace.

Harris, given his own preference, would have equipped his command throughout with Lancaster heavy bombers and Mosquito light raiders, but his expressed wishes were over-ruled due to the large commitment already on British aircraft manufacturers to produce Halifaxes and other types. New, bigger and specialised explosive bombs, incendiaries and other forms of pyrotechnic stores were becoming available in squadron and station bomb dumps; and the early frustrating and, mainly, unsuccessful sorties by the Path Finder Force were now giving way to more accurate, precision spearheading by PFF elements, guiding main force bomber streams onto target.

Thus the near-future prospects for Bomber Command certainly appeared to be brighter than at any period since the start of the war. There still remained the question of pure destructive power : could Harris bring sufficient weight, concentration and precision to be capable of truly devastating a specific target? What Harris needed to finally convince his political (and Service) 'masters' of his Command's potential for defeat of Germany's 'will to resist' was a series of 'knock-out' raids on significant objectives, similar in effect to his '1,000-bomber' raids of 1942 but, he hoped, more intense in devastation and long-term effect. The obvious target was the sprawling Krupps armament complex in the Ruhr – an area so vast in acreage that precision bombing hardly seemed applicable. Nevertheless it was to the Ruhr, and the city of Essen in particular, that Harris turned for the first demonstration of Bomber Command new wave destruction. On the night of 5/6 March 1943, a force of 442 aircraft was despatched to Essen, aided for the first time by guidance to target by Oboe marking technique. Despite the permanent industrial fog and haze hovering above Essen, and its near-legendary heavy defences, 153 bombers rightfully claimed to have released their loads within three miles of the designated target centre, a precision seldom if ever achieved before. The success was certainly attributable to the accurate target-marking of the handful of Oboe-equipped Mosquitos which marked and illuminated the aiming point.

Results of later photo-reconnaissance showed that over 600 acres had been virtually laid waste, including 13 main buildings of the Krupps works gutted by fire and a further 53 seriously damaged. The cost to the bombers was light : 14 bombers missing over Germany, and a further 38 damaged due to various causes. This initial blow to Essen marked the beginning of what has since come to be termed the Battle of the Ruhr, a slight misnomer in that the operations associated with this series of attacks ending on 13 July 1943 did not always include targets specifically in the Ruhr itself.

This opening round of the Ruhr battle against Essen was made with a force representing some 60 per cent of Harris's available air crew strength, and the relatively light losses were not to be typical of the forthcoming months. From a daily *average* of 593 crews ready for operations in February 1943, rising to 787 by August 1943, it could be shown statistically that any loss rate of just seven per cent over a three-month period would effectively nullify operational efficiency; even five per cent would produce an 'unacceptably low' factor in efficiency. Yet of 43 major raids during the Battle of the Ruhr, in which a total of 18,506 individual sorties were made, 872 aircraft failed to return and a further 2,126 were damaged, including complete write-offs in crashes and the loss of crews. Such figures reflect an overall loss rate of at least sixteen per cent, while certain raids saw this tragic figure rise sharply to almost thirty per cent. With rare exception, all such losses were borne by the main force heavy bombers; the almost total immunity of the Mosquito crews, employed mainly for Oboe-marking being in brilliant contrast to their big brothers. Considering that a normal tour of operations for bomber crews of the main force – excluding the PFF – at this time was thirty sorties completed, it needs little imagination to calculate the ordinary crew members' chances of survival until the end of his tour. As might be expected, the first six or seven sorties of any tour were considered the most likely to produce the 'chop'; yet death offered no favours or discrimination in the night skies, and second-tour veterans were as susceptible to the 'Grim Reaper' – the RAF crews' usual euphemism for death – as any first-sortie tyro.

In general it may be said that the Battle of the Ruhr operations demonstrated conclusively Bomber Command's ability to carry out the area bombing principle effectively; assisted by Oboe, main force bomb loads were more than often well concentrated on vital areas, creating widespread damage and destruction. To have expected the same concentration to be narrowed to any specific building or other precise target was at this period beyond the capability of almost any RAF bomber crew. Yet there were occasional exceptions to this generalisation, and without doubt the most outstanding was the over-publicised 'Dams Raid' by 617 Squadron on the night of 16/17 May 1943.

Formed from specially-selected experienced crews, and commanded by the veteran Wing Commander Guy Gibson, DSO, DFC, 617 Squadron initially had a single term of reference: the destruction of several huge water dams within the Ruhr area. On the actual raid Gibson led 19 of the unit's Lancasters to their targets, where their ultra-low level attacks resulted in the destruction of the Möhne and Eder dams, and severe damage to the Sorpe dam. From the 19 crews despatched only eleven returned, five of these having sustained damage. Gibson was subsequently awarded a Victoria Cross, and 33 survivors were mass-decorated.

This unique example of precision night bombing was nevertheless neither representative nor in any way 'normal' in relation to Bomber Command's contemporary methods. The squadron had been formed solely for the operation, manned by hand-picked veteran crews, and had been omitted from the nightly battle order for several weeks while they worked up to readiness state for the sortie – all 'perks' in the context of RAF bombing operations without precedent. The loss rate alone could never have been sustained by any bombing force engaged on continuing operations, while such precision could hardly be expected from the average-experienced crew. As a one-off operation the Dams Raid was unquestionably a brilliant example of outstanding valour, dedication and expertise, while various new methods and techniques devised originally for its execution were to be adapted for more general application later – one such being Gibson's idea for personal control of the raid by VHF radio as a 'Master of Ceremonies', which led later in the same year to Bomber Command's inaugural use of Master Bombers to conduct major raids similarly.

In summary, the Dams Raid was – in the words of an official historian * – '. . . a classic example of the exception which proves the rule'. No one could possibly underestimate the value of such an outstanding feat of arms, yet its true importance in the overall scheme was to come later, when 617 Squadron became a highly proficient pioneer unit for a variety of marking and precision bombing techniques which helped its parent No 5 Group to achieve increasingly successful, often spectacular results during 1944–45.'

By early March 1943 the paper strength of RAF Bomber Command, as it prepared for the opening blow of the Battle of the Ruhr, looked healthy enough. The battle order showed 65 squadrons *in toto*, of which 18 were equipped with Lancasters, 11 with Halifaxes, but a further 16 were still operating on the ageing though doughty Wellington. Many of the squadrons were not strictly speaking firstline bomber units, however, being tasked with other equally vital duties. By this stage of the war the huge contribution of the various Empire countries to the overall RAF effort was clearly evident too. Within Bomber Command at that time were no less than four squadrons of the Royal Australian Air Force (RAAF), two Royal New Zealand Air Force (RNZAF) units, and eleven squadrons of the Royal Canadian Air

* *Strategic Air Offensive against Germany, 1939–45,* Vol II by C. Webster and N. Frankland, HMSO.

Force (RCAF). All but two squadrons of the latter were the full complement of No 6 Group, based mainly around Yorkshire in north-east England. Other 'national' squadrons with Bomber Command included three Wellington squadrons, all based at Hemswell, and crewed by Polish personnel.

Segregation of such different nationals among the ranks of operational bomber units was not a hard and fast rule, however. Virtually every squadron, and almost all crews, tended to be a mixture of nationalities – English, Welsh, Scotch, Irish, even individual Americans, Jamaicans, Australians, etc – a polyglot blending of differing races, colours and creeds which invariably proved to be efficacious in hard practice. Apart from member countries of what then was still the old British Empire, no few numbers of air crews in RAF uniform were patriots of the many European countries over-run and occupied by Germany in the early months of the war. Messes and NAAFIs were often filled with the cacophony of a dozen different tongues and accents, as Belgian mixed with Czech, Free French, Pole, Dutch, Norwegian.

The bomber crews, of whatever background, had several things in common. The vast majority were young – many below the arbitrary legal definition of maturity of 21 years' age – though it was not uncommon to find occasional beribboned veterans of the 1914–18 war hiding behind the guns of a Lancaster turret. All were volunteers – at no time in its history has the RAF ever conscripted men for operational flying duties – and with rare exception each man or boy was wholly dedicated to his designated role. Though all were subject to the general restrictions of RAF book discipline as minutely detailed in King's Rules and Regulations, almost without known exception operational bomber crews, of all nationalities, quickly developed an unbidden, self-created discipline of their own which could not be found in any book.

Each bomber crew was initially formed by an almost random method of selection at Operational Training Unit level, but once posted to an operational squadron developed swiftly into a cohesive, individual community. By common, unspoken consent, and natural practice, the leader of such a tiny band of brothers was the first pilot, the Skipper, whose word in the air – and often even on the ground – was law. Rank was almost irrelevant in this context – non-commissioned skippers often had commissioned officer crew members – and all crews looked to the Skipper for ultimate decisions in matters in any way related to flying. The reason was simple : survival. Any lingering fulsome ideas of the glamour or glory of war were dispelled rapidly after just one operational sortie over Germany, and the uppermost motivation thereafter was the desire to complete the requisite thirty-sorties' tour in one piece – to survive.

Thus every crew set out from the start to weld itself into an efficient, interlocking working team of individual expertise; interdependency and well-practised co-ordination were the essential ingredients of crew efficiency. An American infantryman's cliché of the period declaimed there were 'no atheists in foxholes', but there were no 'foxholes' in the night skies over Germany; survival might ultimately be the prerogative of some Greater Power, but faith in the loyalty and efficiency of fellow crew members was at least a slim hedge against the capricious whims of the Grim Reaper.

As Bomber Command intensified its night offensive against the Ruhr and cities further afield, the Fortress and Liberator crews of the USAAF's Eighth Air Force doggedly persisted with the hope of making daylight bombing pay dividends. During the month of February 1943 aircraft losses in action had amounted to 22, a figure often exceeded by RAF losses in a single night but which represented a quarter of the actual number of bombers usually available for operations by the Americans on any given day.

Chief opponent to American ambitions remained the European weather, as cloud, fogs and haze constantly frustrated bomb aimers over priority targets, but the occasional conditions of clear visibility enabled a few missions to add credence to the overall policy. On 18 March, for example, a force of 97 Fortresses and Liberators dropped three-quarters of its bombs within 1,000 yards of the designated aiming point over Vegesack submarine yards, damaging at least seven U-boats and wrecking sixty per cent of surrounding buildings.

Such successes were, nevertheless, offset by days of near-disaster. On 17 April the Eighth Air Force despatched its largest force to date, 115 Fortresses, to bomb the Focke Wulf aircraft factories at Bremen. As this unwieldy collection of formation boxes began their bombing run over the target, two *Gruppen* of Fw 190s from JG1, ignoring the intense flak barrage mushrooming around the bombers, attacked from head-on in succeeding waves. One Fortress was lost to a direct flak hit, but 15 of the leading Fortress formation went down under the guns of the Luftwaffe fighters, and a further 48 finally got back to England displaying ragged damage mementoes of the furious battle. Yet again American gunners' claims for combat victories were grossly inflated, and the claimed total of 63 was later known to be justified in 10 cases only.

From its initial mission to Rouen on 17 August 1942 until May

1943, the onus of responsibility for the Eighth Air Force's pioneering 'experiments' in daylight bombing had been borne in the main by the 91st, 303rd, 305th and 306th BGs; but on 4 May 1943 these four Groups flew their last missions as trail-blazers, when 79 Fortresses, escorted by no less than twelve squadrons of fighters, bombed the Ford motor works at Antwerp and returned without loss. In previous weeks five more groups had been added to the American presence in Britain, while there was a firm promise of a further seven B-17 BGs to come within the following two months.

Those first nine months of operations by the Eighth Air Force in the ETO (European Theatre of Operations) had been instructive and costly. Aircraft lost in action for the whole period totalled 99, with an equal number severly damaged – in human terms, more than 1,000 air crew men killed or crippled. Fantastic claims for enemy aircraft destroyed in combat, even after careful pruning, still amounted to more than nine times the known 50 or so German fighters lost in such engagements. What had actually been achieved by the bombing had usually been overestimated – the many attacks against submarine yards and pens had created negligible damage, though individual raids against factories and railway depots had been more positive in destruction.

Many invaluable lessons had been learned. The initial brash (to British eyes), over-optimistic eagerness to get to grips with the enemy may have been tempered, even sobered in the harsh light of sheer experience on operations, but no one doubted the will to win of the American bomber crews. It may have been due to a superiority complex which seemed an integral part of the American national character, or simply the normal hardening determination associated with any 'minority' group, intent on proving its worth; yet the fierce *esprit de corps* and dogged courage of the American bomber crews in the face of, at times, dismaying casualties and high odds can only be regarded as wholly admirable. The oft-quoted description of the early USAAF contingents by a war-weary British population as being 'over-dressed, over-paid, over-sexed, and over here' may have been earned by a fringe element of the more extrovert Americans, but the bulk of the 'Hollywood Warriors' – another British insulting description – earned an unreserved applause from RAF veterans who knew only too well the ordeal that these tyro, fresh-faced combat crews faced each time they ventured into German-held air. Nothing appeared to daunt the Fortress and Liberator crews in their quest to achieve equal standing as combat-partners with the vastly more experienced RAF during the first months of the USAAF's bombing offensive. Their striving and sacrifices were to be the rock foundation upon which the Americans continued to build an air strike force which, by mid-1944, became the largest such force ever pressed into battle.

The long-awaited reinforcement of the Eighth Air Force virtually coincided with Harris's opening phase of the Battle of the Ruhr, thereby heralding the dawn of a truly combined aerial offensive against the common enemy, Germany. It would be another year before this offensive would reach the peaks of operational weight and effort intended to blast a path forward for the inter-Allied land invasion of *Festung Europa*, but the interim year was to witness a day and night struggle for supremacy in the skies unprecedented in the annals of military aviation. For the Allied air forces it was to be the beginning of an unrelenting climb to a pinnacle of victory. For the Luftwaffe it would mean an unceasing, and eventually desperate defence of ever-shrinking borders to the German homeland. The heady years of resounding victories for Göring's vaunted air force were by now mere shades of a misty past; the future held only a darkening horizon as the golden vision of Hitler's boasted 'Thousand Years' Reich' wilted, tarnished, and began its decline to oblivion.

CHAPTER EIGHT

Aces All

For the men of RAF Fighter Command the year 1941 had been a period of shifting fortunes. Recovering steadily from the toll of the protracted campaigns in France and then over southern England in the previous year, the command had begun by a determined swing over to the offensive – 'leaning forward' into enemy-occupied territories. By the spring of 1941 the command's slowly increasing strength and fresh equipment appeared to indicate near-future adequate muscle for sustaining and even escalating the offensive pressure on French-based units of the Luftwaffe. Before ever reaching any such state, however, Hitler's invasion of Russia intervened. An immediate consequence of Hitler's move was the decision by Churchill and his War Cabinet to render effective material aid to their latest 'ally', thereby creating an immense diversion of labour and material which might otherwise have been directed into bolstering the RAF's operational capacity, particularly Fighter Command.

Conversely, the Russian invasion campaign, with its consequent transference of the bulk of Luftwaffe strength to the eastern zones, presented Fighter and Bomber Commands with a wide opportunity to attempt a battle of attrition with the relatively weak remaining German units based still in France; hence the inauguration of the Circus style of operations with their supplementary Rhubarb sorties. The outcome of such an attempt was distinctly 'unprofitable', with losses in men and aircraft disproportionate to the results achieved, and, considering the numerical inferiority of the few French-based *Jagdgeschwader*, tantamount to a moral victory for the Luftwaffe's fighter pilots. Yet, while on the one hand preaching caution to Sholto Douglas in respect of such worrying losses, the Air Staff in London could offer little alternative owing to the prevailing war situation. The Battle of the Atlantic necessarily claimed high priority in consideration : without constant replenishment of war materials via the ocean lanes, Britain could not survive, let alone continue a full-scale war. In the air, the early 1941 night bombing blitz against major British cities and industrial centres gradually faded away, but the prime urgency in establishing an efficient and effective aerial night defence force continued, having only recently commenced virtually from scratch.

If the 1941 daylight fighter offensive operations had their gloomier aspects, they also contained plentiful long-term benefits from the RAF viewpoint. Wide scope was afforded for staffs to gain practical experience in large-scale fighter offensive planning and execution, fresh tactical ploys were tested, adjusted and adapted; new concepts in combat direction and control both from the ground and in the air were practised. Equally important, the mushrooming crop of freshly-trained pilots arriving on firstline squadrons were inculcated guardedly to the operational scene, and thereafter gained invaluable hard experience in their daily tasks.

A particularly significant feature of the year had been the real beginning of an unceasing striving for technical superiority in actual fighter designs by both the RAF and the Luftwaffe, apart from a broadening diversification of certain fighter variants for particular roles. Development of any military aircraft has always been an integral facet of its designers' intention from the outset of any new venture, a process often extended over many years before frontline squadrons begin to benefit from re-equipment with the very latest results of such research and testing. The intense pressure of wartime necessity inevitably compressed such lengthy trial parameters in time, and clear evidence of this was first demonstrated in 1941. The Luftwaffe continued to rely almost exclusively on its standard single-seat fighter, the Messerschmitt Bf 109, but modified its 1940 E-version to produce the Bf 109F variant by early 1941. As this version entered firstline service in the spring of that year, a fresh development of the RAF's classic Spitfire also entered the combat lists; the Mark V, which commenced operations at squadron level from March. Both 'new' fighters were chiefly up-rated in engine power and different, more powerful armament in the main, and first clashed in combat over Kent on 11 May 1941, when a 91 Squadron Spitfire V from Hawkinge shot down a Bf 109F attempting a sneak, low-level bombing raid.

The other Fighter Command stalwart, the rugged Hurricane I which had claimed a lion's share of the command's triumph during the 1940 Battle of Britain, also received a face-lift. Recognised as too slow for 1941 standards of high altitude fighter combat, the Hurricane II variants entered service mainly as low-level fighter-bombers. According to version, the Hurricane II had considerably increased fire-power, with 10, 12 machine guns, or four 20mm cannons crammed into its wings, plus strengthened structure to enable the 'fighter' to carry 250lb or 500lb bombs under its wings.

If Fighter Command felt any complacency by the Spitfire V's apparent ability to cope with the improved Messerschmitt Bf 109F, such confidence was soon rudely shaken. On 17 August a Belgian pilot of 609 Squadron, on return from a daylight sortie, reported a combat with some twenty German fighters, one of which he described as '. . . a Messerschmitt with a radial engine'. RAF Intelligence chose to disbelieve the report, but clear evidence of a new fighter of such configuration came from the camera gun film of an escort fighter of a Circus operation on 13 October. It was the Focke Wulf Fw 190, an entirely new design well superior to any contemporary firstline RAF fighter which was to gain for the Luftwaffe a modicum of aerial supremacy over France for many months to come. Except for its superb turning capability, the Spitfire V was outclassed by the Fw 190 in every other combat facet, and British aircraft designers were urgently pressed for a replacement.

While the search for an answer to the Fw 190 proceeded, Fighter Command received two new types of fighter for operational initiation. In September 1941 Nos 56 and 609 Squadrons received their first examples of a stablemate to the Hurricane, the pugnacious-looking Hawker Typhoon. Though first flown in prototype form in February 1940, the 'Tiffie' had a long history of teething problems, many of which were still unresolved when it was pressed into frontline use. The second fresh type was the unorthodox, twin-engined Westland Whirlwind. With a nose battery of four 20mm cannons, and speed in excess of 350 mph at low level, the Whirlwind had first reached 263 Squadron for operations in late 1940, but its relatively poor high altitude performance restricted its eventual use to ground-strafing and escort duties, and only one other unit was equipped with the type, 137 Squadron in September 1941, after which the Whirlwind faded from the operational scene quickly.

Two other events in early 1941 were portents of an entirely new era in not only fighter design but aeronautical history. On 2 April 1941 the German Heinkel He 280 made its first powered flight from Marienhe airfield, the first flight ever made by a turbo-jet-powered aircraft designed as a potential fighter. In England, at Cranwell, on 15 May 1941, the Gloster E28/39 experimental jet single-seater prototype made its first flight. The days of piston-engined aeroplanes were numbered. Germany's lead in turbojet-engined aircraft had really begun on 27 August 1939, when the Heinkel He 178-V1 actually made the world's first flight by an aircraft powered by such an engine, but its relatively poor showing produced little interest among the Luftwaffe's hierarchy, and development was restricted. German research into better-powered fighters by 1941 had also produced the first examples of two Messerschmitt fighters of significance in later years of the war. One was the tail-less Me 163 fitted with a rocket-power 'engine', while the other, the Me 262, though intended for twin turbojet engines, made its initial testing flights with a temporarily-installed piston engine until sufficient turbojet engines became available. The necessary protracted testing, improving, and developing of each of these early bids by both the RAF and the Luftwaffe to enter the jet age militarily meant that first fruits would not be seen until 1944, though the seeds of the new era had been sown.

Whatever the technical improvement might be in any form of aircraft used in combat, however, the ultimate criterion for victory has always been – in the main – the quality and spirit of the man at the controls. In the 1941–42 period both the RAF and the Luftwaffe were well served by their fighter pilots in the contexts of skill, courage, and determination generally. The men of Germany's *Jagdgeschwader* were led by veterans of aerial combat whose dedication to their task cannot be questioned. Their counterparts among the RAF fighter squadrons were equally tested and tried in the white-heat of the combat crucible, and on a par with most Luftwaffe *Experten* in terms of skill and fighting guile.

Training for the rising generations of future fighter pilots in either service was as yet little altered from pre-1939 thorough instructional quality, though slightly more condensed in pure time. Volunteers to fill the fighter cockpits were never lacking, and only the best were graduated from operational training establishments as yet. Even by 1941–42 wartime standards, the RAF's training syllabus for a fully-fledged fighter pilot required at least forty weeks actual instruction, apart from 'non-active' considerations such as leave periods, sickness *et al*. The Empire Training Scheme, whereby thousands of embryo RAF air crews were trained in Canada, USA, Rhodesia, India, etc, was to ensure a constant flow of fresh men for all RAF squadrons as the war progressed, but the same could not be said of the Luftwaffe. Already dangerously impaired by ruthless stripping of the training establishment to bolster its various 1939–40 campaigns, the Luftwaffe's potential future stock of newly-trained crews was already thin by 1941. Expansion and recruiting was hardly a problem in a totalitarian dictatorship, but the lack of a long-view policy for providing future crews was to dog the capability of the firstline units for much of the war.

By 1941 too Göring's lack of foresight – though in this context Hitler and other Nazi hierarchy must be allotted at least equal blame – failed to give Germany's aircraft designers and manufacturers any firm policies or continuing commitments for progressive development of up-dated aircraft designs for the air arm. Much of the immediate blame for such short-sighted policies as were adopted pre-1939 could be laid at the feet of Ernst Udet, Göring's appointed chief of the Luftwaffe's technical departments. As technical supremo, Udet's clearly out-dated ideas on fighter design, obsession with the efficacy of dive-bombing, allied to a character essentially out of place in such high office, left the Luftwaffe at least three years behind in pure technical development by 1941 compared with the contemporary state of the British aviation industry supporting the RAF. While certain avenues of research and experimentation – e.g. turbojet-engined aircraft – were admittedly further along the path to fruition than Germany' opponents, several glaring omissions, such as the cancelled long-range heavy bomber projected development pre-1939, were soon to prove significant.

The final months of 1941 had also seen several important events which would affect the Luftwaffe's immediate future. In November Ernst Udet committed suicide rather than continue as chief scapegoat for all Luftwaffe's failures and problems, and the chief instigator of Udet's downfall, Erhard Milch, was appointed in charge of future aircraft production planning. While flying to attend Udet's State funeral service, Werner Mölders, the Luftwaffe's leading fighter pilot, was killed in a flying accident. Within an hour of Mölders' body being interred alongside Udet and Manfred von Richthofen in the Invalidenfriedhof, Göring appointed Adolf Galland, colourful ace of JG26, as General of Fighters in Mölders' place. Though relatively young in years, Galland was thus promoted to a rank and position of authority which had only two superiors in Germany – Göring and Hitler.

Galland's reluctance to be taken off active combat duty was soon submerged in his attempts to convince the Luftwaffe staff at high level of the crucial need for vast expansion of the fighter forces. Under Milch's driving energy general fighter production was already promising well for the near-future strength of the *Jagdgeschwader,* but the greatest obstacle in all such matters was Hitler's obsession with a clear and, especially, speedy conclusion to the Russian campaign in the east. Thus the Chief of the General Staff, Hans Jeschonnek, had clear orders from Hitler to concentrate the full strength of German forces, especially the Luftwaffe, on the coming spring offensive against Russia which, Hitler was convinced, would solve the eastern threat. Once Russia was defeated, Milch's increasing aircraft production figures would not only replace casualties in the east, but provide ample strength for a renewed offensive in the west against Britain – such was Hitler's conviction. The blunt effect of this priority was to leave the Luftwaffe fighter strength in the west at the start of 1942 with little more than two fighter groups and a few training units, less than 300 aircraft overall with which to face the mounting RAF offensive, and a strength which was to see little improvement in the west throughout 1942.

Galland had hardly time to get accustomed to his new appointment when he was saddled with a responsibility by Hitler which was to stretch his organisational abilities and his under-strength fighter forces almost to their limits. Fearing an Allied invasion or at least strong attack via Norway and Sweden, thereby diluting his intended spring offensive against Russia, Hitler ordered the German raiders *Scharnhorst, Gneisenau,* and *Prinz Eugen* to be moved from Brest to Norwegian water via the English Channel. Vital to the success of such a daring venture was a full escorting protection of the naval force by Galland's fighters, a condition imposed by German naval staff officers and ratified by Hitler. After some three weeks of urgent trials and intricate planning under a veil of strictest security, the three capital ships and their outflanking naval escort set sail from Brest in the late evening of 11 February 1942. Operation Thunderbolt * had commenced.

The emphasis on the crucial importance of aerial protection for the naval force was well appreciated by all German forces involved, yet Galland's total resources amounted to 280 fighters, drawn mainly from JG2, JG6, the Paris Fighter Training School, and sundry units. Of this total at least 30 Messerschmitt Bf 110s were nightfighters, charged with patrols in the early morning or evening periods of the Channel 'Dash'; the bulk of Galland's force were comprised of Bf 109s and Fw 190s. To preserve some form of continuous cover, these were despatched in formations of 16 to 20 machines for set periods, overlapping by some ten minutes with relief guard-formations, while the remainder maintained an immediate readiness state at airfields stretched along the route on the northern French coastline. It was, in all conscience, a relatively small air umbrella for such an important role, but with intricate planning and meticulous timing it could still

* The official code-name, though the Germany Navy, for security reasons, used the code-title *Cerberus*.

succeed. Everything hinged on how quickly the RAF discovered the move, and more significantly, how rapidly the RAF would react in terms of hard opposition.

Awareness of just such a possible move by the *Scharnhorst* and *Gneisenau* by the RAF dated back to April 1941, when Coastal, Bomber and Fighter Commands had received orders from the Air Staff to prepare for a contingency countermove, Operation Fuller. Yet when the German move eventually commenced, it was not until late in the morning of 12 February that the convoy was first seen and reported, by which time the vessels had reached the mouth of the river Somme, virtually the halfway point of their journey. Even after recognising the nature of the activity in the Channel, the RAF was lamentably slow in reacting, owing largely to lack of co-ordination between Commands and an incredibly bureaucratic security blanket being adhered to rigidly by certain RAF and Admiralty authorities even as units were being sent into action. It was not until two hours later than the first British aircraft made any attempt to attack; six Fleet Air Arm Swordfish torpedo-bomber biplanes of 825 Squadron, FAA, temporarily based at RAF Manston, and led by Lieutenant-Commander Eugene Esmonde, DSO, RN. All six were blasted into oblivion by heavy gunfire from the battleships and a swarm of Fw 190s. This suicidal attempt *should* have been escorted by five squadrons of Spitfires, but only one unit, 72 Squadron led by Squadron Leader Brian Kingcombe, DFC, rendezvoused with the Swordfish prior to the attack; the rest were too late.

From then until after 6 pm RAF bombers, fighters and torpedo-bombers made an unco-ordinated, spasmodic series of fruitless attempts to close with the German battleships, and failed to make any impression. As dusk fell, the German naval formation was well clear of any danger from the air, and reached Wilhelmshaven and Brunsbüttel harbours, despite damage from sea mines to two of the capital ships, by dawn of 13 February.

The utter failure of Operation Fuller to prevent the German breakthrough along the whole length of the English Channel was emphasised in the context of the aerial facets by the minor losses suffered by Galland's air umbrella: eleven men and 17 aircraft. As Galland expressed it later: 'The pilots of the RAF fought bravely, tenaciously and untiringly, but had been sent into action with insufficient planning, without a clear concept of the attack, without a centre of gravity, and without systematic tactics'.

At least 30 Fighter Command squadrons had played some part in the fiasco, and hundreds of bombers had also been involved, all to no avail. The official post-mortem inquiry into this overt failure by all RAF and naval forces involved virtually whitewashed most authorities of specific blame, but several senior RAF officers were quietly re-shuffled into less active posts. From a purely naval strategic viewpoint the move of these three German battleships from the North Atlantic seaboard was a vast relief, enabling the Royal Navy to reposition its forces for its many other commitments. For RAF Bomber Command such a relocation was also – in the long view – welcome; the previous year of protracted bombing raids against Brest attempting to destroy, or at least contain, the giant sea raiders had been highly unprofitable in terms of casualties and overall effort. None of these hindsight con-siderations, however, could camouflage the immediate and obvious tactical defeat of Allied air power.

The aftermath of the 'Channel Dash' fiasco was widespread among RAF authorities, but Sholto Douglas, commanding Fighter Command, had several other problems to solve in early 1942. Chief among these was the continuing need to build an efficient night defence system against potential future Luftwaffe repetition of the blitz tactics of the 1940/41 winter months. During the first four months of 1942 German night-raiders had been relatively minor, and Fighter Command had been able to progress, albeit slowly, in its testing of new airborne radar devices, allied with ground control and detection techniques.

The best available nightfighter then was the mighty Bristol Beau-fighter, a rugged design with a lethal punch of four 20mm cannons in the fuselage and up to six machine guns in its wings. Crewed by two men, the Beau seemed ideal for its role, and its success rate had risen steadily over the previous year's operations. In December 1941, how-ever, fresh teeth were added to the nightfighter force, when 157 Squad-ron was formed at Debden to equip with De Havilland Mosquito fighters, fitted with A1 Mk V radar sets. By April 1942 the unit was based at Castle Camps and had 14 radar-equipped Mosquitos on charge, and on 6 April a second Mosquito unit, 151 Squadron, began to exchange its former Boulton Paul Defiants for 'Wooden Wonders', as the Mosquito had already been dubbed by the media. A classic design from its genesis, the Mosquito was of all-wood construction, tough, well-armed, and had a turn of speed superior to any similar contemporary design of twin-engined aircraft.

The arrival of these initial Mosquitos was propitious because on 23 April some 40 Junkers Ju 88s and Dorniers from KGs 2, 100 and 106 launched the first of a series of so-called *Baedeker* night raids against cathedral cities in Britain, a pure terror-bombing ploy aimed at destroying British civilian morale. While the Beaufighters and Mosquitos ranged across Britain's night skies seeking out German bombers, other Mosquito crews were inaugurating yet another role for this ubiquitous aircraft : night intrusion. The first Mosquito intruder sortie was flown by a 23 Squadron crew on the night of 6 July 1942 in the Caen area, and on the following night the same crew found and destroyed a Dornier 217 east of Chartres. For this role Mosquitos were fitted with long-range fuel tanks, thereby adding some ninety minutes to normal endurance and extending operational range to a radius of roughly 600 miles – ample elbow room to indulge in attacks on most Luftwaffe bomber bases within striking range of England. It was the beginning of a role for Mosquito crews which was to become a major facet of RAF night operations over Germany throughout the rest of the war, and the birth of a near-legend in audacity and courage for the men of the night 'Mozzies'.

By day the night fighter offensive of the RAF continued apace, still attempting to suck the Luftwaffe fighters up into a battle of attrition, but plans were already being projected for what amounted to a large-scale 'invasion' of German-occupied France in the summer of 1942. Though planned from the outset as merely a probing exercise, the overall object of this intended foray was as a testing of organisational ability and execution of mounting any such assault – in effect, a rehearsal for the eventual hoped-for real invasion of Hitler's Fortress Europe. The place selected was Dieppe, and the date chosen was 19 August 1942.

The lessons of Germany's failure to invade Britain in 1940 were well recognised by the Dieppe Raid planners, and the need for total air supremacy over the target area was a first priority. No 11 Group, Fighter Command, became the logical controlling authority for the air cover, and this Group was quickly strengthened to a total of 56 squadrons of fighters. In flank support were to be four squadrons of reconnaissance Mustang fighters, five squadrons of twin-engined light bombers – Bostons and Blenheims – for peripheral roles, and further direct help would be afforded by the heavy bombers of Bomber Command and the USAAF's Eighth Air Force attacking Luftwaffe targets inland from Dieppe. The complete air strength of some 70 squadrons was far greater than Hugh Dowding had under his command when he faced the total might of the Luftwaffe in the summer of 1940.

The actual Dieppe 'invasion' began in the early hours of 19 August, when the sea-borne infantry and Commandos were preceded by waves of smoke-screen laying light bombers and Hurricane fighter-bombers smothering the German defensive positions. By 6.30 a.m. the main fighter umbrella had swung into position over the invading forces; a continuing succession of Spitfire and other squadrons maintained an unending presence at layered altitudes above the invasion zones. Luftwaffe reaction was relatively slow until about 7 a.m. when the first heavy clashes occurred between the opposing fighter arms. From then until the early evening the air battle increased in intensity and numbers, and casualties mounted inexorably on both sides. By mid-morning German bombers were put into action but these had to run a gauntlet of RAF fighters if they were to reach any worthwhile target. Many RAF and German fighter pilots flew three, four or even more sorties that day – a succession of shuttle flights to and from the fighting zone, with minimal rest between sorties.

With less than 200 fighters available at the start of the day, the *Jagdgeschwader* – almost exclusively JG2 and JG26 – faced high odds, which increased as the day wore on due to losses, damage etc. Yet by the end of the day the Luftwaffe, had it known the true figures, might rightly have claimed a resounding victory. In one day's marathon combat the RAF lost 106 aircraft overall, while German losses amounted to 48 destroyed and 24 seriously damaged. Contemporary RAF *claims* were, as might be expected, exaggerated, totalling 91 Luftwaffe aircraft destroyed and nearly 200 others damaged.

The air battle over Dieppe, at least in numerical context, was the RAF's greatest air fight. In terms of gross depletion of the Luftwaffe force in direct opposition, the RAF fighters that day scored more heavily than even they realised, because by the dawn of the day following the Dieppe raid, the Luftwaffe strength of the French-based fighter units had been reduced to just 70 serviceable machines. Hypothetically speaking, had the Dieppe air action continued the next day at the same pitch of combat, the Luftwaffe in France would have been rendered effectively *hors de combat*; within forty-eight hours the RAF would have achieved all that it had been attempting to do in its Circus and Rhubarb operations for the previous eighteen months. The RAF's losses on 19 August, though tragic enough, would have been a small sacrifice to pay for any such knockout blow.

Perhaps more significant in the long-term view of the Dieppe action was the scale of organisation, planning and actual effort involved by the RAF. Throughout the day it had flown a total of 2,955 individual sorties, roughly two-thirds of these by fighters; while the much weaker Luftwaffe fighters and bombers had grossed approximately 1,000 such sorties. The myriad lessons learned from the Dieppe operation were to be embellished and enlarged in later larger-scale invasions, such as North Africa, Sicily and, in June 1944, Normandy.

From the German view the Channel Dash had been, in Admiral Raeder's phrase, 'a tactical victory and a strategic defeat'. All three capital ships made no further contribution to the war of any significance, while the Luftwaffe in the west could ill-afford such proportional casualties. Milch's lively expansion of German aircraft production was beginning to produce good numbers of replacement aircraft, but the ever-hungry eastern front ate up much of this production throughout 1942 and early 1943; while the overall priority insisted upon by Hitler was for manufacture of bombers, not fighters. The potential threat of an increasingly strong aerial bombing offensive against the German homeland by the RAF and its latest partner, the USAAF, was of little importance to Hitler. The German Führer's uppermost concern was for the Russian campaign throughout 1942, and in any case his attitude to employment of the Luftwaffe was succinctly summed up in a single phrase : 'The Luftwaffe must *attack* and not defend.'

This obdurate maxim of Hitler's, supported as ever by the obsequious Göring, was to daunt all aspects of the Luftwaffe's operations through the remaining war years. In Göring's case there were highly subjective reasons for glossing over any such shortcomings in 'his' Luftwaffe. Since his failure to subdue the RAF in 1940, his personal credibility among the Nazi hierarchy had badly declined, and only Hitler's personal loyalty to him permitted him to continue in his elevated and privileged status. Having boasted in previous years that no bombs would ever drop on German soil, Göring now preferred to play down any implied urgency for building an effective aerial defence force to face the RAF and USAAF bombers in the west. It was a fairyland philosophy : if one ignored a problem it might eventually go away !

To Adolf Galland, head of the Luftwaffe's fighter arm, the portents of the forthcoming Allied bombing offensive had been crystal clear since 1941, and he maintained a constant campaign of attempts to persuade Göring and the General Staff greatly to increase the western defences, particularly in the context of more fighters. His opinions and exhortations merely fell on deaf ears; only Hitler himself could reverse his orders for priority for the bombers, and Hitler refused to entertain any such idea. The separated organisations for day and night fighter operational commands further complicated Galland's wishes. Both were virtually being employed in piecemeal manner, instead of being co-ordinated as a cohesive defence force for the Reich. While the slender

day fighter units continued throughout 1942 to challange all incursions by Allied bombers and fighters over France and Germany the
main successes lay with the night fighters. By May 1942 the *Nachtjäger* crews had *claimed* some 600 Allied aircraft since the start of the
war, a figure slightly exaggerated but far closer to reality than any
comparable claims by the day fighters, as witnessed by the known
figure of almost 1,300 RAF bombers lost by night over Europe
throughout the year 1942 alone. Such successes were not due solely to
the unquestioned courage and skill of the Luftwaffe's nightfighter air
crews, but had their foundation in the huge ground control and detection .organisation which had gradually evolved by 1942, and which
was to continue to expand and strengthen during 1943–44.

This base-rock foundation of German night fighters defence was due
in overwhelming measure to the foresight and energy of Josef Kammhuber, who despite a multitude of problems, not least the higher
command's antipathy to all matters concerning night defence of the
Reich in the first three years of war, steadily constructed the initial
systems of nightfighter networks. Bedevilled by lack of aircraft and
crews specially trained for this new form of aerial fighting in the early
stages, Kammhuber persisted. When the supply of suitable radar –
both ground and airborne types – began to flow to the Luftwaffe in
1942, he immediately pressed for expansion of his existing meagre
force from (basically) one *Geschwader* to eight nightfighter *Geschwader*
and an extra 150,000 men. In addition he demanded delivery of 600
Würzburg-Riesen radar installations by September 1942, and wide
replacement of existing *Lichtenstein* A1 radar with wider-angle airborne radar of greater acquisition range.

The response to this demand from Kammhuber was a blunt rejection by both Göring and Jeschonnek. Undismayed, Kammhuber
proceeded to achieve at least part of his needs by other methods, recruiting many thousands of men, boys and women from a variety of
German non-operational organisations, including the German Youth
Organisation. By August 1942 he could count some 30,000 personnel
within his signals organisation, a strength which grew to 40,000 by
January 1943; while the operational flying units were also increased
by the close of 1942 to five *Geschwader*, albeit not all to full fighting
establishment.

Considered objectively, Kammhuber's organisation was a minor
triumph of dogged persistence in the light of the many obstacles placed
in his way by higher command. At the outbreak of war defence of the
Reich was almost solely in the hands of the flak guns and associated

searchlights and sound detectors. Nightfighters *per se* were no part of the Luftwaffe's schemes, and in the context of Reich defence, considered superfluous. After the initial RAF raids against targets within Germany's borders – though in trivial numbers, sporadic, and having minimal effect – attempts had been made to at least protect the more obvious industrial objectives and major cities by attaching a handful of Messerschmitt day fighters to the night defences. These fighters, bereft of radar or any other form of target-acquisition devices, relied entirely upon the searchlights to point out raiding bombers. Appointed in charge or this embryo defensive system, Kammhuber adopted two main tactics for his mixed bag of fighters and bombers, allotting single-seat fighters to pure night defence of German territory, and despatching the longer-range Dorniers and Junkers as intruders against the RAF's bomber bases in England.

Hitler's order in October 1941 forbidding further night intrusion operations – despite the obvious success of this form of 'defence' – limited Kammhuber to protection of Germany itself, and he revised his organisation accordingly. The gradual introduction of ground, then air, radar installations offered opportunities for more precise forms of detection, location and therefore destruction of incoming RAF raiders, and Kammhuber set up what came to be code-named *Himmelbett* (literally, 'Four-Poster Bed') defensive belts stretching in a curved line from Denmark in the north to France in the south-west, athwart the main penetration air corridors used by the RAF's night formations. The essence of the *Himmelbett* system was ground-controlled and directed nightfighter defence; it was aided by the close of 1941 by a new airborne radar set, *Lichtenstein*, with its detection range of at least two miles, and the huge ground-control *Wurzburg-Riesen* with its 40-miles ranging. At that time Germany's nightfighters totalled some 300 aircraft in gross, and among the pilots were several experienced *Experten* (German equivalent idiom for the Allied description 'ace') whose accumulating operational skill in fighting in the dark was to form a hard core of future triumphs by the *Nachtjäger*.

Throught 1942 expansion of the 'Kammhuber Line' was painfully slow, and by the end of the year its fighter count stood at slightly less than 400 machines. The bulk of these were Junkers Ju 88s and Messerschmitt Bf 110s, each carrying at least two-men crews, and festooned with the aerial paraphernalia of *Lichtenstein* radar.

The escalating successes of Kammhuber's night defenders were heartening but by no means conclusive by the end of 1942. Moreover, now that the USAAF's Eighth Air Force had joined with the RAF's offensive operations by day, it seemed logical to assume that the Americans would also co-operate with the RAF's night-raiding of Germany. Accordingly, Kammhuber submitted yet another memorandum to higher authority in May 1943, outlining what he considered to be the necessary strength of the Reich's defence force to meet the anticipated joint Allied aerial onslaught. In it he called for expansion of his command to a par with RAF Fighter Command, and argued that the existing force of roughly 500 nightfighters be reinforced to an ultimate total of 2,160 fighters – in effect, a demand for an additional 10 *Geschwader*.

Having obtained Göring's personal unqualified assent to these final figures, Kammhuber went to see Hitler for final ratification – and was blankly refused. Göring, with an entirely typical *volte-face*, then accused Kammhuber of '. . . wanting the whole Luftwaffe' and called him 'a megalomaniac'. From that moment Kammhuber's credibility and influence rapidly lessened with an inevitable co-effect on the fortunes of the only practical aerial defence system the Nazi Reich then possessed.

If the German nightfighters faced increasing difficulties, the much smaller day fighter force in France now had the prospect of ever-larger formations of American Fortresses and Liberators, penetrating even deeper into German skies by virtue of being escorted by long-range fighters. Total escort for every stage of a bomber's route was a long way from being possible as yet, but the latest versions of Spitfire, and the recently-introduced American P-47 Thunderbolt were being modified continually towards greater range and flight endurance. In 1943 two other fighter designs were to join the offensive and eventually prove significant : the twin-tailed, twin-engined Lockheed P-38 Lightning and, later, the P-51 Mustang.

To the less obtuse among the Luftwaffe operational commanders, the day of total escort was perilously approaching its dawning. With the massive industrial capacity of the bombing-proof USA for aircraft manufacture in untold thousands, and Germany's necessarily limited parallel production capability, the obvious conclusion must be total Allied reign in German skies ultimately. Clearly, the Luftwaffe could not hope to survive any all-out, slugging match of pure attrition; the 'arithmetic' was simply against it in any such contest-of-arms. The only real hope lay with technical superiority : new weapons, fresh aircraft types, original ideas in technology which would not require numerical superiority for total effectiveness.

CHAPTER NINE

Reaping the Whirlwind

The various Luftwaffe bombing attacks on civilian-populated cities in the early years of the war once prompted 'Butch' Harris, commander of RAF Bomber Command from 1942 and 1945, to quote Hosea from the Bible, saying, 'They have sown the wind, and they shall reap the whirlwind'. Apart from isolated attacks on Germany, such as the three '1,000-bomber' raids of 1942, however, his command was in no position to carry out Harris's threat until 1943 onwards. With the USAAF virtually commandeering the prerogative of bombing by daylight, the RAF concentrated almost its whole efforts from 1943 on a night offensive against Germany, endeavouring to translate into practice the intentions of the Casablanca and Pointblank Directives of future Allied bombing policy. The year 1943 was to see the first fruits of that practice. As related, Harris commenced his latest phase of operations on the night of 5 March 1943 with a heavy raid on Essen, the opening round of the so-termed Battle of the Ruhr. From then until July Bomber Command flew almost nightly to Germany in relatively high strength, ranging from some 100 to more than 800 aircraft per raid, and suffered distressingly high casualties. New radio and radar aids coming into general use increased *average* efficiency in target location and actual bombing results, but also provided a better measure of pre-warning, and thereby, protection – to the bomber crews from the predacious attentions of German nightfighters.

The parallel race for superior radar devices by both the RAF and Luftwaffe at this period produced a bewildering variety of technical innovations or vast improvements of earlier models of 'black boxes'. Several were parasitic, like the Serrate receiver fitted into some RAF fighters and bombers which picked up radar signals from *Lichtenstein*-equipped Luftwaffe fighter, and therefore offered the British crews a homing source. The earliest examples of Serrate were fitted into Beaufighter nightfighters of 141 Squadron in mid-1943 and contributed greatly to that unit's mounting success rate against the Luftwaffe. The possibilities of such extra 'eyes' in the night war led to a number of Mosquito fighters being threaded in to main force bomber streams bound for Germany, giving yet more protection to the Lancaster and Halifax crews.

One extraordinarily simple device, developed unknowingly in almost exact parallel by the RAF and the Luftwaffe technicians and civilian 'boffins' (scientists), was the strip of aluminium foil of precise length and width related to whatever radar wavelength was intended to be baffled, known to the RAF as Window, and to the Luftwaffe as *Düppel*. The basic idea of these foil strips used to confuse enemy radar location screens had been born several years before, and by March 1942 had been successfully tested in Britain. Only weeks later, however, Sholto Douglas of Fighter Command made an urgent request to Air Ministry for prohibition of the use of Window by Bomber Command until an antidote was developed. His reasoning was that, once used, Window could be easily copied and used by the Luftwaffe for raiding Britain. Accordingly, the Chief of the Air Staff, Portal, issued a virtual ban on use of the foil in May 1942. At almost the same time German scientists had carried out similar testing of their counterpart *Düppel* foil – with identical aftermath. Göring himself, on reading test reports of the disastrous dislocation of radar possible, ordered the cessation of all further experimentation, in case news of it was leaked to the Allies.

The internal controversy over whether or not to use Window operationally raged on within Air Ministry circles for almost a year. The apparently insoluble worry about enemy discovery and eventual counter-use of this weapon was a familiar argument to many British scientists, who had experienced similiar assertions about the use of the H2S radar device in previous years.

By April 1943, however, as the Battle of the Ruhr got under way, the arguments against using Window were being far outweighed by the escalating casualty figures in Bomber Command. British Intelligence suggested that perhaps seventy per cent of bombers lost over Germany were shot down by German radar-equipped and controlled nightfighters, indicating great improvement in German defensive strength and methods, while German bomber strength for possible retaliation against Britain was regarded as rapidly diminished. The first six months of 1943 had cost the RAF a total of 1,110 bombers on night raids alone, apart from a further 2,352 aircraft damaged by flak or nightfighters. Even calculating the number of German nightfighters actually fitted with radar as fifty per cent of those which shot down British bombers, the use of radar-baffling Window was estimated to have been able to have saved some thirty-five per cent of the casualties had it been in use, the equivalent of almost 300 bombers and their crews who might still have been alive and available for operations by June 1943. Such was the hypothesis which weighed most heavily in favour of immediate introduction of Window, and on 15 July 1943 the Prime Minister, Winston Churchill, personally authorised its use over Germany.

Just ten nights later Window was introduced to Germany, when nearly 750 RAF bombers released some 40 tons (or 92 million strips) of the aluminium foil over the ancient city of Hamburg. Ringed by 54 heavy radar-directed flak and 22 searchlight batteries, Hamburg was one of the best defended cities in Germany, as befitted its importance as a port and naval construction centre. Harris selected Hamburg deliberately, code-naming the projected destruction of the city Gomorrah, but warned that Germany's second largest city would not be 'eliminated' in any single raid. 'It is estimated that at least 10,000 tons of bombs will have to be dropped to complete the process . . .'

On the afternoon of 24 July the RAF bomber crews were briefed thoroughly, emphasis being stressed upon the vital need for the *concentrated* use of Window for self-protection, and just before 10 p.m. that evening the first bomber began its take-off run. Within the hour a total of 347 Lancasters, 246 Halifaxes, 125 Stirlings and 73 Wellingtons were airborne, a phalanx of 791 bomb-laden aircraft spread over nearly 200 miles between England and the target. Before the first gaggle of 20 H2S aircraft had arrived over Hamburg to commence marking, 46 bombers aborted their sorties due to mechanical problems, but at three minutes to one o'clock on the morning of 25 July Hamburg's ordeal commenced as the first salvos of blind markers began to fall.

The Hamburg defences – which included direct contact with six nightfighter airfields within combat range – were alerted early; radar warning and radio listening-out posts had detected the massive build-up of the bombers as they formated initially over the North Sea, and first indications of an incoming raid had been given as early as 11 p.m. by a coastal unit. At 12.19 a.m. the first sirens wailed in Hamburg, and at 12.31 a.m. the full *Fliegeralarm* was moaning its discordant tones across the city. The flak and searchlight batteries prepared quickly, while at all six airfields German nightfighter pilots, already strapped into their cockpits, began to take off towards their appointed radio beacon control centres, there to circle and await specific direction instructions for engaging the Tommies winging towards them. They waited in vain – the release of clouds of Window at carefully spaced one-minute intervals from the bombers had commenced, and on the ground radar screens were unable to distinguish the difference between real and phantom aircraft. Confusion mounted rapidly among the defence controllers; master searchlights, the dreaded 'blue' lights which usually pinpointed aircraft with deadly accuracy, meandered all over the sky, predicted flak soon realised the hopelessness of relying on their radar guidance systems and began firing blindly, nightfighter pilots with rare exception were bereft of precise target location and were left to their individual devices.

As the Path Finders completed their initial marking of the aiming point, the first wave of 110 Lancasters from Nos 1 and 5 Groups arrived over the centre of the city at two minutes past one o'clock and released their loads. Within thirty minutes the following waves had laid a seven-mile carpet of incendiaries along the approach leg to the heart of Hamburg, and of the 728 crews who later claimed to have hit the designated objective, at least 306 had dropped their cargoes well within three miles of the aiming point. When the last bomber finally quit the scene, Hamburg was burning with an intensity not seen before, and some 1,500 citizens were already dead. Back at base airfields the Intelligence staffs totted up the cost, and were staggered to realise that a mere 12 bombers had failed to return and 34 others could be classified as damaged, a loss rate of roughly twenty per cent of normally expected casualties for such a raid. Clearly, Window had saved hundreds of air crew men from possible death. The only losses to German nightfighters had been 'stragglers' – bombers flying high above or outside the protecting shroud of the main Window clouds, which appeared starkly obvious on fighter radar screens.

As dawn on 25 July revealed the horrifying carnage of the night's raid, the citizens of Hamburg, dazed and shocked, began to tackle the widespread conflagration which hung a pall of smoke over the crippled city. By early afternoon it was obvious that Hamburg had suffered its greatest destruction by any single night's attack to date, but the ordeal was far from over. At 20 minutes before 3 p.m. that day, Allied bombs were again falling on the Hanseatic city, this time from a formation of 68 B-17 Fortresses of USAAF Eighth Air Force. Though slotted in to the overall Gomorrah plan, this American mission was really one part of a full week of sustained raiding by the Eighth Air Force – known as 'Blitz week' to the crews – in which Ira Eaker made his greatest effort to date. On the first day, 24 July, Eaker despatched a force of 324 bombers to attack targets in Norway, all but one of which returned safely to English bases. The attack on Hamburg on 25

July was simply one prong of a projected three-fold thrust against specific targets in the Hamburg–Kiel areas. The Hamburg-bound Fortresses mostly bombed through cloud, but ran headlong into violent opposition from German day fighters. The savage infighting cost the Americans 14 bombers which fell to the fighters, while five others fell victims to highly accurate flak.

Even before the last shell-racked survivors regained their English bases, a handful of RAF Mosquitos were preparing to visit Hamburg. The latter were virtually 'pot-boilers', intended merely to prolong the tension of the city's defences, because the night's main objective was Essen's Krupps Works. Again, Window was used to great effect in nullifying German radar-controlled guns and fighters, and huge damage perpetrated upon the Krupps factories. The cost, 23 aircraft 'missing' and 67 damaged, represented almost half the loss rate of previous attacks against Essen, another example of the efficacy of the tinfoil 'clouds'. The following day, 26 July, saw the Eighth Air Force again bomb Hamburg in relatively small numbers, while that night the 'pot-boiler' Mosquito force renewed its campaign to keep Hamburg's population and defences alert.

The second heavy raid against the city by the RAF came on the night of 27 July. This time Bomber Command sent a force of 787 bombers and the attack commenced shortly before 1 a.m. on 28 July, when a total of 722 crews claimed to have bombed the target area.

This time the German defences claimed 17 bombers brought down, and damaged 49 others. Window had again been used but the German defenders were already adapting quickly to this menace. The morning following the first raid on the city had seen Göring and other German leaders initiate immediate countermeasures to the latest innovation of the RAF.

Göring's first move was to contact Major Hajo Herrmann, an ex-bomber pilot who had advocated supplementing normal radar-directed fighter defences by 'free-lance' fighters, operating by visual contact only. Ordering Herrmann to set up such a force, Göring thus authorised the formation of the first *Wilde Sau* ('Wild Boar') unit, JG300, a force of some 60 Messerschmitt Bf 109s and Focke Wulf Fw 190s with wide-ranging freedom of operational function.

The effect on Hamburg of the RAF's second major raid on 28 July was devastating. To the still-burning or smouldering havoc caused in the previous three days the main force of bombers added a blanket of incendiary and high explosive bombs, and the city suffered the phenomonon known as the fire-storm. Already heated air rising from the shattered city was accompanied by an incoming rush of colder air underneath, thereby adding oxygen 'fuel' to the existing fires and escalating both the temperatures and intensity of the holocaust. Soon the enormous convection currents achieved super-hurricane force, while air temperatures climbed rapidly beyond the 1000-degree Centigrade mark, an inferno of horror beyond any artist's ability to portray. At the vortex of this fire-storm conditions were beyond human description. People died within seconds of being subjected to the unimaginable heat, dying from oxygen-lack, carbon monoxide poisoning, even incandescence. Buildings, vehicles, even large trees became mere toys as the hurricanes of whirling heat rampaged through the streets of the city. Already devoid of water supplies, telephonic communications, and street access for rescue services from the crippling initial assault on 24/25 July, Hamburg 'died' on that awesome night of 28/29 July. By mid-afternoon of 29 July more than a million survivors of the holocaust had fled the area, leaving behind them some 40,000 dead among the smoking, burning rubble.

Even then the city's agony was not complete, for in the early hours of 30 July came the first glittering 'Christmas Trees' – the German nickname for the RAF Path Finders' pyrotechnic marker bombs and flares, heralding the RAF's third major assault of the 'Battle of Hamburg'. Initially, a force of 777 bombers set out, 700 of which claimed aiming point accuracy, though photographic evidence suggested that only 238 actually released their loads within three miles of the target-centrepoint. Losses for the RAF were higher than in the two previous raids : 30 bombers failed to return while a further 43 were seriously damaged, owing to the improved German fighter tactics. Yet these figures were still well below the anticipated 'norm' for any major RAF bombing attack.

The final blow of the Hamburg battle came on the night of 2 August, when Harris sent out a force of 740 bombers – 329 Lancasters, 235 Halifaxes, 105 Stirlings, 66 Wellingtons and five Mosquitos – to seal the destruction of the hapless city. For the first time weather conditions were by no means ideal – heavy cloud conditions to and over Hamburg, no moonlight, and rainstorms at ground level led to virtually total blind-bombing through the murk. Nevertheless, the bulk of bomb loads descended into the city area, and German nightfighters achieved some successes. Thirty bombers were lost and 54 others damaged, double the loss rate of the initial attack yet still supportable. In these four major actions against Hamburg the RAF had despatched a gross total of 3,095 individual sorties, dropped almost 9,000 tons of bombs – roughly half of these incendiary – and lost just 86 aircraft and their crews; less than ten per cent overall.

What did the Battle of Hamburg achieve? In the period 24 July to 3 August, Hamburg suffered the gutting of some 6,000 acres and almost forty per cent of its civilian population killed or 'unaccounted for'. As an industrial centre of great importance, Hamburg had come very near to Harris's intention of obliteration, and the wider effect of the RAF's concentration upon the city was reflected in the words of the Nazi Minister for Armaments, Albert Speer, who later recorded :

> . . . a rapid repetition of this type of attack upon another six German towns would inevitably cripple the will to sustain armament manufacture and war production. It was I who first verbally reported to the Führer at that time that a continuation of these attacks might bring about a rapid end to the war.

Thus, Harris had ostensibly demonstrated in no uncertain terms his command's apparent capability of foreshortening the war and bringing Hitler's empire to its knees. While no one could question the overall success of the Hamburg operations, certain factors leading to that success could not be depended upon for all future similar attempts to take out a whole city or equivalent large objective. Foremost, naturally, was the surprise use of Window, yet within weeks the German night defences had adapted to fresh countermeasure tactics which were to become at least partially successful. Hamburg was also a relatively easy target to locate and reach, being coastal in location and thereby requiring almost no depth in penetration of German skies. Targets further inland would inevitably incur greater hazards in running a gauntlet of well-prepared defences. And weather conditions, except for the 2 August raid, had been near-ideal for the bomber, leaving such a city as Hamburg peculiarly vulnerable to an incendiary raid of any significant weight. Clearly, only the most optimistic could ever hope for such a combination of good fortunes in any future attempts to obliterate a target – and Harris was nothing if not a realist.

If the Battle of Hamburg appeared to justify the policy of area bombing, its results were not immediately extended to other similar objectives, and RAF Bomber Command resumed its more normal variegation of nightly targets. Within days, however, the command was called upon to obliterate a rather more precise target – a form of bombing not to Harris's taste. Hitler's reaction to the news of the

RAF's first attack on Hamburg on 24/25 July had been violent anger, and on 25 July, pursuing his constant obsession with revenge attacks against Britain, he signed a decree for mass production of Germany's latest revenge weapon : the A4 (or as it was more usually titled, V2) super-rocket. Though it would be nearly a year before the first of these behemoths was to descend from the sky over England, most of the research and experimentation trials of the V2 were centred at Peenemunde on the Baltic coast. The nature of the German activities at Peenemunde had been suspected by Allied Intelligence for many months, and in June 1943 photo-reconnaissance evidence confirmed the presence at Peenemunde of what could only be long-range rockets palpably intended for use against Britain. Accordingly, Bomber Command was given instructions to take out this latest threat, and the crews detailed for the initial raid were told that the target *must* be destroyed at any cost – if the first attack failed, the operation would be repeated, at whatever cost, until success was achieved.

With these grim warnings uppermost in mind, the crews of 597 bombers set out on the night of 17/18 August 1943. Preceding the main bomber force were eight Mosquito bombers of the Path Finder Force who carried out a feint 'marking' of Berlin, as if in preparation for a heavy raid on Germany's premier city. This spoof marking had outstanding success in diverting the main nightfighter defenders away from Peenemunde, and as the first markers descended upon the rocket establishment, some 200 German *Wilde Sau* fighters were circling above Berlin – 100 miles away.

The Peenemunde raid was notable in many respects, not least for the use of a Master Bomber, Group Captain John Searby, to direct actual progression of the bombing over the target area, a technique initiated by Wing Commander Guy Gibson in the famous Dams Raid earlier in the year. The damage caused to Peenemunde was severe and undoubtedly contributed in some measure to delay in actual eventual use of this terror weapon against England, but was by no means as significant as contemporary claims assumed. The operation was also costly. Once the circling nightfighters over Berlin realised that the true target for the RAF that night was Peenemunde, they flew direct to the target area and plunged into the stream of bombers. In all, 40 bombers were brought down and 32 others heavily damaged; about half of which were credited to the 'freelance' fighters. High as this loss was for the RAF, it had been relatively lower than the expected figure. The bombers had been ordered to attack at considerably lower altitudes than normal in order, hopefully, to ensure accuracy – a ploy with inevitable risks from the flak barrage.

The success of the Hamburg operations pointed hopefully to similar devastation in other major German cities, with Berlin as the most obvious prime consideration for such tactics. On 23 August, therefore, Harris launched the first of three heavy attacks against the German capital. In the first, a force of 727 bombers was despatched but their intended objective was correctly diagnosed early by German defences and the *Wilde Sau* nightfighters were in ambush-readiness for the bomber crews even before the latter reached the outskirts of the city. A sprawling succession of combats resulted in at least 33 bombers being shot down by fighters, a further 20 damaged by fighter attacks, and 23 others becoming victims of the flak barrage.

The next two Berlin raids, on 31 August and 3 September, were equally expensive for the bombers. The *Wilde Sau* fighter pilots, now granted higher priority than the flak gunners, claimed no less than eighty per cent of the bombers which failed to return to base. The three Berlin attacks had cost the RAF 123 bombers destroyed by enemy action and a further 114 damaged heavily. Statistically, it was noticeable that in the first two raids the bulk of losses had been sustained by Halifaxes and Stirlings, yet the third raid, an all-Lancaster effort, still suffered slightly more than six per cent losses. The German antidote to RAF Window was, at least temporarily, highly effective, and success for the free-roaming *Wilde Sau* fighters was due in great measure to the very flexible tactics employed. Fighters were not strictly bound to particular airfields during operations, and could land anywhere convenient for refuelling, re-arming, and redeployment during actions.

If the losses during this triple-attack against Berlin seemed daunting, they did not deter Arthur Harris from his eventual aim of destroying the heart of Hitler's Reich. On 3 November 1943 in a minute to Winston Churchill, he wrote :

We can wreck Berlin from end to end if the USAAF will come in on it. It may cost us 400–500 aircraft. It will cost Germany the war.

Such a dramatic promise accorded with Churchill's sense of theatre, and he immediately gave his assent for Bomber Command to prosecute the Battle of Berlin. Historians, in too many cases, have tended to criticise Harris's decision to inaugurate the intense night-bombing campaigns of the 1943/44 winter in particular, usually on the grounds of the high casualties resulting 'balanced' against known *postwar* statistics of damage achieved, strategic importance, *et al*. Nevertheless, wars are not won with hindsight – only contemporary intelligence and intention can be the proper criteria. The three Berlin attacks of August–September had given clear illustration of the *possible* outcome of any further raids against such a heavily-defended target, deep in the German heartland. Yet every night's operations had singular aspects, not all of which were common to any other night effort. The constant and rapid changes in tactics, weapons, radar and radio aids, ever-shifting weather conditions, and a dozen other considerations dictated each separate operation – only unimaginative repetition of well-tried modes of attack or defence brought inevitable disaster.

Although precision bombing, such as the Dams Raid and Peene-munde attack, had brought isolated successes during 1943, it was a form of aerial warfare still elusive to the contemporary Bomber Command crews. Thus the area bombing policy, usually and mistakenly attributed almost solely to 'Butch' Harris, was the only practicable means of destruction open to Harris's crews. The crux of all bombing success was accuracy in, first, marking the aiming point for the main force, and, generally, navigational precision. It was with these two major problems in mind that No 8 (Path Finder) Group had been formed in mid-1942, and by the close of 1943 the PFF had accumu-lated prodigious experience in the role of spearhead. Nevertheless, the PFF, and Bomber Command overall, were still far short of the standard of expertise which might automatically ensure both maxi-mum effect and minimal cost. The Battle of Berlin operations were to give added emphasis to the command's vulnerability. Harris's proviso for USAAF participation in the projected hammering of Berlin was, perhaps, over-optimistic in the contemporary climate of bombing operations. Eaker's Eighth Air Force was neither equipped, trained, or experienced enough for any worthwhile contribution to *any* night offensive; indeed, until mid-1944 even its stubborn adherence to day-light precision attack was to remain questionable. Moreover, RAF bombers could lift more than double the average bomb-loads of the American Fortresses and Liberators, an effective weight ratio of de-livered bombs which argued strongly in favour of an all-RAF offensive on the more vital targets.

Harris's chief weapon for the Battle was intended to be the Lan-caster, though in the event the contribution of the Halifax was far greater than originally surmised. With the Stirling and Wellington being almost phased out of firstline bombing operations, the pre-1939 ideal of an all-heavy bomber force almost reached its fruition during the Berlin Battle. The one outstanding exception was the astonishingly versatile DH Mosquito bomber. Capable of lifting a 4000-lb 'Cookie' blast bomb as far as Berlin, the Mosquito possessed superlative qualities of speed and manoeuvrability, assets reflected in its overall loss rates usually well under one per cent. Yet throughout the Berlin operations Harris had less than 60 Mosquitos at his disposal at any given time, compared to a heavy strength varying between 800 and almost 1,000.

By late 1943 it would have been impossible to alter the long-standing intention of converting RAF Bomber Command to a force basically equipped with four-engined, long range, strategic aircraft but the efficiency of the Mosquito, particularly demonstrated in the Berlin operations of 1943/44, at least justified speculation of a more balanced mixture of such aircraft. As it proved, the relatively tiny Mosquito force made contributions far greater than its quantitative strength implied. Operating in small formations or, often, singly, Mosquitos were used for feint, diversion raids and pot-boiling interim sorties between major attacks, apart from an increasingly important role in the initial marking phases of main force raids.

On the night of 18 November 1943 Harris despatched 444 bombers to Berlin, the first of sixteen major operations against the city between that night and 24 March 1944. Collectively, these sixteen raids constituted the greatest attack against a single target ever launched to date by the RAF, involving a gross total of 9,111 individual sorties, of which 7,256 were flown by Lancasters, 1,643 by Halifaxes, 162 by Mosquitos and 50 by Stirlings. In addition, sixteen minor pot-boiling raids were made on Berlin by totals of 186 Mosquito and 22 Lancaster sorties. At the outset Harris had declared that his force might lose '400 to 500' bombers, and in this prophecy he was to be almost a hundred per cent correct. Casualties for the whole Battle included 111 Halifaxes and 376 Lancasters missing; a further 944 'Hallies' and 'Lancs' were seriously damaged, many of these becoming write-offs. In human terms, the effort cost almost 3,500 air crew members killed, missing or prisoners of war, the toll of just *part* of some eighteen weeks' bombing offensive. And it is stressed that the Berlin sorties were only slightly less than half the overall effort flown against Germany during those weeks, because interspersed with attacks against the 'Big City' were nineteen raids against at least twelve other important German centres, involving a total of 11,113 individual sorties. These, and other non-major sorties over the same period, accounted for a further 641 aircraft classified as missing, almost 4,500 more air crew men lost to the command. It might truthfully be said that those four and a half months' operations cost RAF Bomber Command the equivalent of its complete firstline strength as it stood before the opening attack against Berlin.

Contrary to Harris's expressed conviction, however, the Battle of Berlin failed to achieve its stated purpose. Huge tracts of Berlin acreage were razed to rubble, especially in the western sectors of the city, but by no stretch of the imagination was the capital city 'wrecked from end to end'. Moreover, the adopted tactic of increased density of concentration of main force bombers over the actual target area – devised to get the crews through the most dangerous section of the whole operation in the shortest possible time – proved to play into the capable hands of the Luftwaffe's nightfighters. Acting now under voice ground control, instead of pure radar or individual guidance (the *Wilde Sau* tactic, later supplemented by other similar methods of direct control evolved in 'answer' to the Window problem) the fighter force could be readily concentrated in mass onslaughts against any detected incoming bomber stream, providing the ultimate target had been deduced early and correctly. Combat engagements over the actual target area occurred more frequently, while on some occasions interception took place before the bombers even reached the coastline on their approach routes. During the five months of November 1943 to March 1944 inclusive, German nightfighter pilots were officially credited with slightly more than 1,000 *confirmed* victories, despite the many shortcomings of 'non-radar' directional control – a figure remarkably close to the known RAF losses to fighter attacks, and most probably a slight underestimation.

The *Nachtjäger*'s greatest triumph came on the night of 30/31 March 1944. That night the RAF despatched an overall total of 999 British and ten American aircraft to Germany, 795 of which were the prime striking force sent to bomb Nuremberg. The ensuing operation, dismally planned and dogged by much more than a normal ration of misfortunes, witnessed a virtual massacre of the strung-out bomber stream as Luftwaffe nightfighters made the most of bright moonlight, 'fighter flares' dropped above the bombers to mark their path, and the 250-miles long undeviating run-up by the bombers to their final turning-point onto target-bearing. The Allied target had been deduced relatively early, and fighters were assembled in ample time to intercept. By the early morning of 31 March no less than 94 bombers had been shot down – 79 by fighters – while eleven more crashed on return to England; a loss rate of almost 14 per cent, and the highest single loss figure for the RAF throughout the war. It had been a 'fighter night' *par excellence* – German losses only amounted to five aircraft – while one pilot of NJG1, Oberlutnant Becker, claimed seven bombers alone. Nuremberg undoubtedly marked the pinnacle of German nightfighter successes, but for the men of RAF Bomber Command this particular operation became a byword synonymous with disaster – it had been their greatest single defeat.

The Nuremberg debacle also marked the close of Bomber Command's year-long attempt to pursue the Pointblank Directives's aim of 'bludgeon-bombing' German industrial and suburban centres, because on 1 April 1944 Harris's command came under the aegis of the American General 'Ike' Eisenhower, appointed supreme commander of all Allied forces about to assemble or participate for the projected land invasion of Europe in mid-1944. Henceforth, emphasis for bombing attacks was to be, in the short-term, confined to objectives in France, a softening-up campaign intended to pave the path forward for the invasion troops once these had established a foothold on the Continent.

Even without this priority the possibility of continuing the heavy offensive by night against Germany was speculative. Shortening nights during the spring and early summer meant added hazards for any bomber force attempting to penetrate German defences as deeply as Berlin, while the obvious ascendancy of the Luftwaffe's nightfighters, exemplified grimly at Nuremberg, added plentiful argument against any continuance of such mass attacks. Another avenue of argument against continuing the Pointblank-style of aerial bombing was concerned with pure achievement. Throughout Bomber Command's long and bloody year of applying sheer weight of attack, its crews flew almost 75,000 individual sorties against major objectives; from this 2,864 aircraft had been lost – in human terms, more than 20,000 men killed or missing. In balance, some 26,000 acres spread among 43 German cities had been devastated. Yet German war production had hardly been dented; indeed, fighter production rose in the period 1943–44. Crushing raids, such as the Hamburg Battle, had severely shaken German civilian morale, but any initial disruption of such vital production centres as Essen had been quickly rectified by a masterly, urgent dispersion of production facilities throughout Europe. The 'pause' in pursuing the area bombing principle from April 1944 gave further opportunity for the German war production to recover and even escalate. Whatever the pros and cons, however, the combined Allied night and day offensive – primarily – had by early 1944 accomplished one hugely marked reversal in the tenor of the whole war; it had forced Germany onto an irrevocable defensive stance, a desperate fighting 'rearguard' posture which would only cease when Hitler's Nazi empire finally lay in ruins.

While Harris's crews were making history in a saga of unwavering fortitude and bloody sacrifice in the night skies over Germany, their gritty courage and determination was being matched by the Fortress, Liberator and Marauder crews of Eaker's USAAF Eighth Air Force by day. Ostensibly slotted into the day-gaps in the RAF's bombing forays, in fact the 'Mighty Eighth' was in essence pursuing an entirely different and virtually separate form of offensive. With the exceptions of its four pioneering bombardment Groups, the Eighth's crews were mostly raw in hard battle experience, and the year 1943 was used mainly to expand in size and to 'experiment' with various forms of attack methods. Though only a fraction of the size of RAF Bomber Command at that stage, the Eighth Air Force was determined to achieve parity in quality of achievement. Thus, in the period May to October 1943, it passed through its most crucial testing time. During those months almost every mission flown meant that the bombing formations were, to all intents, literally 'on their own'. RAF diversionary raids were often laid on with the hope of attracting Luftwaffe fighter opposition away from the American bombers' routes, while contemporary versions of Spitfires and P-47 Thunderbolt fighters provided aerial escort to shallow depth into enemy-held territory.

Once beyond the combat range of their fighter cover, the bombers were devoid of outside protection, and survival depended on maintaining position in the overlapping, carefully-blueprinted 'box' formations, which thereby provided an interlaced trelliswork of defence from the hydra-headed barrage of fire produced by the defensive gunners. German fighter pilots had learned quickly the futility of tackling these gun-bristling box formations with normal anti-bomber tactics; a box of 100 Fortresses meant they had to plunge through the crossfire of more than a thousand .50-inch calibre machine guns pumping out shells. Instead the Luftwaffe interceptors adopted a wide variety of ploys. Chief amongst these was the multi-fighter head-on assault, particularly against the leading groups which contained bombing leaders. Others favoured targets were the lowest formations, and especially any bomber which had wavered out of the protection of its fellows; stragglers seldom survived when isolated.

Throughout that fateful summer the Fortress and Liberator crews fought a no-quarter battle against weather, fighters, flak, and an ever-increasing toll of aircraft and men. Luftwaffe fighter strength had slowly increased during mid-1943, as the defences of the Reich became a high priority for Göring, and these occasionally inflicted savagely high casualties on particular American missions. On 17 August 1943 – the first anniversary of the USAAF's first-ever operations from England – a two-pronged mission in great strength was scheduled to attack two separate objectives; the Messerschmitt aircraft factories at Regensburg, and the ball-bearing manufacturers at Schweinfurt, both targets being deep in Germany. The original plan was for both forces – 147 Fortresses to Regensburg and 230 B-17s to Schweinfurt – to attack almost simultaneously, thereby dividing Luftwaffe opposition. In the event, the Schweinfurt force was delayed in take-off by weather condtions over its English bases and did not get away until the Regensburg formations were deep into enemy territory. P-47 Thunderbolts detailed for escort to the German borders accompanied the Regensburg Fortresses until fuel states dictated their return to base, whence they were then immediately turned round to protect the Schweinfurt bombers.

The Luftwaffe reaction to both raiding forces was violent and in large numbers. As the Fortresses were just fifteen minutes from the Belgian coast plunging inland, the first German fighters struck at the lowest, rear Group. Only minutes later the P-47s were forced to turn for home; the bombers were on their own. For the next one and a half hours the Fortresses were subjected to a continuous onslaught by a horde of German fighters which attacked from every possible angle in force, and the bombers' track to target became littered with the wreckage of 47 Fortresses brought down and a handful of Luftwaffe fighters. The unceasing combat was described by one lead bomber pilot as '. . . fantastic; it surpassed fiction.'

Finally reaching their objective, the surviving Fortresses bombed from 17,000 to 19,000 feet with excellent precision, causing major damage to two-thirds of the workshops and, incidentally, destroying most of the fuselage jigs for the still-secret Messerschmitt Me 262 jet fighters being built there. For another half-hour after leaving the target, the bombers were again subjected to fighter attacks, but instead of swinging back across Germany, as expected by the Luftwaffe, the surviving formations headed across the Alps south-westerly, crossed Italy and the Mediterranean, and finally let down at North African Allied bases. Total losses were 24 Fortresses, of which five had ditched in the sea, one crashed in Italy, and two had been forced to land in Switzerland; the rest lay in Germany.

The Schweinfurt raid penetrated Germany along much the same path as its predecessors, but turned north-east near Mannheim for the ultimate run-in to target. Against them was pitted an even greater fighter force than the Regensburg bombers, when at least 200 German fighters provided a running battle to, over, and from the objective. As the last survivors finally reached sanctuary over England, they had left behind them a tragic trail of 36 Fortresses shot or forced down. Thus the day's toll amounted to 60 bombers missing for the two raids; some 700 men gone within a few hours, apart from the many other dead and wounded brought 'home' in flak-scarred, shell-racked aircraft. An indication of the intensity of the combat engagements was the gross total of 288 German fighters claimed by Fortress gunners that day, whereas in fact Luftwaffe losses amounted to merely 25 destroyed. Though significant damage had been caused to both objectives in these missions, a loss rate of almost one in five bombers was prohibitive in any long-term offensive; nevertheless, the Eighth Air Force continued its assault on the Reich.

For nearly six weeks after the Schweinfurt–Regensburg epic battles the Americans restricted raiding to targets in the Channel coast areas of France; partly due to weather conditions over Europe which prevented any major strike against Germany being worthwhile, but also as part of the pre-invasion deception plans attempting to persuade German commanders that such an invasion would be launched in the Pas de Calais area. One attempt to mount a major raid with 338 B-17s against Stuttgart on 6 September was foiled by heavy cloud, and then savaged by German fighters, losing 45 bombers; but serious raids against German target only recommenced in October, when several days offered good visibility for precision attacks. By then too the first long-range P-47 Thunderbolts were becoming available, enabling a fighter escort to remain with the bombers for some 300 miles. The Luftwaffe opposition had, however been vastly increased by that time, with almost 800 fighters available, the bulk of these stationed within Germany itself. The German fighters were also carrying heavier and new forms of armament, devised particularly for attacks on the B-17s, including extra 30mm cannons and 21cm rockets. Against these, the Fortress squadrons began receiving new models of the B-17, the B-17G variant, fitted with extra armament protection and, most importantly, a power-operated chin turret up front to combat the Luftwaffe's head-on tactics.

October 1943 brought a series of heavy-numbered missions, with daunting casualty figures. On 8 and 9 October the Eighth Air Force lost 30 and 28 bombers respectively, but on 14 October the Fortresses returned to Schweinfurt, scene of their greatest loss on the previous

17 August mission. A force of 291 bombers were initially despatched against the ball-bearing factories, and these met an overall opposition of some 400 German fighters en route. The sprawling gunbattles which ensued saw no less than 60 bombers brought down, while on return to England 17 others either crashed or were written-off due to battle damage, and 121 others needed plentiful repair. Some 600 men were missing, while five dead and 43 wounded men were taken out of returning bombers. Damage caused to Schweinfurt was extensive, halting full production until six months later, but such losses could not be sustained indefinitely by any air service.

The long-held 'sacred cow' theory of the self-defensive bomber was now recognised as a faulty doctrine by USAAF senior commanders. In future long-range bombing missions would depend on long-ranging fighter escort to obviate the continuing massive German fighter onslaughts. By the close of 1943 this latter concept was becoming possible. The P-47 Thunderbolt could already stay with the 'big brothers' for some 300 miles, while the recently introduced P-51B Mustangs, fitted with external supplementary fuel tanks, could stay with the heavy bombers almost all the way to any target in Germany. A third fighter recently brought to the European theatre of operations was the Lockheed P-38 twin-engined fighter from which much was expected, but technical troubles with its engines in the cold, dank European climate nullified the design's operational usefulness, at least for the moment.

As the shortening days and increasing murk of the 1943/44 winter clamped down over England, the USAAF's Eighth Air Force recuperated, replenished, and began preparations for a renewed day offensive in the new year. Meanwhile RAF Bomber Command opened its Battle of Berlin campaign, and steadily increased its weight of destruction across the German border. For the Luftwaffe 1943 had been a year of very mixed fortunes in Europe. The incessant calls upon its overall strength for the Russian and Mediterranean theatres had made deep inroads on existing aircraft and crews, but thanks to the prodigious efforts of General Erhard Milch's production drive, by January 1944 overall Luftwaffe numerical strength had risen to some twenty per cent more than the appropriate figure in January 1943. In particular, much emphasis had been placed on fighter production, while a large proportion of ostensible bomber designs were now being produced, modified and employed in defence of the Reich. By the end of January 1944 the German nightfighter force could list a total of almost 1,000 aircraft, the bulk of these being Junkers Ju 88s and Messerschmitt Bf 110s, festooned with the latest radar devices and heavy armament.

Improved fuel stocks and newly-designed aircraft shortly coming into service, added to the obvious successes of the Reich defences over the RAF and USAAF throughout the year, might have tended towards a feeling of euphoria among Luftwaffe commanders at the start of 1944. It was only to be a matter of a few weeks before any such dreamworld was rudely cracked open.

CHAPTER TEN

They Also Served

To most civilians – and indeed no few servicemen or women – the prime facets of the aerial war of 1939–45 were the daily-publicised achievements of the fighter and bomber arms of each nation's air forces. The pseudo-glamour of fighter combat with its inherited charisma of 'duelling aces', and the awesome destructive power of the bomber, impinged directly upon populations whose routine lives were often affected starkly by the ramifications of one or both of these particular aspects of the air war. Compounded by the constant attention given to the exploits of fighter and bomber crews by the radio and press media of the period, such emphasis tended to obscure other equally significant, even vital roles undertaken by the men of other aspects of the struggle in the air. Two such 'silent services' in particular were the constant endeavour of maritime airmen over sea and ocean, and the necessarily cloaked activities of the photo-reconnaissance branches of each air service. Neither attracted much public attention or even a proportional 'ration' of service recognition in terms of honours or awards, yet both were instrumental in ensuring the eventual outcome of the war.

As an island Britain had always depended for its existence on imported goods and raw materials, and in wartime the ocean life-lines became the arteries of the nation's war effort. Without such constant replenishment by sea Britain could never have sustained its role as a base for continuing opposition to the grandiose ambition of world conquest envisaged by the Nazi hierarchy. Thus even before war with Germany had been legally sanctioned, Britain's Royal Navy and RAF Coastal Command swung into action in a protective role for the ocean-bound mercantile convoys and other shipping. Apart from the individual enemy capital ship as an ocean raider, the prime enemy was the submarine, the U-boat (*Unterseeboot*), which could roam the oceans almost at will and, in the early stages of the sea war, was almost undetectable in its approach to any intended shipping target. The vast canvas of the seas gave surface ships little hope of any permanent solution to such a threat, but the aeroplane offered, ostensibly, a far wider range of countermeasures. From the air could be watched a vista far beyond the capability of any surface vessel, while any attack could be delivered within minutes and from any angle. This constant, hovering threat to any U-boat became an effective deterrent and deadly hazard for all German submariners throughout the war. Outside their purely protective duties, Coastal Command crews also pursued a constant offensive role against other German shipping. As a partially landlocked country, Germany too depended heavily on imported raw materials for its war industries, and merchant shipping intended for Axis ports became prime targets at all times for roving Coastal aircraft.

Though the major part of Coastal Command's war during the first four years of the conflict was concerned with the Battle of the Atlantic – and therefore outside the parameters of this book – no little activity was concentrated around Britain's coastal waters, especially the English Channel, the Bay of Biscay, and the North Sea. These were the main hunting grounds for Coastal Command's strike squadrons where any surface vessel was legitimate prey for RAF attack. The command's actual capability for such operations at the outset of war was, frankly, minimal. Of its 20 available squadrons of all types of aircraft, only two were designated as torpedo-strike units, and these were equipped with obsolete Vickers Vildebeeste biplanes. In November 1939, however, the first examples of a new, twin-engined monoplane torpedo-bomber, the Bristol Beaufort, reached 22 Squadron; while by early 1940 a number of Blenheim and Wellington bombers had been diverted from Bomber Command to Coastal for anti-shipping sorties. With these few and hastily converted aircraft the Coastal strike crews attempted to scour British coastal waters throughout 1940, a task which assumed greater importance after the fall of France, when Germany acquired control of coastlines stretching along France, the Low Countries, Baltic and northwards along Norway. Such occupation gave German naval units open access to the Atlantic for sea-raiders, while the Norwegian fiords and harbours became bases from which to harass any Allied shipping in the North Sea. Existing Coastal Command aircraft were incapable of any truly long-range offensive, and Bomber Command was therefore called upon to devote a substantial part of its effort then to attacks against naval targets, such as Brest, the Channel ports of northern France, Belgium, Holland, and Germany itself. By June 1940, of the 500 aircraft available to Coastal Command for all facets of its role, only a handful of Sunderland flying boats were able to operate beyond 500 miles from base.

The continuing lack of sufficient or suitable designs for Coastal

Command's anti-shipping sorties throughout 1941 meant involving yet another command, in this case Fighter, for the role. Additionally, No 2 Group's Blenheim crews of Bomber Command were detailed to concentrate on all enemy shipping between Brittany and Germany, with peripheral patrols over the northern sections of the North Sea. The Blenheims commenced these duties in March 1941 and continued such operations until November. The ultimate cost to 2 Group was frightening, rising to thirty per cent on occasion, and for relatively small achievement overall. These operations, made mainly in daylight, involved the Blenheim crews in ultra-low level attacks in the teeth of fierce flak, while the range at which many attacks were made meant that fighter escort could seldom be provided to soften up opposition effectively or cover the bombers from Luftwaffe interference.

As the appalling casualties mounted among the Blenheim crews, the morale of the survivors was severely taxed; yet they returned to the fray almost daily and never once flinched from pressing home attacks at the closest quarter irrespective of the intense fury of the opposition. Though the main operations flown by 2 Group at that period, the bomber crews interspersed these Channel Stop – code-name for the anti-shipping duties –sorties with direct bombing raids against ports and harbour installations along the enemy-occupied coastlines of France, Belgium and Holland, raids also involving deck-level flying through murderous barrages of flak and high casualties. Returning aircraft, often riddled with shell damage, commonly bore evidence of their 'grass-height' aerobatics with pieces of cable, trees, and other debris adorning wing-tips and bellies.

New designs of aircraft for Coastal Command filtered slowly into the squadrons during 1941–42. The Atlantic battle was reinforced by the addition of the first Catalina flying boats, while the anti-shipping units began to receive first examples of a twin-engined, rugged design evolved from the Beaufort: the pugnacious Beaufighter. With an armament punch of four 20mm cannons and six machine guns, the 'Beau' was strong and heavy, with long-ranging potential destructive power. First to receive the Beaufighter within Coastal Command were 143 and 152 Squadrons, but it was several months before these became even moderately effective in the strike role. The first Strike Wing came into being in November 1942 at North Coates, comprised of Nos 143, 236 and 254 Squadrons, each squadron had a separate role as fighter, fighter-bomber, and torpedo-bomber respectively and thereby (in theory at least) was self-protecting. The wing's first strike operation on 20 November proved to be a fiasco, however; for three ships of a convoy claimed as damaged, the wing lost three Beaus in the action, and four others which crashed or force-landed on return. The wing was immediately taken off operations for intensive training and did not re-enter the lists until April 1943. The overall intention was to equip Coastal Command with 15 Beaufighter squadrons by April 1943, and in May the North Coates wing received its first rocket-armed Beaus, using these operationally as a wing for the first time on 22 June 1943. Meanwhile, the effectiveness of a Beau's three-inch rocket projectiles had been firmly established by Flight Lieutenant 'Mike' Bateman of 236 Squadron who attacked the *U-418* on 1 June and sank it.

By May 1943 the Beaufighters of Coastal were joined by another classic aircraft, the De Havilland Mosquito. On 10 May 1943, the first Coastal Mosquito unit was formed at Leuchars, when 333 (Norwegian) Squadron was 'born' from a nucleus of No 1477 Flight. The Mosquito's longer range, faster speed, and equally heavy armament meant that the Beaufighter would eventually be superseded by 'Mozzies', but in the interim the two types flew in complementary roles. Prime targets for both Beaufighter and Mosquito crews were all varieties of surface shipping, rather than U-boats, and in this role their depredations knew no limits. Ranging far and wide over the North Sea to Norway's fretted coastline, all along the northern European coastline, or south across the Irish Sea and, especially, the notorious Bay of Biscay; they pounced on any vessel flying the crooked cross of Hitler's Germany. Opposition from the Luftwaffe was frequent and often violent, and many pitched battles occurred between the Coastal crews and Junkers Ju 88s and Focke Wulf Fw 190s over the restless seas. Although their main task remained the harassment of enemy shipping, Coastal Beau and Mosquito crews were often called upon – usually at minimal notification – to act as pure fighter cover for Allied merchant ship convoys in danger of Luftwaffe attack. Once arrived above their designated charges, the crews were as often as not greeted with a distinctly unfriendly gun barrage from Royal Navy escorts to such convoys. Throughout the war the naval gunners earned notoriety for their 'shoot first, ask questions later' quickness on the trigger against any aircraft within range; in itself an unconscious tribute to the potential destructive power of aircraft. Such unfriendly gestures were stoically accepted by Coastal crews as part of the job, and their ever-ready willingness to assist their web-footed comrades-in-arms remained unwavering.

The wide use of cannon-armed, rocket-carrying, Beaus and Mosquitos against surface shipping – and later U-boats – did not imply any lack of faith in the air-dropped torpedo as an effective weapon. The courage and determination of Coastal's Beaufort crews during 1940–41 had proved the efficacy of the torpedo against ships of any size, though Beauforts were relatively few in number on operations, and the design had insufficient performance range to exploit such a tactic to its limits. Nevertheless, the airborne torpedo required conditions of use seldom encountered in the rough and tumble of operations, and was essentially a 'one-shot' weapon, permitting no second chance of success should the initial launch be inaccurate or wrongly placed. The ubiquitous armament fitted in Beaufighters and Mosquitos offered far more varied opportunities for attacking almost any form of target, in virtually any sort of conditions. An example of the magnificent Mosquito's ubiquity was the installation of a 57mm Molins cannon in the FB XVIII variant. Only a dozen of these 'Tsetse' Mosquitos were actually built, and the first two were sent to 248 Squadron at Predannack in October 1943. The 'Tsetse' version had been developed quickly as an additional anti-submarine weapon, and though the type continued on operations until well into 1944, no U-boat was actually sunk by an FB XVIII.

The bulk of Coastal strike squadrons remained equipped with the Beaufighter throughout 1943, and their operational versatility was perhaps best exemplified by those who attacked enemy shipping along the Norwegian coast. Such sorties involved a long haul across the coldly inviting waters of the North Sea, often through conditions of cloud, fog, rain or even snow blizzards, and called for precise navigation to make landfall on some relatively insignificant fiord or inlet. Once over the Norwegian coastline, the Beau crews then needed to search among a myriad of possible hiding places for enemy vessels among the thousand or more fiords. Inside most fiords the Beaufighters had little room to manoeuvre, being usually hemmed in on two or even three sides by towering, vertical cliff-faces which could spell disaster for any ill-calculated manoeuvre. Enemy ships often anchored as close as possible to the fiord sides, thereby diminishing even further any attacking aircraft's freedom of action. Thundering through the menacing rock faces at 250 mph or faster, with target acquisition confined to mere seconds, called for delicate and highly concentrated skills – and no small courage as the Coastal crews ran gauntlets of raw nature and man-made flak opposition. Once within range of the coastline, whether approaching, over, or leaving, Beaufighter and Mosquito crews were always susceptible to Luftwaffe fighter attack from the nearest German airfields in Norway. The only escape route was the open sea; five or six hundred miles of the North Sea to be crossed with steadily reducing fuel states, apart from the not uncommon problems of shattered engines or airframes or control surfaces racked by cannon or flak shells.

Apart from the obvious value of harrying and destroying Axis shipping, the Coastal Command unceasing offensive around the North Sea, Channel and Biscay zones had the desirable effect of forcing the Luftwaffe to retain fighter and bomber units in Norway and France which might otherwise have been added to the night defences or the campaign in the east against Russia. By June 1943 the Luftwaffe's equivalent anti-shipping forces stood at their lowest ebb, due in great measure to the attrition of German torpedo-bomber and other anti-shipping units in the Mediterranean area during 1942–43, and by mid-1943 there remained only two *Gruppen* – some fifty Junkers Ju 88 torpedo-carrying aircraft fit for operations, backed by a miscellany of day fighters and a handful of the four-engined Focke Wulf Fw 200 long-range types. With the certain belief that the Allies would attempt an invasion of France in the near future, some attempts were made in 1943 to expand the Luftwaffe's ability to attack shipping. The ultimate aim was to form at least five *Gruppen* of torpedo-bombers by June 1944, apart from enlargement and re-equipment of existing forces. Fresh equipment included the Heinkel He 177 four-engined bomber, Dornier 217s carrying Hs 293 glider-bombs or *Fritz-X* radio-guided missiles, while one outlandish project attempted was the *Mistel* ('Mistletoe') pick-a-back combination of a crewless Ju 88 stuffed with high explosive surmounted by a Bf 109 fighter; the pilot in the latter controlled the whole unwieldy contraption and was able to 'drop' the Ju 88 at close quarters against Allied naval targets.

Hopes for an eventual force of some 450 specialised aircraft and crews for anti-shipping operations by mid-1944 never reached fruition. The increasing priority accorded to fighter production for defence of the Reich, and a proportionally high casualty rate among anti-shipping units during late 1943 and early 1944, left the force with less than 250 aircraft by April 1944, and far less than 200 by June of that year.

If the roles of the opposing coastal air services tended to be individualistic in operation and barely publicised, an even lonelier – and unpublicised – facet of the aerial war was the Trojan work of the photo-reconnaissance crews. Apprehension by the German General Staff of a forthcoming Allied land invasion of northern Europe had been evident from 1941, resulting in the gradual construction of a vast, impressive line of ground fortifications along the French coast facing the English Channel. An appropriate expansion of a Luftwaffe force to support such defences was, nevertheless, never accomplished in significant strength. The many other commitments of Germany's air arm – in the east against Russia, in Italy against the slowly advancing Allied armies, and a dozen other lesser priorities – imposed a steady drain on French-based air strength by the start of 1944. This relative weakness was exacerbated by the general lack of pre-intelligence of Allied intentions gathered by the Luftwaffe, particularly about the size and locations of possible invasion forces assembling in southern England in early 1944.

That the Luftwaffe should be so deprived by 1944 might, at first sight, appear surprising. In pre-war years no small amount of time, money and enthusiastic energy had been invested in creating a wide and efficient – for its designated purposes – organisation for photo-reconnaissance. The Luftwaffe's High Command, backed by Göring personally, was well appreciative of the value of photo-recce; indeed, in 1938 the contemporary Army commander-in-chief, von Fritsch, had declared, 'The military organisation that has the best photographic intelligence will win the next war'. In pursuance of this principle, the Luftwaffe, by the outbreak of war in 1939, possessed sufficient photo-recce units and personnel to account for almost one-fifth of its overall establishment. However, this strength was almost wholly decentralised among the various army formations, with no real central 'filter bank' to gather, process, interpret, store and disseminate any gathered intelligence to Luftwaffe commanders in general.

Like its parent Luftwaffe organisation, the photo-reconnaissance service was strictly linked to the needs of the army on a purely tactical plane, and therein lay its weakness. The essence of German army thinking at the outset was geared to the principle of *Blitzkrieg*, with speed and on-the-spot immediacy in operations over-shadowing any long-term strategic needs or views. Accordingly, German photo-recce units, and the information they gathered, tended to be confined to individual army formations; any broader, interlinked network of intelligence accumulated by the airborne camera crews was seldom immediately available to any other neighbouring formation. Such centralised organisation as was inaugurated by the middle years of the war was confined mainly to the creation of a mere administrative paper factory, rather than any focal store of operational intelligence for use by any unit needing or requesting same.

The counterpart photo-reconnaissance organisation in the RAF had very different beginnings, developing with an entirely different outlook on the use of such services. Clandestine photographing of Germany had been undertaken by the French air services throughout the 1920s and 1930s, albeit in crude forms; while the Luftwaffe bomber crews of 1939–41 were usually supplied with air photographs of many of Britain's chief aerodromes, civil and military, originally obtained by the civil Lufthansa airliner crew of the late 1930s. Broadly speaking, all such efforts at 'aerial espionage' were piecemeal, rather than part of any deliberately planned, overall intelligence scheme.

Within the peacetime RAF, despite the enormous lessons of the 1914–18 air war in the context of the value of aerial photography, no form of basic photo-recce organisation *per se* even existed until early 1938, when a department of air intelligence to co-ordinate photographic intelligence in the RAF was established by the Air Ministry. The need for such an organisation had not been without its enthusiastic advocates: in 1937 the commander of Bomber Command, Sir Edgar Ludlow-Hewitt, had proposed the creation of suitably modified long-range reconnaissance aircraft for photo-recce, but the financial resources available for such 'one-off' design developments were virtually nil, as the RAF hastily expanded its standard force of aircraft for more normal roles.

The needs of the army were already considered to be well catered for by such specialised aircraft as the high-wing Westland Lysander; while the requirements of Bomber Command could be fulfilled by normal bomber crews, whose observers were part-trained in the use of aerial cameras. This latter view regarded cameras as merely one more form of impedimenta able to be carried and operated by regular bomber crews, rather than basic instruments of any entirely individual role in warfare.

The possibilities for specialised aerial photography were exemplified by a civilian, Sidney Cotton, in 1938–39 when, as part of a British Intelligence agency, he calmly flew a civil Lockheed 12a airliner over Germany, ostensibly as a businessman, and obtained many photos of German military airfields and fortifications with his own camera installations. Nevertheless, on the outbreak of war Cotton's small civilian organisation was at first almost ignored, and the RAF relied on the Blenheim bombers of No 2 Group, Bomber Command to gather any photographic intelligence. The total unsuitability of the standard Blenheim IV bomber for such a role became quickly evident. Of the first 48 Blenheim recce sorties of the war, eight aircraft were shot down, while eight other sorties had failed to bring back photographs, owing

mainly to weather conditions. Such patent failures, compared to
Cotton's continuing successes, resulted in Cotton being enlisted as commander of a tiny – and very secret – photo-reconnaissance unit, based
at Heston and in the aegis of No 11 Group, Fighter Command from
late September 1939.

Cotton's first priority was for aircraft suited to the peculiar needs
of the role – ideally, a 'cleaned-up' Spitfire able to penetrate German
skies in depth, and fast enough to obviate any need for armament for
self-defence. Going directly to Hugh Dowding, AOC-in-C Fighter
Command, Cotton requested the 'loan' of two Spitfires in October,
and received them the following morning. Both were gutted of superfluous equipment – armament *et al* – and then cleaned externally to a
high speed surface. The immediate result was a boosting of the Spitfires' nominal maximum speed from 360 mph to 396 mph. Tripling of
fuel capacity also extended the operating ranges from some 400 to
1,500–1,800 miles. Spitfire PR sorties commenced in November 1939.
After only 15 sorties these had photographed twice the amount of
territory covered by some 89 Blenheim sorties – and without a single
casualty.

Officially titled as the Photographic Development Unit (PDU), the
Heston unit was more familiarly referred to as 'Cotton's Circus'; an
indication of the outstanding energy and complete disregard for official
channels held by Sidney Cotton as he made every effort to expand and
improve the quality of photo-reconnaissance. Throughout the Phoney
War and the subsequent *Blitzkrieg* of May–June 1940, Cotton's pilots,
operating from Heston and France, provided an almost nonstop series
of photographic sorties, bringing back on-the-spot intelligence for the
Allied air and ground commands. Yet when they were forced to
evacuate to England in June 1940, no PR sortie had resulted in
casualties, whereas the French air service counterpart unit, *Groupe* 2–
33, had suffered the loss of 17 out of 23 crews in just three weeks'
action.

Hardly had Cotton returned to England from France, however,
than he was somewhat summarily removed from command of the unit
he had diligently nurtured and built. The patent value of the work of
the Heston unit had become well recognised by other Commands, who
now jostled for inclusion of the PR facility within their own aegis. The
question of official 'parenthood' was settled in June 1940, when operational control of the PDU was allotted to Coastal Command, and
within a week Sidney Cotton, virtual founder of RAF photographic
reconnaissance in World War Two, was relieved of his command; his

only 'thanks' from officialdom being a stiffly polite letter of gratitude and the award of an OBE.

Command of the PDU now passed to Wing Commander G. Tuttle, DFC; on 8 July 1940 the unit was retitled as the Photographic Reconnaissance Unit (PRU), and on 27 December its base was moved from Heston to Benson, Oxfordshire. Now well established as a 'regular' operational organisation, possessing a supportive Photographic Interpretation Unit at Wembley, the PRU's terms of reference were blandly defined as '. . . deep penetration into enemy territory . . . and heavily defended areas which could not be carried out by ordinary reconnaissance aircraft.' In addition, as the invasion possibilities escalated during the summer of 1940, the PRU was called upon to provide '. . . regular and systematic air reconnaissance over all areas in which the seaborne expedition might be prepared, and from which it might sail.' In practical terms, Tuttle's men were expected to obtain coverage of enemy-occupied coastlines stretching from western France to northern Norway, some 2,000 miles of coastline alone. For such a gigantic task Tuttle could only provide eleven PRU Spitfires, plus a handful of modified Lockheed Hudsons, and a few communications-only aircraft. Accordingly, he split the PRU into four (eventually, five) detached flights, basing two of these at Wick, Scotland and St Eval, Cornwall, and retaining the others at Heston, later Benson.

Though daily tasks and priorities were always issued by Tuttle's headquarters to each flight commander, once received these were interpreted and executed according to the conditions pertaining at each detachment. The very nature of PR work called for highly individual responsibility, and such was always the tenor of RAF PR operations throughout the war. Flying alone, at great altitude, in an unarmed aircraft, deep into hostile skies, a PRU pilot was almost fighting a private war. Help in any emergency was simply not possible – only by his own skill, courage, and cool-headed decision could he hope to survive. Such operational sorties had no parallel in the work of fighter pilots or bomber crews; not only did the PRU pilot run the constant gauntlet of possible flak and fighter opposition, but his value depended entirely on his being able to bring back the required photographs. Whereas a bomber crew's offensive purpose ceased once a target was reached and bombed, the PRU pilot's task only began at that juncture. Having made all necessary runs over the objective area, it was equally vital that he deliver the results to the PIU in England. To endure the isolation and freezing temperatures of high altitude operations called for qualities of temperament and attitude – and physical resistance –

seldom required to such continuing extent in most other forms of war flying.

In addition, a PRU pilot's long-range sorties called for better than good skills in the matter of aerial navigation; wireless silence, to preserve security, was paramount, thereby depriving him of any outside help in obtaining a location fix in the event of becoming lost in cloud. The lonely environment of the PRU crews was, if anything, the ultimate test of mental endurance. Disorientation from the earth and familiar landmarks often imposed an unreal aura, calling for total concentration of mind to even preserve reality, a constant mental battle which had no counterpart in any other form of operational flying.

The advantages – including virtual immunity from fighter attack – of ultra-high altitude sorties were not overlooked by the Luftwaffe. In early 1940 several much-modified prototypes of the pre-war Junkers Ju 86 were tested, each having a pressurised cockpit for a two-man crew, which could achieve operating heights around 40,000 feet. No defensive armament was fitted – at that altitude no Allied fighter of the period could even reach the Junkers – and several Ju 86Ps flew solitary reconnaissance sorties over Britain in the summer and autumn of 1940. Later versions were used over the Russian and Mediterranean fronts in 1941–42, and a few high altitude bomber variants were also produced and used against England in 1942. Though few in numbers, these high-flying Junkers were virtually the only such operational aircraft employed by the Luftwaffe throughout the war in that role, an omission in strategic air power which might otherwise have proved of huge assistance to Luftwaffe High Command planning.

In general, the Luftwaffe depended on standard bomber designs, suitably modified for accommodation of necessary cameras *et al* for the air photographic reconnaissance duties, utilising in the main 'stretched' versions of Dornier 217s, Junkers Ju 88s and Heinkel He 111s. The German air hierarchy's overall attitude to the need for any specifically designed aircraft for air reconnaissance in pre-war days is overtly reflected in the saga of the experimental Heinkel He 119 produced in 1937. Designed from the outset as an unarmed, high speed recce machine, the He 119's superbly streamlined configuration gave it an immediate maximum speed of more than 350 mph, a ceiling in excess of 26,000 feet, and an operating range of some 1,500 miles, a performance 'envelope' far superior to any RAF bomber of the era.

In spite of the obvious potential of such a design, the Luftwaffe's technical staff chiefs could not accept the simple idea of an unarmed

reconnaissance aircraft, relying purely on speed for evasion of attack.*
Instead they insisted on installation of gun turrets, thereby reducing
the aircraft's performance considerably, and in the event the He 119
was destined to complete its existence as merely a flying test vehicle,
never entering operations in the role intended.

It would be easy with hindsight to condemn such 'obtuseness' among
the German air staff, yet their attitude was shaped by the whole concept of German air power at that time. The Luftwaffe was constructed
from the start as an *offensive* force, allied to swift, massive *Blitzkrieg*
tactics; long-term strategic valuations were irrelevant under such terms
of reference. While RAF photo-reconnaissance was developed from the
beginning as strategic operational instrument of war, the Luftwaffe, by
virtue of its genesis, only grasped such a role seriously much later in the
war, too late to derive any lasting benefit from such a source of positive
intelligence.

From 1940 the RAF's PRU came to be used particularly for
'follow-up' photography over the various targets claimed to have been
bombed by Bomber Command's Wellingtons, Whitleys and Hampdens. Enthusiastic reports of huge damage caused made by bomber
crews at de-briefing – made in absolute good faith in almost every case
– were given a sobering lie the following day after PRU photographs
of the *designated* targets revealed the true state of damage. The crux
of such a paradox lay in the generally inaccurate state of air navigation practised by RAF bomber crews of the period. By mid-1941 careful analysis of PRU photographs of 100 separate bombing raids over a
seven-weeks' period revealed that only ten per cent of bomber crews
dropped their bomb loads within five miles of the actual target aiming
point in the Ruhr area; and over Germany generally some 75 per cent
of crews failed even to reach the briefed objective. Such evidence was
backed by the night cameras fitted in about one in ten bombers by
June 1941; these were used to photograph the *actual* targets bombed,
and thus co-relating to the PRU photographic evidence of damage at
the *designated* targets. The solution to Bomber Command's problem
was, of course, outside the PRU's control, but the continuing use of
PR aircraft to assess bomb damage led to a steady accumulation of
target intelligence at the PIU which would eventually provide
Bomber Command with a ready library of German target information
when planning future raids, a process of gathering, sifting, interpreting

* Such a decision had its parallel when the Air Ministry 'experts' failed to
foresee the startling potential of the all-wood, unarmed De Havilland Mosquito
for RAF operational use at the start of the war.

and co-ordinating photographic intellligence which has continued in ever-increasing sophistication to the present day within the RAF.

July 1941 saw the introduction to the PRU of the first PR-version of the DH Mosquito, and by September PR Mosquito crews were beginning operations in the 'Wooden Wonder'. The early versions offered a ceiling of at least 35,000 feet, a range in excess of 2,000 miles, and – equally important – a maximum speed not far short of 400 mph. Nevertheless, the needs of Bomber Command and other considerations restricted any significant flow of Mosquitos to the PR units until well into 1942, and the PR work continued to be mainly accomplished by PR Spitfires. By early 1942, too, more emphasis on the use of PR was allotted to Bomber Command activities, rather than the previous priority given to the Admiralty for keeping a watchful eye on German naval vessels.

Throughout 1942, however, the limited range and performance of the delicate blue-painted PR Spitfire led to a rising casualty rate as Luftwaffe fighter defences for the Reich increased in numbers and expertise. The only real solution appeared to be the Mosquito, and in early 1943 the Air Staff agreed that the PR establishment would in the near future aim at a ninety per cent Mosquito strength in aircraft. This decision was modified shortly after, and a compromise adopted which would see the PR force equipped in roughly equal proportion with the latest Mosquito PR IX and Spitfire PR XI variants, each of which could comfortably outpace a Focke Wulf Fw 190 either in speed or sheer ceiling. Each type of aircraft had its individual advantages in particular styles of operations; together they proved to be the blood-brothers of the RAF's photo-reconnaissance operations throughout World War Two.

By June 1943 the RAF's PR organisation had grown not only physically but in status, and all units, including by then the USAAF's 7th Photo Group, were amalgamated under the title of 106 PR wing, still under the purely administrative control of Coastal Command but in practice continuing to serve many 'masters'. Its importance for strategic planning was further recognised in May 1944 when 106 PR Wing was 'married' to the Allied Central Intelligence Unit to become a full Group; it was still under the aegis of Coastal Command for paperwork but virtually a lone wolf in terms of tactics, routine, and employment by many of its customers. Chief among the PR requirements continued to be liaison with Bomber Command's mounting night offensive against Germany, providing stark 'evidence in camera' of the bomber crews' swathe of destruction across the Reich, photographic confirmation which was used diligently by 'Butch' Harris, Bomber Command supremo, in his dogged campaign to prove the supreme efficacy of his bomber offensive as the ultimate key to victory. If PR photo-evidence had originally been undeniable proof of the bomber crews' failure to deliver the goods, by 1944 the same photographic witness illustrated only too vividly the awesome destructive power of Harris's bludgeon.

By the start of 1944 the PRU's central processing and interpretation services at Medmenham had become a veritable Aladdin's Cave of intelligence treasures, with superbly interlinked pre-intelligence about virtually every facet of German military, naval and industrial efforts and progression. No item was too small to escape the vigilant, patient eyes of the photo-interpreters whose accumulated experience slotted each tiny segment of information and deduction into its appropriate place in the gigantic jigsaw of Allied knowledge of the common enemy. Even a single aircraft photographed on a remote airfield could be classified as to its wing, fuselage and even root wing chord measurements with amazing accuracy.

Sheer experience over the years gave some interpreters almost a 'second sight' about their particular specialisations in subject matter; progressive photographing of specific types of objective built up a 'history' of the subject which immediately highlighted each new facet. Such inborn knowledge and methods, nevertheless, could unwittingly nurture delusions. Bombing results were consistently overestimated throughout the war by Bomber Command staffs and the Allied intelligence systems, resulting in faulty conclusions being drawn as to the state of German war material production levels and capacities.

Now that photographic evidence was in huge abundance, with ever-widening horizons and increasing depth of minute detail, a form of overconfidence, allied to near wishful thinking, tended to be applied to overall interpretation of what photographs actually portrayed. Aerial photography, though by far the finest type of intelligence, was not self-productive. It required knowledgeable interpretation based on *objective* viewpoint; it was not to be used as an excuse for merely confirming hoped-for trains of thought. The normal human weakness of seeing only that which is wanted to be seen, dismissing anything thought to be irrelevant, simply created delusions. And such was, too often, the case with the Allied higher command's conclusions based on PR 'evidence' in the latter years of the war. This was no fault of the PRU's interpreters at Medmenham, however, and their patient observations were to uncover many hitherto unsuspected facets of German intentions from 1943 to 1945 which were to be vital to the Allies.

CHAPTER ELEVEN

Day of the Robots

In the early hours of 13 June 1944, a 'flying object' was reported as crossing the North Downs of Kent by a Royal Observer Corps post, and at 0418 hours this object keeled over and dived into the ground near Gravesend and detonated an explosion. Three similar objects also crashed and exploded at Sevenoaks, Bethnal Green and in Sussex shortly after. The age of 'robot' warfare had arrived over England. The objects were Fieseler 103 crewless flying bombs, known in Germany as *Vergeltungswaffe 1* (Reprisal Weapon No 1), or more commonly in Britain as simply V1. These first four V1s were part of a salvo of ten launched that day, but six crashed shortly after take-off, a tiny proportion of an originally envisaged barrage of 500 flying bombs intended to open the V1 assault on England.

The V1 came as no surprise to Allied defence chiefs in England. Evidence of German development of new weapons had been fragmentary for many, many months, and had been patiently pieced together – an amalgamation of photo-reconnaissance based on ground intelligence from a dozen sources, interpreted step by step and slowly translated into a vague overall analysis. What the Allied intelligence failed to confirm before the arrival of the first examples was the actual form and variety of such new revenge weapons.

Unbeknown to the Allies was the fact that Germany was developing at least three separate revenge measures for attacking England; the V1 flying bomb, the intercontinental rocket A4 (more commonly titled V2), and in ultra-long range form of gigantic 'gun' in northern French sites to pound England by shellfire. The Air Ministry in London received its first genuine indications of German rocket development in a report on German technical developments given to a naval attaché in Oslo, which was passed to London in November 1939. Among many other details, the report mentioned that 'large rockets' were being developed, and that a major experimental research station was being constructed at Peenemunde on the Baltic coast. The Oslo Report was to prove remarkably accurate in many of its forecasts of German weaponry under experimentation, yet virtually nothing was done by British authorities to follow up its findings for several years.

The first significant reconnaissance sortie over Peenemunde did not take place until 15 May 1942, when Flight Lieutenant D. W. Steventon, on a photo-recce flight to cover Kiel and Swinemunde, found himself with 'spare' film still in his cameras and used this up photographing Peenemunde. His photographs revealed a number of circular earthworks, though these were given little attention by interpreters at that time.

During the following nine months Allied intelligence received a number of isolated reports of trials of a long-range rocket specifically linked with Peenemunde, so old photographs were re-examined and up-to-date reconnaissance photos taken for comparison. By April 1943 suspicions of the existence of such a rocket had hardened into near-certainty among Allied chiefs of staff, but scientific advisers – working solely on supposition – offered the opinion that any such missile would be of some 60 tons' weight (based on an assumption of its propellant being mainly cordite-based), and such a behemoth would require massive horizontal or sloping launching sites. Thus the PRU interpreter staff were led into scanning all photographs for evidence of non-existent site-launch equipment and, indeed ,mythical 60-ton monster rockets; whereas the A4 actually weighed less than 13 tons fully fuelled, was highly mobile by road or rail, and was launched vertically from any convenient concrete hardstanding.

This confusion among the Allied researchers was further complicated by a steady stream of reports from European-based sources which included references to 'remotely-controlled pilotless *aircraft*', a description clearly unconnected with any form of large rocket missile. Still unaware of the true nature of either weapon – indeed, still not realising that the two were distinctly separate projects – the Allies stepped up photo-reconnaissance over Peenemunde in June 1943. A sortie on 2 June revealed an A4 rocket standing vertically on its launch pad, while on 23 June a clear picture of A4 rockets lying horizontally on road transporters within the 'earthworks' so casually noted in the previous year was a godsend to the photo-interpreters at Medmenham. Even then such positive proof was not universally accepted by British scientific advisers to the government, but such evidence at least led to a decision to attack Peenemunde in strength.

Accordingly, on the night of 17 August, 597 bombers were despatched to strike at the German research establishment. Acting as Master of Ceremonies was Group Captain John Searby, DFC, OC 83 Squadron, PFF whose cool direction of the progression of main force bombing that night led to an immediate award of a DSO. Eight Mosquitos from 139 Squadron carried out a feint raid on Berlin as a deliberate ploy to attract Luftwaffe nightfighters away from the Peenemunde area, but their sterling effort was only half successful. The bright moonlight and rapid reaction from German fighter controllers resulted in the loss of 40 heavy bombers and a single Mosquito, mainly to nightfighters and mostly in the third and final wave of attacking bombers.

The surface destruction accomplished by the RAF bombers was, at first sight, conclusive. The raid had cost the staff at Peenemunde a total of 735 lives lost, including several of the more senior scientific engineers, yet essential damage to key plants and test buildings – though heavily concentrated in places – was by no means as crippling as was assumed by the Allies. Leaving main material damage on the surface untouched to fool RAF photo-reconnaissance, only vital buildings were repaired immediately under good camouflage from the air, and the really important facets of the research projects were only interrupted for some six weeks. The main effect of the raid was to cause most testing trials thereafter to be transferred to Blizna in Poland in respect of the A4 rocket, though V1 development was hardly affected. The main omission in the Allied plans was the failure to repeat the raid against Peenemunde for many months, giving the Germans ample time to recuperate; but facile condemnation of such 'omissions' usually fail to recognise that in August 1943 the Allied intelligence had yet even to identify the exact form of the A4 rocket and was, as yet, ignorant of the V1 flying bomb and its relationship to Hitler's oft-pronounced threats of revenge weapons.

The Allied picture was further confused by the many reports being received from Europe of other 'secret weapon' sites. Peenemunde was merely one of a string of establishments mentioned; equal emphasis was also being given to German constructions at Watten, Sottevast, Equeurdreville, Siracourt, Wizernes, Lottinghem and Mimoyesques – all apparently connected in some way with the 'Terror weapon' programme. Each required some attention from Allied bombers, and on 27 August, for merely one example, the USAAF sent the Eighth Air Force's 4th Bombardment Wing of B-17s to Watten. Heavily escorted by fighters, the Fortresses returned without loss, then repeated the raid in smaller numbers on 7 September. The bombing was accurate and highly destructive, effectively rendering the base useless for rocket-launching and leaving it to become merely a production centre for liquid oxygen.

Meanwhile the investigations into the precise purpose and forms of German weapons continued, and it was not until the last days of November 1943 that the V1 flying bomb was finally identified, when a WAAF officer, Constance Babington-Smith, 'found' a 'midget aircraft' on a Peenemunde reconnaissance photo taken the previous June. Two weeks later a PRU pilot brought back a photograph showing one of these midget aircraft in place on its long launch ramp – the V1 pilotless aeroplane had finally been identified for what it was.

Immediately connected with many previous photos of similar launching ramps at many other sites, this evidence revealed over 90 such sites along the northern coastline of western Europe, and on 5 December RAF Bomber and Fighter Commands were given supplementary tasks to raid each one of these 'ski sites', as they had been provisionally dubbed. Though Bomber Command's heavy bomber force was already mainly committed to Harris's Battle of Berlin by then, elements of the light bomber force, in conjunction with the USAAF's Ninth Air Force, undertook these operations in strength. On Christmas Eve 1943, for example, an overall total of 672 American 'heavies' released 1,472 tons of bombs on 24 ski sites.

The importance of eliminating the flying bomb menace was exemplified by the weight of bombing attacks made upon the ski sites and other suspected bases during the opening phase of operations. More than 3,000 tons of bombs were aimed at these sites in December 1943 alone, and the following six months saw a further 28,000 tons fall on rocket and flying bomb bases. Such raids were, nevertheless, not accorded absolute priority for aerial operations. By late 1943 preparations and massive reorganisation of the Allied air forces based in Britain were well under way as the eventual invasion of Europe began to reach its final stages of planning. Not until April 1944, when Arthur Harris's Bomber Command would henceforth come under the aegis of the Allied supreme commander, Eisenhower, could the RAF's main bombing offensive power be brought to bear on the secret weapons' menace.

As part of the pre-invasion reorganisation Britain's traditional home defence air arm, Fighter Command, was split into two distinct new commands from 15 November 1943. On that date Fighter Command *per se* officially ceased to exist, and its functions were divided between a retitled home defence force named Air Defence of Great Britain (AGDB), comprised of ten day and eleven night fighter squadrons, commanded by Air Marshal Roderic Hill, and a total of 32 fighter squadrons which were transferred to the newly-created 2nd Tactical

Air Force (2nd TAF), commanded by Air Marshal Sir Arthur Coningham. The 2nd TAF was literally that, a *tactical* air force specifically tasked with protection and support of the land invasion forces intended for the European venture, and both 2nd TAF and the ADGB came under the overall command of Air Chief Marshal Sir Trafford Leigh-Mallory.

From November 1943 until June 1944, when the invasion of Normandy finally got under way, Roderic Hill's ADGB held a dual responsibility. Continued metropolitan aerial defence against the Luftwaffe remained its obvious role, but Hill was also given the onerous task of providing total protection of the unprecedented mass of Allied troops and material being gradually concentrated in England's southern counties for the projected invasion of France. At all costs the Luftwaffe had to be prevented from photographing or otherwise learning of the massed invasion forces. From 6 June however, Hill's secondary duty of providing an air cloak for 2nd TAF and the Allied armies virtually ceased as the invading forces surged forward into Normandy, and 2nd TAF aircraft began to use French landing strips as operational bases. Just seven days after the first Allied troops waded ashore in Europe, Hill's ADGB was brought to full alert as the first V1 flying bombs descended in Kent, harbingers of the latest Luftwaffe assault on England.

Pre-warned of just such a possibility, the British home defences had drawn up a hastily prepared contingency plan, code-named Diver, but the initial feeble assault on 13 June did not seem to Hill to justify full implementation of this plan. Then, on 15 June, late in the evening, a total of 55 sites in France began launching a continuous avalanche of V1s in the general direction of London, and within twenty-four hours a gross total of 244 V1s had left their launch ramps heading north-westwards. Of these, only 144 actually reached the English coast, and 33 were destroyed by the quickly alerted defences of fighters and anti-aircraft guns. Hill immediately initiated the full Diver plan, and also requested the loan of a wing of Mustang III fighters from Coningham's 2nd TAF reserve. By 15 July Hill could muster 13 squadrons of single-engine fighters and eight squadrons of Mosquitos, by which date the Germans had launched 4,361 of the cruciform robot 'aircraft'. Of the latter, some 3,000 crossed the English coast, and the defenders destroyed 1,241 – 924 of these by ADGB aircraft.

On the face of it, the V1 was a perfect target for either anti-aircraft guns or fighters. It flew an unwavering flightpath at reasonably low altitude, and was simple to detect. However, its small configuration

– wings spanned only 17 feet six inches – and cruising speeds of any figure from 300 mph to more than 400 mph made it difficult to destroy by any normal fighter tactics. In addition, its filling of 1,870 lb of Trialen high explosive was violent enough to devastate anything within hundreds of feet if detonated – a constant danger for any pursuing fighter who closed to normal firing range. The sheer speed of a V1 offered problems for interception by conventional aircraft, but by mid-1944 the ADGB was part-equipped with Spitfire Mk XIVs and the aesthetically-pleasing Hawker Tempests; each design was quite capable of catching a V1 in full flight.

The main question for ADGB pilots remained how best to destroy the ugly little robot invaders. Once the lethality of an air explosion had been recognised, most pilots chose either long-range cannon-fire, or resorted to pure flying manoeuvres : flying close to the V1 and then creating turbulence in its flightpath, or even formating with the flying bomb, then tipping it with a wing-tip to topple it from its course. Whichever method was used, the fighter pilots ran dreadful risks. One Tempest unit, No 486 Squadron, achieved a reasonably high tally of V1 kills eventually, but paid the price of three pilots killed, ten others seriously injured, and a total of 17 Tempests destroyed or damaged beyond repair.

The full countermeasures to the V1 contained in the Diver plan embraced fighters, anti-aircraft guns, balloon barrages, and a host of individual forms of armament. Collectively these defences were to account for a high proportion of V1s reaching English air space, but the real antidote could only be destruction of the launching sites in France and the Low Countries. From April 1944 RAF Bomber Command switched its priority from raiding the Reich to preparing the way for the Allied invasion, and in conjunction with the USAAF's Fortresses, Liberators and Marauders Harris's crews began a series of strikes at coastal batteries and fortifications all along the French, Belgian and Dutch coasts and concentrated even more on German and French railways, canals, highways and traffic centres; a deliberate campaign to disrupt and devastate all types of ground communication or supply routes in north-west Europe. Once the land invasion gained impetus from June 1944, the armies' progressive liberation of enemy-occupied territories also swallowed up V1 launching sites. This initial stage of over-running V1 sites, especially in the Pas de Calais area, led to a temporary lull in the robot assault on England.

From 16 July to 5 September anti-aircraft guns in Britain had destroyed 1,198 V1s, while ADGB fighters had accounted for a further

847; indeed, since the very first Vi had been launched against England, Britain's defences had destroyed almost one in three of all flying bombs despatched. One significant addition to ADGB weaponry had been the formation of the RAF's first-ever jet-engined aircraft unit. On 12 July 1944 No 616 Squadron, based then at Culmhead, received its first Gloster Meteor jet fighter, and two weeks later, on moving base to Manston, had seven Meteors on charge. Jet operations commenced on 27 July, and in August the first Vi was brought down by a Meteor pilot. By early September the jet fighters' tally of Vis reached 13 destroyed.

By 1 September British and Canadian troops had reached the River Somme in their plunge northwards, and on that date the German Vi crews fired their last robot from a French site before hastily evacuating to Belgian territory. There followed almost two weeks' lull in the Vi offensive, and the British government and Air Ministry stated publicly that the flying bomb need engender '. . . no further fear of danger'. This statement was rash and premature, and the following seven months saw a renewed Vi offensive from sites in Holland, resulting in a further 2,000 flying bombs at least descending on England. A number of these attacks were by air-launched Vis carried by Heinkel He 111s of KG53, and often by night, a fresh form of attack which was, nevertheless, soon challenged by ADGB Mosquitos and the ever-ready anti-aircraft gun crews.

The KG53 participation lasted from September 1944 to January 1945, after which the unit was withdrawn to Germany. Its crews had launched several hundred Vis, but lost 41 aircraft; about half of the latter to ADGB fighters and the remainder to accidents or other causes. The gradual ascendency of the English defences over the robot bombs was perhaps most marked during August and September 1944. On 28 August, for one example, a total of 97 Vis survived launching and approached the English coast. ADGB fighters shot down 23, while the AA gunners accounted for 65. Of the surviving nine bombs to reach London's outer suburban areas, two more collided with barrage balloons, three failed to descend on the metropolis, leaving a mere four to plunge into the city itself.

The last Vi flying bomb to be launched towards Britain left its ramp on 29 March 1945. From June 1944 until that date, a gross total of some 9,000 Vis had been launched, of which approximately 2,000 crashed soon after take-off or miscarried from their intended courses. Of the remaining 7,000, the ADGB, anti-aircraft guns and balloon barrages claimed the destruction of 3,955. Only slightly more than a quarter of the total V1s sent actually penetrated the defences, mainly reaching the greater London area, an overall tonnage of high explosive equivalent to about two per cent of the HE tonnage of bombs expended by the RAF and USAAF against suspected launching sites from December 1943 to early 1945. The tally of V1s destroyed by the Diver defences was shared almost equally by anti-aircraft gunners and Roderic Hill's ADGB fighter crews: 1,878 and 1,846 respectively, with the balance of 231 credited to balloon barrage aprons.

In view of such officially confirmed statistics, it was, to say the least, petulant of the Prime Minister, Winston Churchill, to attempt to downgrade the work of the air crews. In a memorandum to the Secretary of State for Air, in March 1945, Churchill wrote:

> You have no grounds to claim that the Royal Air Force frustrated the attack by the 'V' weapons. The RAF took their part, but in my opinion their efforts rank definitely below that of the anti-aircraft artillery, and still farther below the achievements of the Army in clearing out all the establishments in the Pas de Calais . . .

Even as the V1 menace was reaching its peak, the ADGB was presented with a second and deadlier opponent. Almost since the outbreak of war, Allied scientists had suspected that Germany might be developing some form of huge ballistic missile, a rocket capable of intercontinental trajectory which, patently, could be adapted easily to include an explosive warhead of considerable destructive potential. Until 1944 the mainstream of Allied intelligence had been aimed at confirming and locating such a rocket though – as has been related – with little accuracy. The arrival of the V1 buzz-bombs in June 1944 did nothing to obviate Allied anxieties about such a rocket being launched in vast quantity against London and other British population centres, but the advancing Allied invasion armies through France offered more than a modicum of hope that all possible launching sites for such rockets would be quickly captured.

Such an optimistic view was pure underestimation of the rocket's performance, especially in terms of operational range, and led to the Director of Intelligence (Research) in London declaring on 2 September 1944 that any rocket threat would be nullified '. . . when the area in northern France and Belgium 200 miles from London was neutralised by the proximity of our land forces and the operations of our Tactical Air Forces'.

This overconfident prophecy was reinforced by the Vice-Chiefs of

Staff only four days later when they opined that 'Rocket attacks on London need no longer be expected'. Just forty-eight hours later, at 6.43 p.m. on 8 September, an A4 rocket screamed out of the sky to detonate in Chiswick, killing three people and injuring ten others; it was followed within ten days by 26 more A4s in various areas of London.

The A4 rocket, more usually referred to as V2, was an interconti-nental missile weighing 12.7 tons, 46 feet in length, carrying a war-head of 1,650lb of high explosive, which could reach 50 miles in extreme altitude and achieve a maximum speed approaching 3,600 mph. On its final plunge to earth it descended vertically at a speed of 2,000 m.p.h. In blunt terms, the A4 was impossible to intercept by any existing means of defence then available to the Allies. Thus, the only feasible solution to the A4 was swift and complete destruction of its launching bases.

This remedy was urgently put to Bomber Command and 2nd TAF by the ADGB commander, Roderic Hill, only to meet a marked reluct-ance on the part of both of those formation commanders. Harris's command was already heavily committed to deep penetration and other more tactical operations in support of the Allied armies in France, while 'Mary' Coningham much preferred to continue using his 2nd TAF air power for its original purpose – on-the-spot tactical back-up for the invasion armies as they advanced across Europe. What amounted to token sorties were indeed undertaken by both Bomber Command and 2nd TAF aircraft against some identified or suspected A4 bases, but the onus of responsibility for any air offensive against the rocket sites was mainly shuffled back on to Roderic Hill's shoulders.

With only medium- or long-range fighters at his immediate dis-posal, Hill was in no position to carry out any worthwhile bombing operations against A4 sites; in any case, many of these were located beyond his fighters' operational range. A further difficulty lay in actual location of such sites : the A4 needed relatively little space from which to be launched, unlike the V1 with its long take-off ramps and other ancillary paraphernalia. It was a dilemma for Hill which was never fully to be resolved until the Allied ground forces on the Continent finally over-ran all possible launching locations in Holland and along the Baltic coast.

Radar detection of incoming A4s was barely possible in time to initiate ample warning to the civil population – an A4 took barely five minutes to travel from its bases in the Hague to London. Yet Hill's repeated requests for heavy bomber attacks on A4 sites continued to go unheeded, even after one particularly tragic incident on 25 November when an A4 struck a crowded building in the New Cross area of London, killing or injuring 268 people in a single explosion. Hill continued to despatch his fighter-bombers against the rocket sites – in December 1944 alone, nearly 400 individual sorties over the Hague dropped some 40 tons of bombs – but to relatively little effect. Hill's only consolation, a purely negative one, was that the quantity of A4s descending on Britain was nothing like the avalanche of missiles originally expected by Allied Service chiefs. Throughout the A4 campaign, arrivals on English soil varied between six and eight per day on average, rising to no more than ten per day even in the later stages. Moreover, the actual effects of an A4 exploding on impact – though impressive enough – tended to be highly localised. Deep initial penetration of the impact point restricted blast effect on the surface to a much smaller area than the cruder V1 flying bomb's aftermath.

As the new year 1945 opened, Hill intensified his fighter-bomber assault on rocket sites, and in the first two months his crews flew 1,143 sorties, dropping 216 tons of bombs. In March the pace intensified, with the fighters flying more sorties than in the previous four months added together and dropping about 600 tons of bombs. In relation to the casualties and damage caused to the German rocket personnel and sites, however, much of this overall effort bore little significance. The only real salvation for the long-suffering British civil population still lay with the imminent occupation of German-held territories in northern Europe, and a consequent cleaning-out of all tenable rocket and V1 launching areas.

Fortuitously, this cleansing was not long in being accomplished, and on 27 March the last A4 to fall on British soil exploded in Orpington, Kent. From September 1944 a total of 1,403 A4 rockets had been sent against England, the vast majority being aimed at London. Of these, 349 failed to reach Britain, while the rest were distributed almost half-and-half between London and other parts of England.

The toll in human lives of the combined V1 and A4 robot offensive against England was heavy. From June 1944 to March 1945 (inclusive), 8,938 civilians were killed and a further 24,504 civilians were seriously injured by one or other type of weapon; collectively, almost a quarter of all civilian casualties caused by direct bombing or shelling of Britain throughout the entire war. The great bulk of the robots' victims resided in the Greater London area, while the capital city also suffered the largest proportion of material devastation.

Yet Hitler's declared purpose for the use of his mechanical reprisal or revenge weapons – to break the morale of the British people – was never achieved. Shortly after the first V1s began to descend on southern England in June 1944, the shock of being bombarded by automatic bombs resembling something out of the pages of cheap novels on science fiction created something of an exodus of civilians from the London metropolitan zones at a rate of some 100,000 people per week over a period of nearly three months, all seeking haven in the more westerly countryside areas. Once the menace had become a more routine fact of war, however, this evacuation was reversed, and from the autumn of 1944 the same civilians were moving back to their former homes in London at a rate which reached almost ninety per cent by the end of the year; despite the additional threat of the A4 rockets. 'Business as usual' became a national catch-phrase, recalling for many the defiant cheerfulness so evident among London's residents during the worst days and nights of the 1940–41 blitz.

From the German viewpoint, the use of the V1 and A4 gained little beyond propaganda value to an increasingly battered and disillusioned populace. The immense amount of effort, time, and resources expended upon the V-Weapons projects might well have been more usefully employed in bolstering the Luftwaffe, though it remains a moot point if *any* expansion of the air arm could have really been achieved to any significant level owing to Germany's chronic lack of fuel resources and personnel recruitment by 1944. Certainly, the robot weapons could achieve no strategic advantages, while the use of such expensive items for mere tactical purposes would have been entirely wasteful and, to a great degree, pointless.

The V1 flying bomb was, in effect, a blind alley in weapon research and potential development – relatively easy to detect and counter – but the A4, if nothing else, represented the practical dawn of man's space age. Created as a weapon of pure destruction, it parented the vehicles which carried man on his first faltering probes into the surrounding universe and cosmos only decades later.

CHAPTER TWELVE

Overture and Beginners

The prospect of an Allied invasion of Europe had first been considered, somewhat unrealistically, almost immediately after the French surrender in 1940. Considering the state of Britain's forces then, any such venture could only be regarded as a pipe-dream by non-participating armchair warriors. In any case, the desperate defence of the United Kingdom against an imminent German invasion occupied all priorities throughout 1940 and well into 1941. The lessons of the Battle of Britain, nevertheless, sowed the seeds of recognition of the vital necessity for air supremacy being paramount as a pre-requisite for *any* form or sea or land invasion of another country.

Hitler's switch of offensive might eastwards for his intended conquest of Russia in 1941 eased the pressure on Allied forces in Britain, permitting a gradual re-strengthening of land and air power, and the RAF's tentative air offensive over German-occupied countries provided, at least, a tasting of the basic problems involved in any such use of the air weapon. The entry of the USA into the war against the Axis powers in December 1941 gave huge promise of a future offensive power of combined military and industrial resources, and the question of an invasion of Europe again came into the limelight in 1942, when Russia, grimly staving off a renewed German onslaught, called upon the Allies for a second front behind the German armies to relieve pressure in the east. Beyond the practice run at Dieppe that year, however, Allied Service chiefs were only too aware that any full-scale invasion attempt at that time could only result in disaster; and despite mounting calls for such a venture in press and Parliament, set their faces against such a folly.

By mid-1943, with American power well in being, and the mounting RAF bombing offensive agains the Reich, the possibility of such an incursion was not only considered seriously but even mooted by some members of the British government and service staffs. Had those views prevailed the Allies might well have suffered a crippling defeat. Though by then committed to fighting a multi-front war with consequent dilution of its forces, Germany was still able to increase its war production levels, while the Luftwaffe's fighter defences in Germany and France were being steadily expanded, even to the detriment of its bomber arm. Fortunately, the many opponents of any such Allied expedition, one of the most vigorous being Bomber Command chief Arthur Harris, prevailed and any thought of a 1943 invasion attempt was, for the moment postponed.

Harris's objections were not solely altruistic. Though convinced that the Allies were as yet in no position to undertake such a massive undertaking, he maintained his view that his strategic bombing offensive against Germany must be allowed to demonstrate his firm conviction that German war potential could be destroyed, or at least vitally crippled by sheer air assault. Any lengthy interruption to the offensive he was at that period pursuing would simply give German industry an opportunity to recuperate quickly, and thereby nullify any results already obtained by the bomber crews. Ever a practical realist, Harris wholly recognised that any invasion attempt must utilise exclusively the entire Allied air power based in Britain to support the ground forces. His main worry was just how long his bombers would then be 'diverted' from what he regarded as their prime role : the destruction of German industrial power. Even a few months of exclusive army co-operation would undo everything achieved to date by the bombing offensive.

Initial plans for the eventual invasion of France were begun in April 1943, though elements of preparation in embryo had existed long before then. At first the air aspects of preparation and actual cover for the invasion forces were placed under the aegis of the commander-in-chief of RAF Fighter Command. By July 1943, the basic plan was set into motion, and the tasks of the RAF and USAAF elements were defined to be carried out in four main phases. The first phase was Harris's strategic bombing offensive against Germany, co-ordinated loosely with the USAAF's Eighth Air Force's daytime assaults on the Reich. The next phase called for a preliminary concentration of bomber and fighter offensives against all types of objectives in France linked in any way with the proposed land assault : railway centres, coastal defences along Hitler's vaunted 'West Wall', airfields, harbours, and the like. The third phase concerned the actual assault, including total protection of the land and seaborne forces en route to France across the Channel and on the beaches of Normandy. Thereafter, the air forces were to repeat the objectives of the first two phases, disrupting all possible reinforcement routes for the Germans at the coast, destroying rail centres and repair yards, breaking major bridges, and generally offering a supreme aerial umbrella to the ground forces up to 150 miles from actual beach-head locations.

On 15 November 1943 Air Chief Marshal Sir Trafford Leigh-Mallory was appointed as supremo of a newly-created Allied Expeditionary Force (AEAF). His command comprised three main elements: the USAAF Ninth Air Force (a tactical formation), and the two formations into which the former RAF Fighter Command was reorganised within forty-eight hours, the 2nd Tactical Air Force and the Air Defence of Great Britain (ADGB). The 2nd TAF, commanded by Air Marshal Coningham, included thirty-two former Fighter Command squadrons and a number of army co-operation units; this left Air Marshal Hill of the ADGB with 21 fighter squadrons to defend Britain by day and night, as well as protecting the amassing forces in southern England prior to the actual invasion date.

Once the invasion got under way, 2nd TAF would go with the forces into France and remain their immediate tactical air support force for the future land campaign. Bomber Command and the Eighth Air Force, however, were left under their existing commanders and the continuing strategic air offensive remained a top priority, an arrangement which was not favoured by Leigh-Mallory but one which he was, for the moment, powerless to change. Both Harris and the newly-appointed commander of the US Strategic Air Forces in Europe, General Spaatz, were distrustful of any policy of using their heavy bombers for purely tactical support of the armies; both men were committed to the principle that only strategic targets were the heavy bombers' legitimate role and purpose.

Leigh-Mallory, renowned for his persistence in his own views, set up an AEAF Bombing Committee in January 1944 which presented a plan for using the heavy bombers for wholesale destruction of the French and Belgian railways systems as a preliminary to the invasion, increasing in scope as the actual invasion date drew nearer to include all other types of enemy communications leading to the proposed Allied beach-heads. Both Harris and Spaatz protested at what they regarded as misuse of their bombers, but by mid-April 1944 the Transportation Plan' was confirmed as policy by Air Chief Marshal Arthur Tedder, deputy supreme commander of the invasion forces.

Throughout the preceding months to the invasion, Bomber Command and the Eighth Air Force maintained a programme of mixed operations, devoting a large measure of effort steadily to reducing the rail communications in Europe to a parlous state of efficiency, but continuing to attack purely strategic targets deep into Germany by day and by night.

By early 1944 Germany was on the defensive on all major fronts, a position emphasised by the increasing priorities given to the Luftwaffe's defence of the Reich against the escalating pounding of American bombers by day and RAF heavies by night. The Luftwaffe's fighter arm soon dominated all production quotas, being supplemented in no small degree by the conversion of many standard bomber designs to a nightfighting role. The Allied bombing of Germany's aircraft industry in particular had created something of a crisis in overall production figures by the close of 1943, with fighter production reaching some of its lowest levels of the war; but a decisive reversal of this trend commenced in early 1944 when Reichsminister Speer founded the *Jägerstab* (Fighter Staff) in February and set in motion a fresh production programme with heavy emphasis on the manufacture of fighters, and the monthly output of fighters doubled between March and June 1944. Equal priority was given to day and night fighters, and on 31 May the nightfighter force, including a number of modified bomber designs, had no less than 1,156 aircraft available for defensive operations overall.

The unceasing bombardment of Germany by Allied heavy bombers throughout 1943 merely increased Hitler's constant obsession with retaliatory revenge bombing of Britain, and on 7 December he issued a directive to Göring to prepare 'a massive blow' against London. This renewed bombing assault on England, code-named *Steinbock* ('Ibex'), was initially intended to employ at least 500 bombers, including the first operational use of the troublesome Heinkel He 177 four-engined design. By mid-January the *Steinbock* units were moving to airfields on the French and Baltic coasts, and on the night of 21 January a total of 227 bombers set out for London.

If the veteran crews among this force still retained memories of previous, relatively unopposed attacks on England, they were to be surprised by the vastly improved countermeasures now available to the British defence system. By dawn next day the Luftwaffe had lost 18 bombers to RAF fighters, even more to anti-aircraft guns or other defences, and a further 18 aircraft due to non-action reasons. This 'Baby Blitz', as the minor offensive was quickly nicknamed by the British, continued until May 1944; during this time British civilian casualties – mostly in the Londan area – amounted to 1,556 killed and almost 3,000 seriously injured. The cost to the *Steinbock* force, however, was prohibitive, with more than 300 bombers lost during the same period, an insupportable casualty rate. In a dozen raids the *Steinbock* crews had dropped some 2,000 tons of bombs -- a fraction of the bomb damage dropped by Allied aircraft on Hamburg in a single week.

Though a relatively minor operational effort, *Steinbock* marked the demise of the Luftwaffe's bomber arm as an effective war weapon. It also marked the final conversion of Hitler from his obsession with bombers as the priority in Luftwaffe operations, though the Führer's *volte-face* was still a tardy and reluctant decision to concentrate more on fighters as the salvation of his Reich. While placing undue faith in the imminent V1 and A4 robot terror-weapons to vent his spleen on Britain, his long-held aversion to fighters as the premier tool of aerial warfare was well reflected in his personal attitude to the various latest fighter designs reaching production status in Germany. Several promising new fighter designs had been in embryo for a considerable time, notably the Messerschmitt Me 163 *'Komet'* rocket-propelled defence fighter, and the twin-jet Messerschmitt Me 262 *Schwalbe* ('Swallow'). Nevertheless, until mid-1944 the Luftwaffe's industrial support factories had concentrated mainly on standard designs, particularly the Bf 110, Bf 109, and Junkers Ju 88 of long-standing use. Only when Speer instigated his new broom throughout the industry in early 1944, sweeping aside wasted efforts on outmoded or unnecessary aircraft types, did the latest designs assume any priority in production. The Messerschmitt Bf 109, Bf 110 and Junkers Ju 88 still dominated the Luftwaffe's day and, especially, night fighter strengths, with the Focke Wulf 190 a close rival.

On the other hand, potentially good fighters like the Heinkel He 219 nightfighter, the unconventional Dornier Do 335 fighter with its tandem-engine configuration, and others now received much more attention. The first of the new-wave fighters to see operational use, the tail-less Me 163 *'Komet'*, was blooded on 16 August 1944 against an American bomber formation, but despite its potential the Me 163 was to prove ineffective. Its stable-mate Me 262 had a chequered pre-operational career. Originally ordered into production in June 1943, with an intention of supplanting the Bf 109 on Messerschmitt's production lines, subsequent bombing by the Allies of factories, and a lack of enthusiastic support from non-operational Luftwaffe chiefs like Erhard Milch, delayed any possibility of early introduction to the operational units. The tardiness was further protracted when, on 26 November 1943, Hitler witnessed a demonstration of an Me 262 V6. Impressed by the speed of the jet aircraft, Hitler immediately ordered its modification for use as a carrier for bombs for attacking England!

One major factor in the general interference with German aircraft production in early 1944 was the intensified bombing offensive centred upon aircraft manufacturing centres and their support depots. In particular, the week of 19 to 25 February witnessed the most concentrated efforts to date by the USAAF to eliminate its chief opponent's resources, the Luftwaffe fighters' production and repair factories; seven days of no-quarter combat with the Luftwaffe over Germany thereafter referred to as the Big Week. Supplemented by the 15th Air Force bombers from bases in Italy who flew over the Alps to deliver their part in missions, the Eighth Air Force flew a total of 3,300 individual sorties during Big Week and dropped sixty per cent of the overall 10,000 tons of bombs carried by the American heavy bombers. They created havoc at various vital fighter production centres, notably at Regensburg and Augsburg, causing an immediate – if temporary – diminution of production.

The first full mission on 20 February gave indication of the scale of the USAAF attacks, when a force of 1,028 heavy bombers set out, escorted by 832 USAAF long-range fighters, supported by 16 RAF fighter squadrons. Luftwaffe opposition was fierce, but overall USAAF losses were surprisingly light: just 21 bombers missing in action. The long-range P-47 Thunderbolts and P-51 Mustangs, now able to escort the bombers all the way to the target, were largely responsible for such relatively light losses to the bombers. Ranging at will well above any bomber formation, the eager American fighter pilots could deliver devastating diving attacks on any German fighters attempting to intercept; as on 20 February when the P-47s of 'Hub' Zemke's 56th Fighter Group bounced a 24-aircraft gaggle of Bf 110s of III/ZG26 and desstroyed 18 of these.

To counter the American onslaught that week, the Luftwaffe day fighters amounted to 1,000 aircraft, intended to cover all and any incursions into Reich air. Less than half of this number were operationally available at any given moment, and the German fighter crews rose to intercept knowing too well the tremendous odds against them. Allied air supremacy above the Reich was by now almost total, and the ultra long range capabilities of the latest Mustangs and Thunderbolts meant that thereafter German defenders would be running a double gauntlet of fire from the awesome bomber boxes' combined firepower and the high-flying American fighters every-ready to attack from superior altitudes.

Notwithstanding such odds, the determined German fighter crews seldom failed to tackle the massive bomber arrays, making breath-taking head-on assaults or plunging from height with cannons and rockets. Successes were achieved on occasion – as on 24 February when the 25 B-24 Liberators of the Eighth Air Force's 445th BG, detached from the main force, left the Gotha Bf 110 factory ablaze but were singled out by Luftwaffe fighters on the return journey. Within an hour of bombing, 13 B-24s had been shot down, while nine others arrived eventually in England displaying grim evidence of the aerial battle.

By the close of the Big Week, the USAAF had suffered the loss of 226 heavy bombers and 28 fighters – nearly two and a half thousand young men killed, prisoner, or just missing in action. These represented barely six per cent of the total forces despatched, an 'acceptable' rate in the eyes of Allied air commanders. As a deliberate attempt to eliminate the Luftwaffe's fighter strength – a vital pre-requisite to the intended launching of Operation Overlord, the Allied invasion of France in June 1944 – the Big Week operations at least amply demonstrated the ability of Allied air power to operate in broad daylight over deepest German with near-impunity.

The main outcome of the Big Week operations for the American bomber crews in particular was the sure knowledge that never again would they need to operate beyond the fighting range of a fighter escort. With Mustangs, and later Thunderbolts, now capable of flying and fighting to Berlin and even beyond, the Fortress and Liberator crews could undertake deep penetration raids in daylight without automatically inviting crippling casualties from Luftwaffe opposition. It did not mean absolute immunity, or for that matter supreme superiority in every situation or circumstance. In the year ahead casualties, occasionally high in number, would inevitably occur as local engagements favoured the German defenders; while the lone straggler bomber or formation remained highly vulnerable.

Nevertheless, the maximum effort of Big Week was a vital contribution to the aerial struggle over Europe, initiating the final downfall of Luftwaffe defence of the Reich and exposing the heart of Hitler's empire to a day bombing assault which would continue to gouge the heart out of Germany and, alongside RAF Bomber Command's night offensive, pave the way to ultimate triumph in the air. Moreover, with their capability of wide-ranging activities, the USAAF'S long-range fighters now adopted an even more aggressive, *offensive* role over Germany. No longer shackled solely to bomber-shepherd roles, the American fighter pilots sought out the Luftwaffe, in the air and on the ground, in a deliberate battle of sheer attrition. While a proportion of the fighters continued to keep a watchful eye on their bomber big brothers, the bulk of USAAF fighters now began to roam around Germany, attacking targets of opportunity and seeking out the Luftwaffe wherever it could be found.

Meanwhile RAF Bomber Command doggedly pursued Harris's Battle of Berlin on every possible night while the hours of winter darkness still offered a cloak of protection from the flak and *Nachtjäger* ever-waiting above Germany. The moonlight battle for mastery was an entirely different conflict to that of the daylight war being waged by the American bomber crews. By day a bomber crew could see their opponents from afar and prepare accordingly. Once combat was joined the Fortress and Liberator gunners had a visible, recognisable enemy to deal with. In the raven-black of night the aerial war was an elaborate spider web of deception, hide-and-seek movements, a sneak-thief fight in which victory usually went to the man who could catch his opponent unaware and destroy him before he could react. A high proportion of bomber crews died in a holocaust of flaming petrol or explosive blast without ever knowing who or what was responsible. Protection from other bombers' gunners was never possible; every night crew was essentially on its own, fighting virtually a private war each time it ventured into enemy-held skies. In such circumstances every bomber crew became an interlinked, efficient team, a tiny community of brothers knitted together by the common will to survive. Only by such a cohesion of thought and action could any crew hope to emerge alive, given a fair ration of good luck. Even so, sheer experience was no guarantee of ultimate survival. Death distributed its net indiscriminately, gathering veterans and tyros with complete impartiality.

If the USAAF had gained a marked supremacy in the skies of Europe by day, the same could never be said of the RAF's plodding, stubborn assaults by night. By January 1944 the RAF's bomber offensive was meeting an increasingly efficient and successful Luftwaffe nightfighter defence. In that month Bomber Command launched nine major operations: six against Berlin and others against Stettin, Brunswick and Magdeburg. Accurate flak and, especially, nightfighters accounted for 306 bombers shot down en route, while dozens of others arrived back at base bearing wounded or dead crew members and livid scars of cannon and shell damage.

Typical of the period's operations was a raid aimed at Leipzig on the night of 19/20 February. A force of 816 heavy bombers and 25

Mosquitos took off from England and crossed Holland before setting course eastwards towards Berlin. The Luftwaffe controllers decided that Berlin was the main objective and therefore ignored the various light diversionary attacks on several German fighter airfields and feint thrusts at Dresden and Aachen; they infiltrated some fighters into the main bomber stream near Bremen but concentrated most fighters in the Berlin area. In all 294 German fighters were airborne that night and these cut a swathe through the heavy-laden bombers as they neared Berlin and then turned southwards to their proper target Leipzig. By the time the last bomber had crossed the Channel heading homewards, 74 bombers had been shot down by nightfighters and four others were lost, presumably to flak. Of the defenders, 17 fighters were destroyed.

Whether encountering predicted flak, controlled nightfighters, or in-filtrated opponents, the night bomber crews had one constant foe – the weather. Unpredicted winds could scatter a main force of bombers over hundreds of miles from any intended routing, and left the straggling gaggle of Lancasters and Halifaxes prey to determined flak gunners or roving *Nachtjäger*. Just such conditions were met on the night of 24 March when Bomber Command despatched a final major attack against Berlin. The now-usual diversionary feint raids failed to attract notice from the nightfighter controllers, but unpredicted high winds scattered the main bomber stream over a wide area, pushing many bombers over heavily defended areas where the flak gunners seized their opportunity to inflict heavy casualties. At least 50 of the 72 RAF bombers lost that night were claimed by flak, though the German fighter pilots made claims for 84 'kills' as against fighter losses of 14 aircraft. Two night later, 705 bombers were sent to Essen and only nine failed to return, while 20 nightfighters were lost.

If such a reversal in fortune gave momentary hope to the bomber crews, the sudden fluctuations in the nightly battle were grimly ex-emplified on the night of 30 March. The target was Nuremberg, the true 'heart' of Hitler's Nazi movement, and Bomber Command des-patched 795 aircraft to destroy the ancient city. A combination of bad routing, clear skies, and well-alerted defences wreaked a fearful toll of the bombers who lost – in all operations that night — 108 aircraft. Of this total, eleven crashed on return to England, but eighty per cent had been shot down en route by German nightfighters. It was RAF Bomber Command's greatest single operational disaster in the context of pure casualties. It was equally the zenith of the Luftwaffe's night-fighter effort. Such a victory may have temporarily heartened the

Luftwaffe, but in the long term it could no longer prevent the inevitable decline of Germany's air defences. Isolated examples of success would still occur, but the 'writing on the wall' was all too plain.

By April RAF Bomber Command had in essence ceased its year-long night assault on Germany in pursuance of Arthur Harris's hope to cripple Germany's will and ability to fight. Even Berlin, the nub of Harris's final phase of operations, was by no means destroyed despite its long ordeal. It would be incorrect to say that Harris had 'failed'. Throughout his reign as the RAF's bomber supremo, Harris had been forced to fight for the separate existence of his command against the many pressures being applied to segment and dilute the RAF's only true strategic striking force. Even after he had managed to dispel any notions of breaking up the command into small parcels for tactical use by other commands, Harris was never given the sufficiency in sheer numbers and suitable types of aircraft necessary to wage any war-winning strategic bomber offensive. Once the Lancaster bomber became available for operations, Harris pressed hard for total Lancaster equipment for his heavy bomber units, only to be denied. As he has stated :

> The Lancaster was so far the best aircraft we had that I continually pressed for its production at the expense of other types; I was even willing to lose nearly a year's industrial production from the Halifax (bomber) factories while these were being converted to produce Lancasters. I did not get my way in this . . .*

It was merely one facet of Harris's unceasing striving to be allowed to prove the true potential of strategic bombing power; a battle with 'higher authority' which was continually frustrated by having to divert substantial proportions of his available bombers to duties and operations unconnected with the offensive against German cities and industries.

If Harris's offensive failed to bring German to its knees, it had not been for want of intention. Nor had it been any fault of the thousands of young men, so many still barely out of teenage, who returned nightly to the clandestine battle of the night skies over Europe. Every air crew member of Harris's command – indeed, of the entire RAF – was a volunteer; at no time in its long history has the RAF ever 'pressed' men into operational flying. Thus the bomber crews willingly placed

* *Bomber Offensive* by A. T. Harris : Collins, 1947.

their unfulfilled lives on a borderline of possible sacrifice each time they climbed into their aircraft and ventured abroad.

A glance at the statistics for merely one year of the RAF bombing offensive reveals a measure of the effort – especially the human cost – of those crews. From April 1943 to the end of March 1944 inclusive, Bomber Command initially despatched an overall total of 69,548 individual sorties. Of that tally, 2,703 bomber aircraft failed to return and were officially listed as missing; the equivalent of almost exactly 19,000 air crew men either killed, prisoner of war, or simply lost in unsolved circumstances. In even simpler terms, the rough equivalent of at least 130 complete Lancaster squadrons, more than the total force of squadrons available to Harris in April 1943. It would be difficult to discover a comparable record of losses proportionate to any equivalent fighting formation in any of the other services.

Perhaps their finest tribute was made by the man responsible for ordering them into battle night after night, Arthur Harris:

> There are no words with which I can do justice to the air crew who fought under my command. There is no parallel in warfare to such courage and determination in the face of danger over so prolonged a period, of danger which at times was so great that scarcely one man in three could expect to survive his tour of 30 operations . . . it was, moreover, a clear and highly conscious courage, by which the risk was taken with calm forethought, for aircrew were all highly skilled men, much above the average in education, who had to understand every aspect and detail of their task. It was, furthermore, the courage of the small hours, of men virtually alone, for at his battle-station the airman is virtually alone. It was the courage of men with long-drawn apprehensions of daily 'going over the top' . . . such devotion must never be forgotten.*

With the cessation of the Battle of Berlin, RAF Bomber Command began to concentrate on the Transportation Plan, the wrecking of French and German railway routes, depots, repairs centres and other means of conveying troops and machines to the Channel coast. Throughout April and May 1944, the RAF's heavy bombers sustained this plan with increasing weight and success, and by the first days of June had dropped more than 42,000 tons of bombs on targets stretching back from the Channel to Paris and beyond. In order to avoid

* *Bomber Offensive* by A. T. Harris: Collins, 1947.

such sorties being recognised as pure pre-invasion tactical bombing, additional heavy raids against strategic objectives in Germany were interspersed among the transportation sorties.

The overall emphasis on disruption of the French railway system also meant a shift in emphasis from the area bombing principle hither-to pursued vigorously by Harris to precision bombing of specific targets, a form of bombing which even Harris himself was unsure his command was capable of doing with the degree of accuracy necessary to justify such a switch in tactics. In fact Harris's doubts proved ill-founded. During 1943–44 the Path Finder Force primarily, and the 'independent' path-finding elements of various Bomber Command Groups (notably those of No 5 Group) had demonstrated clearly their ability to find, mark and destroy precise targets. Moreover, the change of pressure in bombing from Germany to France had an immediate effect on Bomber Command's casualty rates. With the bulk of German night defences concentrated on protection of the Reich itself, the Lancaster and Mosquito crews found reduced aerial opposition over France. Of the total of 21,226 sorties flown by Bomber Command by night in April and May 1944, 488 aircraft were listed as missing, a tragic enough toll but a figure which would have undoubtedly been far higher had Harris been directed to maintain the pace of operations, and therefore casualties incurred, in 1943–44 over Germany alone.

The USAAF's Eighth Air Force, which by the end of the Big Week operations had reached numerical parity with RAF Bomber Command, also contributed to the Transportation Plan, albeit on a much smaller scale than the RAF. Its prime purpose, however, remained the battle of attrition against the Luftwaffe and its back-up industries and resources, a task it was by now more than adequately armed in strength and hard experience to pursue to its inevitable conclusion. Although broad, agreement about the necessity for complete integration of American and British air power for the forthcoming invasion of Europe had been reached in the early planning stages, the actual command structures and directive responsibilities for such a combined air offensive were still a bone of contention among service and political chiefs as late as mid-April 1944. General Spaatz, the American air commander, bluntly refused to take orders from the appointed AEAF supremo, Leigh-Mallory, while Harris continued to argue for his convictions that Bomber Command was best employed in continuing its area attacks on German cities and industrial centres. Both commanders were most reluctant to surrender their existing status of 'independent' bomber formations with esoteric roles. Both men, though conceding the need for some participation by their heavy bombers in the Overlord programme, preferred to 'adjust' their existing aims and policies for their respective commands rather than become mere segments of an overall air plan and be subordinated to the directives of men like Leigh-Mallory who had no practical experience or esoteric knowledge of modern strategic bombing.

The various views and disagreements on functional control of the air power available to support Overlord were soon resolved by the insistence of the appointed Supreme Commander, General Eisenhower, who 'demurred at anything short of complete operational control' of the whole of Bomber Command and the USAAF's bomber forces based in Britain. His deputy, Sir Arthur Tedder, whose unequalled experience as an air force commander in the Middle East had embraced tri-service operations, was uniquely qualified in joint service warfare, and his appointment as Eisenhower's immediate deputy gave him the authority of a supreme air commander in relation to Overlord operational control and direction. Accordingly, he issued orders to Spaatz and Harris outlining the proposed priorities of their forces. This directive, issued on 17 April, defined priorities for the various bombing formations of Bomber Command, the Eighth Air Force, and the light bombers of the 2nd TAF as facets of a combined, overall plan, rather than three separate objectives. The USAAF was allotted the 'primary objective' of destruction of the Luftwaffe in every facet, while Bomber Command was given non-specific authority to '. . . continue to be employed with their main aim of disorganising German industry'. Many specific differences of opinion continued to be discussed and argued, but the broad plan for Overlord was now set.

For Bomber Command the pre-invasion operations it undertook now assumed an entirely fresh direction. While some seventy per cent of its efforts in March 1944 was directed against targets in Germany, in April less than a third of the monthly bomb tonnage was dropped in Germany as emphasis changed toward the French railway system. In May some seventy-five per cent of bombs fell on French targets, while in June – the invasion month – barely a tenth of the bomber loads fell on German soil. Thereafter, with only occasional exception, the bulk of Bomber Command operations were devoted to support of the Allied armies in Europe, and on an ever-increasing and more devastating scale than had been achieved in previous years of the offensive in the air. The Eighth Air Force too now found itself in the position it had originally striven for – virtual mastery of the daylight skies of Europe, with the consequent capability of defeating the Luftwaffe and opening the way for unhindered destruction of Hitler's Germany. The only remaining effective arm of the Luftwaffe to be undefeated was its nightfighter force. Night bombing of the German homeland never achieved the same degree of immunity from aerial attack which was soon to characterise the daylight bomber operations, and only when the advancing Allied armies flushed out German occupation forces in France and the Low Countries – with the consequent over-running of much of the Luftwaffe's early warning radar sites – did the Reich night defence system finally begin to crumble.

While the activities and redeployment of the British and American bomber forces proceeded during the pre-invasion months, the many other direct and indirect air formations soon to be involved were gathering strength for the fateful re-entry into Europe by Eisenhower's forces. The principal formation was, of course, the 2nd Tactical Air Force, inaugurated specifically for immediate tactical support of the invading armies. Commanded in the field by Air Marshal Sir Arthur Coningham, 2nd TAF was initially composed of three main Groups, Nos 83 and 84, each comprised of Spitfire, Typhoon and Mustang squadrons, and No 2 (Bomber) Group of medium and light bombers which had, in fact, been detached from its parent Bomber Command as early as June 1943. In addition, No 34 Wing – two reconnaissance squadrons – was based at 2nd TAF headquarters at Hartford Bridge. Until the actual invasion day, the squadrons remained allied to functional liaison with Fighter Command for operational purposes, and therefore participated largely in the attacks against suspected V1 robot flying bomb ski sites, while 2 Group's light bombers – mainly Mosquitos and Mitchells – maintained a series of well-executed, on occasion daring operations against specific targets in France and the Low Countries.

By early 1944 the 2nd TAF fighter pilots commenced specialised training for their intended roles in the forthcoming Overlord operations. Broadly speaking, these amounted to two prime purposes. Primarily, they were to secure complete air superiority over the Luftwaffe, in order to permit unrestricted reconnaissance and tactical bombing by appropriate units in direct support of the land forces. Secondly, though merely a slightly later stage of an equal priority, the fighter and fighter-bomber pilots were to be ready at all times to offer immediate support for the earthbound infantry on a day to day basis. While the bulk of 2nd TAF pilots and ground crews roughed it on their respective toughening-up training, a fourth formation was added to 2nd TAF strength, that of No 85 Group, comprised of Beaufighters, Mos-

quitos and Spitfires, and tasked with the defence of 2nd TAF units
– by day or night – during the build-up to invasion date.

On the eve of invasion, 5 June, 2nd TAF's order of battle showed
80 fighter squadrons, 12 light bomber units, four reconnaissance and
meteorological squadrons, and seven other units on attachment for
other roles. It was an impressive array of aerial might, backed by the
bombers and fighters of Bomber Command and the USAAF's Eighth
and Ninth Air Forces. Yet even this aerial armada was but part of the
whole Allied air strength available and involved in some aspect or
other of the invasion planning. Protection of the vast seaborne fleet of
invasion barges and landing craft which would bear the invading
infantry across the Channel to Normandy was of crucial importance.
The Royal Navy was fully prepared for its traditional surface watch
and ward role, particularly in regard to any possible intervention by
German E-boats or light vessels and the distinct possibility of U-boat
attacks in the Channel itself.

To the Royal Navy's role was added the considerable strength and
maritime expertise of 51 squadrons of RAF Coastal Command, plus a
further dozen squadrons on attachment from the Fleet Air Arm. The
principal task of the maritime squadrons was encapsulated in the overall code-name for their activities – Operation Cork; they were to seal
off the English Channel in every way from infiltration by German
naval or air forces, putting a cork in each end of the slender waterway
by constant patrolling and instant reaction to any form of enemy
activity.

The Cork operations were supplemented by some Coastal squadrons
based further afield whose role was to prevent or, at least, pre-warn
of any German naval movements out into the North Sea or Atlantic or
via the Irish Sea and the Western Approaches. For the seaborne invasion armada actually in the Channel, five squadrons of Fleet Air
Arm Swordfish torpedo-bombers were allotted the close support role,
with back-up force available from rocket and cannon-armed Beaufighters and Mosquitos if needed.

The value of photo-reconnaissance had been fully appreciated well
before the initial preparations for Overlord, and in fact the earliest
gathering of intelligence towards an eventual Allied re-entry into
Europe had commenced in late 1940, albeit an a very small and highly
individual plane. More serious attempts to gather up-dated knowledge
of the French coastline and thereby German defensive preparations
were initiated from May 1942, and by the spring of 1944 all PR units
were very heavily committed to the invasion preparations. Low-level

oblique photography was the chief ploy of the PR Spitfire pilots who patiently built up a virtual mountain of photographic evidence of German gun batteries forts, beach defences, radar sites and other obstacles facing any invading troops. Actual beaches were meticulously photographed and mapped, though to disguise the actual intended landing areas the PR crews covered ninety-one separate areas of northern French coastal zones on their sorties. Careful watch was kept on all Luftwaffe airfields, and any open fields likely to provide landing space for airborne troops were noted and located. All photographic evidence continued to be fed back to the PR Interpretation headquarters at Medmenham, where in addition to the seven million photo prints being issued daily, the Medmenham staff were meticulously building large-scale models of every possible useful site or area in France, each being up-dated daily with added details from the latest PR survey.

One particular line of intelligence vital to the invasion armies was the precise location and size of German coastal gun batteries within range of the proposed landing beaches; an equally important enemy defence system, his pre-warning radar installations in northern France, also needed to be identified and, if possible, nullified. The photo-reconnaissance centre at Medmenham accordingly provided the army and naval commanders with complete, up-dated lists of every German early warning station or site, complete with large-scale photographs and indications of their vulnerable points. This 300-page report was then kept up to date until the eve of invasion. It also provided the basis for a systematic destruction of the German radar sites by RAF and USAAF fighters, backed by relatively heavy but precise bombing operations. This series of strikes commenced in May 1944 and by 6 June all six of the German long-range warning stations south of Boulogne had been put out of commission, while fifteen others had been rendered useless. By that date less than twenty per cent of German radar apparatus in north-west France was operative, and on 6 June – 'D-Day' – no more than five per cent was active. Thus, as Leigh-Mallory was to report later :

The enemy did not obtain the early warning of our approach that his radar coverage should have made possible. There is, moreover, reason to suppose that radar-controlled gunfire was interfered with.

This nullification of the German pre-warning radar network was to contribute greatly to the crucial surprise element of the actual invasion. The week preceding 6 June saw the air forces step up their assaults on the heavily protected coastal gun sites – sorties undertaken in the main by the heavy bombers – while precision attacks by Lancasters eliminated several important enemy communication centres; in particular the German Signals Intelligence Service headquarters at Urville-Hague, near Cherbourg, which received more than 500 tons of bombs from a force of 99 bombers and was effectively wiped out. Its destruction unquestionably caused much of the delay in reaction from the German defenders during the first hours of the Allied landings on the Normandy beaches.

Among the many side-show deception ploys perpetrated by the air crews prior and during the invasion, perhaps one of the most notable, both for its precision and undoubted success, was Operation Taxable. Sixteen Lancasters of 617 Squadron, led by their commander, Wing Commander G. L. Cheshire, DSO, DFC (later VC), in conjunction with 18 small ships, patrolled the Channel between Dover and Cap d'Antifer from dusk on 5 June to dawn on 6 June. Their purpose was to simulate on German radar screens the appearance of a large convoy advancing on a 14-miles frontage, heading for France. A similiar operation was also being carried out off Boulogne by 218 Squadron. Flying at precisely 3,000 feet, in a series of mathematically calculated elliptical courses, the crews released bundles of the anti-radar metal foil (Window) at exactly 12-second intervals with precise regularity.

It was a monotonous, exacting role for the pilots and, especially, the navigators, but achieved its aim in diverting attention from the genuine seaborne convoys setting out from England on 6 June. Elsewhere Halifaxes and Stirlings released dummy parachutists and pyrotechnics simulating rifle and other gunfire near the village of Yvetot in northern France to convey a realistic impression of an attempted landing by airborne troops. Again, success attended their efforts, with a degree of confusion being created among local defences.

The use of airborne troops on the first day of actual invasion to secure the flanks of the main army advance, and to commandeer vital bridges north-east of Caen, was envisaged early in the planning. To convey these troops Nos 38 and 46 Groups RAF were detailed to lift the 6th Airborne Division, while American aircraft provided the transportation of US Army paratroops. Many weeks of intensive rehearsal and training were undertaken from early in the year, and continued almost to the eve of battle. Then at a few minutes after 11 p.m. in the evening of 5 June, the first 'pathfinder' Albemarle transport aircraft lifted off the runway at Harwell, bearing the 22nd Independent Parachute Company to their dropping zones in France, the advance spearhead of the mightiest invasion force ever assembled in the centuries-old saga of human warfare. Elsewhere, a total of 1,136 heavy bombers of Bomber Command began raining 5,267 tons of bombs down onto ten of the foremost German coastal batteries directly opposing the intended invasion beaches, stunning (if not actually destroying) the defensive gunners into partial immobility. Operation Overlord – the long-awaited return of the Allies to European soil – was under way.

CHAPTER THIRTEEN

Dawn of Victory

As the greyness of night brightened reluctantly into a pale sunshine of early morning on 6 June 1944, Oberleutnant Joseph 'Pips' Priller and his *Kaezmarek* (Wing-man) Heinz Wodarczyk from JG26 *Schlageter* dipped the noses of their Focke Wulf Fw 190s and slid through the lowest layer of mists hovering over the mouth of the river Orne, north of Caen, heading westward along the French coastline. The scene below them astonished both pilots. On the beach, code-named *Sword* by the Allies, a teeming, pulsating ant-hill of men and vehicles of the 3rd British Division and 27th Armoured Brigade covered the whole beachline, while off-shore stretching out of sight northward across the Channel in apparently unending procession lay a veritable armada of landing craft and naval vessels churning the water in furious activity. The Allies had landed!

Swiftly dropping to a mere fifty feet altitude, Priller and his No 2 swept across the panorama of khaki-clad infantry, firing long, raking bursts of cannon and machine gun fire, and then climbed frantically for cloud cover as a terrifying barrage of defensive fire reached for them from every angle. The surprise and shock registered on the two Luftwaffe pilot's minds exemplified the reaction of virtually every German defender that morning. An Allied invasion of France had been expected for many months; only the place and date remained in doubt. Yet when the actual invasion forces first scrambled onto French soil on 6 June they caught the German forces unawares.

Priller's lone sortie was also characteristic of the local Luftwaffe's initial moves on that first day of Overlord. Immediately facing the invasion areas stood *Luftflotte* 3, whose aircraft strength on that day amounted to some 815 of all types; only some sixty per cent of these could be regarded as operationally ready, and no more than 100 of these were fighters. Facing this relatively weak force the Allies had overwhelmingly superior strength, sufficient enough to despatch an overall total of 14,674 individual sorties above the invasion forces during the first twenty-four hours of action. The mere handful of individual sorties flown that day by Luftwaffe crews resulted in the loss of three Junkers Ju 88 bombers and a single Fw 190, but the vast majority of Allied fighter pilots found no aerial opponents during the daylight hours.

German reaction by anti-aircraft (*flak*) gunners was more positive, claiming almost all the 113 Allied aircraft brought down during the same twenty-four hours. A contingency plan for immediate reinforcement of the Luftwaffe units directly facing any Allied invasion attempt was initiated on 6 June, and within thirty-six hours slightly more than 200 fighters were flown in to *Luftflotte* 3's area, followed by a further 100 on 10 June. In addition, 135 bombers, torpedo-carrying Ju 88s and others were detached to the battle area within the first week. Specialised ground attack aircraft and crews, of which there were at most seventy-five in France in early June, were never reinforced, despite the blatant need for such types of operational strike types. The reason lay not with any lack of such aircraft, but in Hitler's unshakeable policy decision that the force of some 550 ground attack aircraft then assembled along the Russian front were to remain in the east in preparation for an unexpected Russian offensive in strength.

Thus, by the end of the first week's savage fighting the Luftwaffe opposing the invasion areas could count rather more than 1,000 operational aircraft of varying types; about one-third of these being fighters. The patent lack of ground attack aircraft led to pure fighters being hastily adapted to carrying bombs and, despite the fact that their pilots were untrained in such tactics, no less than 150 such 'fighter-bombers' had been 'converted' by 10 June. The results obtained from such a hasty measure were poor enough to have Berlin issue a directive on 12 June ordering all single-engined fighters to be reverted to their normal function. Virtually all attempts by German bombers to attack the Allied-held beaches were frustrated by the massive and constant aerial umbrella, by day and by night, put up by the AEAF. From 14 June, in view of the impossibility of penetrating such a massively strong air shield, the Luftwaffe bombers were used to mount widespread mine-laying operations in the Channel and its near approaches, in a bid to at least halt or delay Allied reinforcement of the landed forces. During the following six weeks such sea-mining was carried out every night, amounting to almost 2,000 sorties and 'sowing' between three and four thousand mines. It was a useful contribution to the Germans and caused no small inconvenience to the re-supply naval traffic plying between England and Normandy, but could have no more than a nuisance effect on the overall battles.

As the battle of Normandy entered its second week the cumulative effect of constant fighting by the Luftwaffe's fighter units began to tell. Several units fell in strength to little more than sixty per cent, and replacement aircraft were slow in delivery due to the withdrawal of the Le Bourget and Toul depots further east to avoid Allied air attacks. Mounting casualties reduced the overall fighting potential alarmingly, and five single-engine fighter units were actually withdrawn in June for re-equipment. The only immediately available fighter replacements were those of the Reich defence forces and as some of the latter were sent to France the already inadequate Reich defence was inevitably further depleted – this at a time when the USAAF's daylight bombing offensive against strategic targets in Germany was increasing appreciably. Only in southern Germany, where roughly one third of all Reich defence fighters were based to counter the now-regular incursions of Italian-based Allied bombers, was the German defence maintained at near-adequate strength.

This direct side-effect of the early days of the invasion upon the fighter forces defending the German homeland was to be felt even more after July. Once the initial footholds gained in Normandy had been transformed into permanent lodgment throughout much of northern France, the RAF and USAAF's heavy bombers could be released from their temporary duty of tactical support in the field and quickly resumed their original strategic role against German industry.

In the third week of July the British and Canadian forces finally succeeded in breaking out from the initial lodgment area and advanced south-east of Caen and east of the Orne river. By then Luftwaffe resistance, though to continue sporadically for several weeks, was patently having little real effect. From 10 June Allied fighters had been steadily occupying rough airstrips 'constructed' in the narrow Allied beach-head zones, and by mid-July nearly eighty such advanced 'airfields' had been established and brought into immediate operational use by 2nd TAF fighters. These fighters, with occasional interruptions of air combat, expended their efforts in close tactical support of the army, being controlled by RAF and USAAF air crews attached to forward army units who could call down the fighters to deal with any German obstacle or resistance; an instant flying artillery. Elsewhere RAF and Ninth Air Force, USAAF fighter-bombers roamed the enemy's back zones, destroying all and any rail or road movements detected and thus delaying considerably all enemy attempts to reinforce their defences. Such 'freelance' marauding occasionally brought unrealised 'bonuses', as on 17 July when Squadron Leader J. J. Le Roux, leading his 602 Squadron's

Spitfires, strafed a staff car near the hamlet of Ste Foy de Montgomerie. The car overturned and its occupant, Generalfeldmarschall Erwin Rommel, the German commander in Normandy, suffered a fractured skull.

The complete co-ordination of the USAAF and RAF operations was perhaps particularly exemplified on 7 August, when – on direct orders from Hitler – five German armoured divisions launched an intensive attack at Mortain in an effort to cut off the American tank force of General Patton which was then engaged in rolling up the German flank. Since the USAAF fighters possessed no effective armament for attacking heavily armoured tanks, rocket-armed Typhoons of Nos 83 and 84 Groups RAF were instantly switched to this new threat. At mid-day 19 squadrons of Typhoons roared into battle, hammering and blasting the *Panzer* force, and within the next two hours claimed 81 tanks destroyed or seriously crippled. Further attacks on another small force of German tanks claimed five more victims, and by dusk the Typhoons had fired more than 2,000 three-inch rockets and dropped 80 tons of bombs.

This hundred per cent co-ordination of army and air force operational effort was the key to the overwhelming air superiority established from the outset of the invasion. It was a technique tried and tested in the campaigns of North Africa, Sicily and Italy under the aegis of the 1944 invasion's supreme air commander, Tedder, and was now employed with a precision unprecedented in dimension and scope. Backing the silk-like inter-organisation was a pure quantitative strength in firstline operational aircraft which heavily out-weighed any force put up by the Luftwaffe. In particular, the AEAF's ability to replace wrecked or damaged aircraft almost within hours contrasted hugely with the Luftwaffe's capability for replacing or reinforcing its frontline units. Ironically, this stemmed not from any lack of factory-fresh stock of fighters – production of fighters in German industry during 1944 actually reached its highest monthly output figures of the whole war – but was due solely to the extreme difficulties of actually delivering such fresh aircraft to operational *Geschwader*.

The Allied air concentration prior to the invasion on disrupting and wrecking French rail and road routes to Normandy was largely responsible for this state of affairs, but the escalating strategic bombing assault on German oil refineries and depots – the kernel of the USAAF's Eighth Air Force's operational effort in mid-1944 and thereafter – was inexorably reducing the oil and fuel reserves of Germany's military forces to critical levels.

This bombing offensive produced almost immediate results. Production of aviation fuel fell in June 1944 to a third of the previous month's output, while July saw production down by a third of the June figure. In August 1944 even that figure was halved, and September produced a mere 7,000 tons, some five per cent of the May total. Reserve stocks also quickly diminished as these were used to plug the gaps for firstline operations. The situation became so serious that on 11 August 1944, *Luftflotte* 3, on direct orders from Berlin, issued orders for heavy restrictions on all types of flying activity. Henceforth, fighters despatched to tackle the daily Allied bomber assaults on Germany held first priority on fuel, while *all* other forms of operational flying were specially limited to '. . . such actions as could be considered decisive after the closest scrutiny'. It was the first time in the war that a general curtailment of Luftwaffe operational activity had been imposed. It was, in effect, the beginning of the end for the Luftwaffe as an effective fighting formation.

The fuel-restriction general order had wide ramifications on the overall Luftwaffe organisation. First to suffer was the flying training organisation, a vital facet which had already borne too many inroads from past 'emergencies'. Many flying training units were simply closed and their student air crews dispersed among infantry or other non-flying sections of the army. The bomber arm was also severely cut back. Already at its lowest point of operational use, the bomber force was drastically reduced in priority status and equipment. Air reconnaissance units became of secondary importance. Only the fighters acting in direct defence of Germany retained any importance, having little if any restriction as long as they were engaged in tackling the awesome bomber formations now parading boldly in the skies over the Reich daily. The only other types of aircraft to enjoy unrestricted fuel supplies were the jets, which ran on a form of low grade fuel available in ample quantity for the moment.

By September 1944 the general outlook for the Luftwaffe seemed dismal. The Allied air supremacy in the west was now acknowledged by most Luftwaffe chiefs as almost irreversible, and morale throughout the air arm was at one of its lowest levels. Yet, with an astonishing capacity for revival that was demonstrated on several occasions during the war, the German air force was about to re-establish itself as far from a spent force; only to be crippled again by its misemployment during the 1944/45 winter land campaign on the direct orders of Hitler.

From June to October 1944 the Luftwaffe casualties rose alarmingly, both by day and by night. As the German ground forces began to pull back into France, the pursuing 2nd TAF fighters, fighter-bombers, and medium bombers maintained their constant pressure by devastating, low-level attacks on anything German which moved on the ground, and swamped any air opposition. On a single operational sortie Boston and Mitchell bombers of No 2 Group destroyed 1,800 of 2,000 vehicles and killed almost 6,000 German troops; while American fighters of the Ninth Air Force, tackling Luftwaffe aircraft attempting to protect German troops retreating across the Seine of 25 August, claimed 77 aerial victories and 49 other aircraft on the ground. By night No 85 Group's crews claimed almost 200 victories between D-Day and the end of August 1944.

The rapidity of the Allied advance south and eastwards soon saw the Luftwaffe quit French soil by the end of August, moving into Belgium and Holland where the fighters were then placed virtually at maximum operational range from the troops they were expected to protect. An Allied invasion of southern France, commencing on 15 August, further jeopardised the remaining Luftwaffe forces in south and west France, and these could offer only token opposition for a week before being hastily withdrawn to Metz and Germany. By early September the Belgian-based German air units were forced to withdraw again, this time to Germany, losing many more aircraft as these were abandoned or destroyed by Allied fighters.

If the declining numerical strength of the Luftwaffe in the west was fast approaching critical level, fighter production within Germany was already building up a substantial reserve. As the general war situation for Germany produced a contraction of the 'ring' around the Reich, the pulling back of Luftwaffe units to the homeland increased the density of day and night defences. Fuel restrictions continued to thwart any effective overall operations, but day fighters continued to be granted primary consideration in their continuing battles with the Allied heavy bombers. It was at this juncture that the Allies despatched Operation Market-Garden, commencing on 17 September. The operation was designed primarily to isolate German troops occupying Holland and to free the port of Antwerp in order to facilitate resupply of the most forward elements of the advancing armies. Accordingly, a triple airborne assault was intended to capture Arnhem, Eindhoven and Nijmegen-Grave, with special objectives of capturing the bridges across the lower Rhine, Waal and Maas rivers. Meanwhile No 30 Corps of General Dempsey's 2nd Army was supposed to penetrate from the south and link up with the paratroopers and airborne soldiers. On paper, the plan looked good : in practice it proved to be a disaster.

Ideally the whole airborne forces were to be lifted in a single day's operations, yet there were insufficient troop transport aircraft availiable for such numbers. Instead, it was decided to convey the troops on three consecutive days – 17, 18 and 19 September – an arrangement which eventually proved to be a prime factor of the failure of the Market-Garden venture. The whole operation was planned and controlled from London, rather than in co-ordination with No 83 Group of the AEAF, whose front included the Arnhem zones, and in this way 2nd TAF was only used in the operation almost as an afterthought. Luftwaffe opposition to the airborne venture was intended to be heavy, with nearly 600 fighters – including some 350 from Reich defence units, apart from other outside zones – set to fling back the Allied airborne invasion. In the event, weather conditions, fuel shortages, and unsuitable airfields reduced the Luftwaffe opposition considerably. Only after 25 September – when the Allied commanders recognised the failure of Market Garden and began a withdrawal of troops – did the Luftwaffe appear in any real strength. When it did so, it was met with fierce opposition from 83 Group Spitfires, which accounted for 46 German aircraft on 27 September, and a further 27 victories two days later.

The Allied heavy bombing offensive against Germany's oil production and reserves had begun in May 1944 as a distinct and deliberate strategic ploy. On 12 and 28/29 May the USAAF Eighth Air Force dropped over 2,500 tons of bombs on main synthetic oil plants at Leuna, Pölitz, Bohlen, Lützkendorf, Magdeburg, Zeitz and Ruhland; these targets collectively produced some forty per cent of the estimated total output of synthetic fuel. In June RAF Bomber Command and the Italy-based USAAF 15th Air Force joined with the Eighth Air Force in the 'oil plan', and within three weeks had caused the loss of more than ninety per cent of fuel production. If such operations proved so effective, they were by no means the only form of aid given to the invasion forces by Harris's and Spaatz's heavy bombers.

In the early stages of the Normandy fighting a brief series of devastating heavy bombing sorties had blasted gaps in the stiff German resistance for the ground forces to exploit; as at Caen and Colombelles on 18 July when a total of nearly 2,000 heavy and medium bombers dropped 7,700 tons of bombs on the stubborn German defenders preventing the Allied advance. Such awesome demonstrations of the sheer weight of Allied air power readily available to support ground forces totally demoralised the opposing German troops, leading their commander von Kluge, who had succeeded the injured Rommel, to report to Hitler on 21 July : 'There is no way by which, in the face of the enemy air forces' complete command of the air, we can discover a form of strategy which will counter-balance its annihilating effect unless we withdraw from the battlefield'.

In just six major attacks in July–August, the heavy bombers drenched the German defenders with a downpour of 24,300 tons of bombs. On at least two of these occasions, however, inaccuracy in aiming caused a percentage of the bomb load to fall among Allied forward troops, causing heavy casualties. Such raids were essentially 'one-off' occasions; the use of the heavy bombers for such diversions from the strategic offensive against oil targets in Germany found little favour with Harris and Spaatz. Nevertheless with a virtual absence of Luftwaffe opposition by day, the heavies continued to be sent in as a preliminary barrage on several occasions as the Allied armies continued their advance into Belgium and Holland threatening the north-west borders of the Reich.

One such diversion was carried out on 3 October, when a force of 247 Lancasters and Mosquitos of RAF Bomber Command attacked a dyke near Westkapelle on Walcheren in daylight. Releasing their bombs from 6,000 feet or lower, the bombers immediately breached the dyke at its thickest section, letting the sea through and flooding out German defence positions. Further attacks on dykes elsewhere on the island finally opened the way for Allied occupation, and the first landing on the island, at dawn on 1 November, was preceded and accompanied by wave after wave of Typhoons, Mitchells and Spitfires of 2nd TAF. By 8 November, when the final German resistance had melted away, the 2nd TAF crews had flown over 10,000 sorties, fired 11,637 rockets, dropped 1,558 tons of bombs, and lost 50 aircraft and 31 pilots.

While the encircling Allied forces closed the ring around the Reich, the daylight and night combined offensive by bombers maintained its destructive and progressive pressure on Germany itself. German fighter opposition encountered remained intense, claiming relatively high casualties, but the overall effect on the Allied bomber formations was almost negligible. Despite such apparent failure to stem the Allied bombing onslaught, German aircraft production by late 1944 had reached unprecedented quantity in pure numbers; this near-miracle of recovery was unsuspected by Allied air commanders whose previous campaigns against German industry had been regarded as crippling.

Adolf Galland, the Luftwaffe's fighter commander-in-chief, was already planning a *Grosse Schlag* ('Great Blow'), the assembly of a huge force of fighters and fighter-bombers, including a number of the latest jets, for a series of truly telling attacks on the daylight bomber formations. Detailed planning for this 'Blow' included an intention of deploying some 2,000 fighters in mass attacks against any sizeable incoming Allied formation, with the aim of destroying between 400 and 500 bombers in the one engagement, a casualty tally which, it was hoped, would decisively weaken and deter any further mass raids. It was calculated that such a 'blow' would cost the Luftwaffe perhaps 400 aircraft and about 100 pilots, but the healthy state of fighter production in late 1944 promised – at least, in theory – ample replacements for any lost machines; the sacrifice of so many pilots was not so easily replaced but was accepted as necessary.

On 12 November Galland was able to report to Berlin that his 'Blow' was ready to be launched just as soon as weather conditions became favourable enough to ensure success – a total of 3,700 aircraft and crews, the bulk of which were fighters. Galland's carefully husbanded and trained force was never to be used to its intended purpose. In reply to his 'Readiness' report, Galland received orders to prepare his force for close combat aid to the German troops being assembled for an imminent ground offensive in the Ardennes region!

In spite of outspoken objections to such a misemployment of his fighter force, Galland was given blunt orders to transfer all but two *Gruppen* to the west on 20 November. It was yet another example of the piecemeal direction of Germany's war by its Führer, Hitler. The offensive through the Ardennes had been planned since July 1944, at which time Hitler personally reassured his generals that the ground assault would receive 'maximum fighter support' – yet his 'General of the Fighters', Adolf Galland, was never consulted or even informed of the Ardennes offensive until mere days before it was launched. Galland's 'Big Blow' force had been specifically raised, trained and equipped for its intended anti-bomber battle to come; to convert its crews to ground support duties and disperse its units to – in so many cases – entirely unsuitable airfields in the west invited disaster. The bulk of the fighter crews were young, ill-trained, and fresh to combat conditions, a circumstance which might be used fairly effectively in pure fighting interception roles against massed Allied bombers over Germany, but which boded ill for any low-level battle role. Such a move automatically resulted in a substantial depletion of the Reich's day fighter defenders remaining in Germany. Paradoxically, the nightfighter defence for Germany was then at its strongest, with an establishment of 1,170 fighters at the end of November 1944. Indeed, in the following month the *Luftflotte Reich*'s nightfighter establishment was to reach its wartime peak strength of 1,355 aircraft, of which total 982 were available for immediate operational use.

On 16 December Germany launched its last and most intensive land offensive in the west, when the 5th *Panzer* and 6th *SS Panzer* armies – some 24 divisions comprised of roughly 200,000 men – smashed through the Anglo-American lines in the forest areas of the Ardennes, intending eventually to recapture Antwerp and to split the Allied armies. Weather conditions of fog, mists and rain undoubtedly added greatly to the initial surprise and success of the ground assault, but at the same time prevented any aerial activity in strength. Thus, the planned knockout blow against Allied airfields during the opening phase of the offensive was impossible to achieve. Thick fog conditions prevailed for the first eight days and it was not until Christmas Eve that the Luftwaffe could venture forth in any strength. It was immediately countered by heavy 2nd TAF opposition and during the next three days lost heavily in a series of head-on clashes. On Christmas Day the American armies began their counter-offensive and the German advance ground to a halt immediately. Within forty-eight hours the German armies began to regroup and retreat. Then, on New Year's Day, the Luftwaffe had its final fling, when Operation *Bodenplatte* ('Ground Plate') was initiated.

For *Bodenplatte* – an all-out attempt to destroy the 2nd TAF on its airfields – every available aircraft was employed; a total of more than 800 machines of all types. On 1 January 1945 the 2nd TAF's aircraft were occupying many airfields in Holland and Belgium in great numbers, with congestion of up to six squadrons at particular airfields. It was a tempting target, and at shortly before 0930 hours that morning, spearheaded by pairs of navigational 'pathfinder' Ju 88s, waves of Luftwaffe fighters and fighter-bombers struck at 17 different Allied airstrips in successive waves. Roaring in at tree-top heights, the German crews created havoc among the tightly packed Allied aircraft. The attack achieved complete surprise and 144 2nd TAF aircraft were destroyed, while 84 more were seriously damaged. Buildings, fuel and stores dumps, vehicles were set aflame, and Allied personnel casualties amounted to 46 killed and 145 wounded or injured. The cost to the Luftwaffe was equally severe, with nearly 300 aircraft being lost with their pilots, including nearly 60 unit or flight commanders. Many of these losses accrued from the sheer inexperience of the many younger pilots. Air collisions, bad evasion tactics against highly accurate air-field anti-aircraft gun defenders, and generally poor flying ability prob-ably accounted for at least half the total tally of victims.

Hitler's insistence on a maximum employment of the Luftwaffe for the support of his last, desperate attempt to ward off the Allied advance on Germany from the west was, in Adolf Galland's words, 'the final dagger thrust into the back of the Luftwaffe'. The accumulated aircraft strength achieved by near-miracles of industrial organisation throughout 1944 was swiftly and tragically dissipated almost overnight, leaving only a remnant of a once-proud and powerful air force to offer token resistance to its many opponents on all fronts. Drained fuel resources, lack of supply lines and virtually all forms of facilities whittled down the Luftwaffe's power to fight; the only remaining spark was the much-reduced home defence fighter force. Aircraft production continued almost to the very end of the war, and at the final surrender the existing shell of the Luftwaffe could still muster some 3,500 aircraft. Such numerical strength was a hollow 'muscle-power' – nearly all were bereft of fuel, ammunition and crews to fly them by then. Even so the German fighter pilots fought on until almost the last day of hostilities, not in the much distorted Allied propaganda view of 'fanatical Nazis who would never surrender', but as veteran, experienced, professional military men obeying their orders and their clearly defined duty until forced to lay down their arms.

Perhaps no finer example of such men, devoted to their duty as professional officers, existed than the elite band of fighter pilots of *Jagdverband* 44 (literally, 'Fighter Unit 44'). Formed in January 1945 at the express wish of Hitler, JV44 was an 'independent' fighter force equipped with Messerschmitt Me 262 jet aircraft, tasked with home defence against Allied daytime bombing raids. Its original commander was Adolf Galland, recently 'sacked' from his post as General of Fighters by Göring, who was given free rein to select his pilots. Accordingly, Galland gathered together a galaxy of star pilots of huge combat experience, men such as Johannes 'Macki' Steinhoff (176 victories), Gunther Lützow (108), Gerhard Barkhorn (301), Walter Krupinski (179), Hohagen (55), Schnell (72) and others of equal prowess. Nearly all displayed Germany's highest gallantry awards on their uniforms or around their throats, many had survived multiple crashes and wounds, all contributed years of combat experience to a fighting combination unique in fighter annals.

Moving to Munich-Riem on the last day of March 1945, JV44 flew a series of interception sorties throughout April, gaining 50–60 victories but steadily paying a high price for success. On 18 April Steinhoff crashed and sustained horrific burns, while Lützow 'failed to return'. Then on 26 April their leader Galland, after scoring two victories was caught by a Mustang, crashlanded and was hospitalised. His place was taken by Heinz Bär, whose final war tally of 220 victories included 16 from the cockpit of a jet fighter, but Bär's command was destined to be brief. On 3 May, while based at Salzburg, JV44's Me 262s were deliberately destroyed in situ as Allied tanks first appeared over the far perimeter of the airfield.

None of JV44's pilots had ever thought that their task would have any significance in the air situation over Germany; it was simply their clear duty to fight on. Almost without exception, however, the JV44 pilots merely wanted to finish their war – just for once – in a unit possessing a clear technical superiority over the common enemy; a situation for Luftwaffe pilots seldom accomplished in the latter war years.

If the men of JV44 epitomised the fierce pride and dedication of the Luftwaffe crews still fighting in early 1945, they were not the sole examples. For merely one indication of the determination of the German defenders, on 30 April a mass engagement resulted in the fighters of 83 Group, 2nd TAF claiming the destruction of 37 German fighters without loss to themselves. In balance, however, in the last week of February 1945, a handful of Me 262 jets of III/JG7 destroyed no less than 45 heavy bombers and 15 fighters; while on 18 April a total of 37 Me 262s from I and II/JG7 tackled some 1,250 bombers and their massive Mustang escort. In less than thirty minutes of furious combat the jets claimed at least 19 Mustangs and many of the 24 bombers lost on this sortie.

The overt superiority of the Me 262 twin-jet fighter over any existing Allied fighter was clearly demonstrated on 7 April, when the German pilots, for a change, concentrated on attacking the American fighter escorts rather than the bombers. With few losses to themselves, the jets of JG7 alone claimed 28 American fighters, apart from a share in the seven bombers shot down. Though a clear-cut victory, the Me 262s' tally was the only ray of hope on a day which saw the Luftwaffe lose no less than 183 fighters to the roving American Mustangs and Thunderbolts; with No 1 Air Corps losing 133 of these, including 77 pilots killed. Just three days later some 1,200 USAAF bombers carpet-bombed all Me 262 bases in the Berlin area, forcing the jet units to withdraw further afield. It was in essence the swan-song of the superb Messerschmitt Me 262, but even with the golden advantage of hindsight, it is permissible to ponder what effect this jet fighter might have had on the Allied aerial bombing offensive – indeed, on the whole air war over Europe – had it been given top production priority as a *fighter* from its inception. Massed numbers of Me 262 *Jagdgeschwader* which might well have been thus available even before the Allied invasion of Normandy in June 1944 could have jeopardised the whole Allied effort. Its relegation to the unsuitable role of *Blitz* bomber by Hitler in his maniac obsession with offence rather than defence left the Reich to bear untold suffering and devastation from an Allied aerial supremacy which, by 1945, was undeniable.

A measure of the Allied air supremacy during the latter stages of the European conflict was the increasing near-immunity to aerial opposition. Though losses continued to occur until late April 1945, the *casualty* rate declined steadily after August 1944. By September 1944 RAF Bomber Command had been 'released' from General Eisenhower's supreme command to the extent that it could, in the main, resume its former role of strategic bombing of German towns and industrial resources. With the USAAF's Eighth Air Force now committed to attacking Germany's oil refineries and depots, the RAF's night bombers continued to adhere to Arthur Harris's creed of area bombing, interspersed with daylight precision raids when required by the invading forces in France and the Low Countries. The shrinking night defences of the Luftwaffe meant a higher survival rate among Harris's crews by the close of 1944. On 14 October, for example, 1,063 heavy bombers attacked Duisburg in broad daylight and lost just 15 aircraft, but that some night 1,005 bombers dropped 4,547 tons of bombs on Duisburg with a loss of only six aircraft. Part-reason for such light losses was the heavy use of Mosquito 'intruder' and escort fighters along the bomber stream's flightpath, apart from a number of feint attacks which helped to divert and confuse German nightfighter controllers. The month of December 1944 saw RAF Bomber Command despatch a total of 15,333 aircraft over Germany, and suffer a loss of 135 machines – a casualty rate below one per cent.

By early 1945 German oil and fuel production had already diminished to a relative trickle, and emphasis on destruction of German transportation facilities was given almost equal target priority. Even so, Harris's force continued to single out particular cities for attention in the continuing bid to break the German population's will to fight and sustain their war effort. Probably no other such raid executed, with the possible exception of the previous razing of Hamburg, created so much controversy as the brief series of attacks made against the ancient city of Dresden on 13/14 February 1945. Two waves of RAF bombers, complemented by two more raids by the USAAF's Eighth Air Force, decimated the city and razed more than 1,600 acres of the city to a fire-scorched 'desert' of death and horror – almost three times the acreage of London wrecked by the Luftwaffe throughout the entire war.

Civilian casualties were conservatively estimated at some 135,000 at first, though subsequent research revealed figures of slightly more than 18,000 killed and a further 35,000 as 'missing'. Contrary to many repeated statements in various histories of the air war, this was not the *first* bombing attack made against Dresden – the USAAF Eighth Air Force had bombed the city on 7 October 1944 – but it was certainly one of the most destructive 'area bombing' sorties of the whole war. Again, in contrast to past published assertions, Dresden was by no means the 'last' of the RAF's major raids against German cities; indeed, such raids occupied some thirty-seven per cent of Bomber Command's overall operational targets from January to May 1945.

Nevertheless, on 6 April 1945 a fresh policy directive for RAF Bomber Command called for a halt in the area bombing style of attacks and thereafter the bulk of the command's efforts were turned against Germany's transportation systems and fuel resources. Such objectives had been an adjunct to the command's main operations almost since the start of the war, particularly since the pre-invasion period of May–June 1944. Railway marshalling yards, canals, ports, harbours, viaducts had all been pounded at intervals, though usually with little lasting effect. By mid-1944, however, German capacity for repairing such vital communications links was lessening, and the increased weight of attacks often meant complete crippling of specific targets. On 14 March 1945 a 617 Squadron Lancaster dropped a single 22,000 lb DR (Deep Penetration) bomb on the Bielefeld viaduct and effectively put this vital link out of service, the first use of this type of bomb. Similar precision attacks, using 12,000 lb *Tallboy* and 22,000 lb *Grand Slam* bombs, on such deeply protected targets as U-boat pens were equally successful while long-battered objectives such as the Dortmund-Ems and Mitteland canals were finally put out of commission for the rest of the war.

As Bomber Command entered its final weeks of operations, a number of targets selected bore no great significance to the prime policy but were certainly objectives which the bomber crews regarded as 'choice' targets. The best example of such sorties were those undertaken by a force of 359 Lancasters on 25 April against Hitler's private fortress retreat, the so-termed Eagles' Nest, high in the mountains at Berchtes-gaden. That same day a further force of 482 Lancasters, Halifaxes and Mosquitos sought out the coastal gun batteries on Wangerooge Island. Even as these daylight raids were accomplished, a third force of 107 Lancasters accompanied by a dozen Mosquitos bombed oil refineries and tanks at Vallo, Tonsberg during the night – the last occasion when Bomber Command heavies attacked the enemy during World War Two.

It was not the final operation, however; this 'honour' fell to some 303 Mosquitos and other back-up aircraft which set out on the night of 2/3 May to raid such targets as Kiel, Eggebeck airfield and Husum airfield; while 44 other Mosquitos spent the night strafing various enemy troop concentrations and transports. At 1.41 a.m. on 7 May 1945, an agreement for the unconditional surrender of Germany to the Allies was signed at General Eisenhower's headquarters at Rheims, and the following day – 8 May – was officially declared to be VE Day – Victory in Europe Day. The remains of a devastated Europe were – for the moment – officially at peace.

CHAPTER FOURTEEN

Aftermath

The rapidly decreasing opposition, by day and by night, offered by the Luftwaffe to the Allied air incursions from east, west and south during the final few weeks of the war epitomised the dying spasms of a once-proud force. After 10 April 1945 no further attempts had been made to repulse the day bombing formations, while the nightfighter force was reduced to no more than a handful of sorties per night. The only real effort made to use German air power consisted of last-gasp attacks against Allied troops along the Elbe and advancing upon Nuremberg. By 26 April American and Russian advance troops had linked up at Torgau – the circle was complete. Frantic reorganisation of the Luftwaffe high command during the weeks preceding surrender were moves of base and paper control which bore no relation to the realities; the Luftwaffe was by then a completely confused, piecemeal collection of unco-ordinated units, scattered far afield, with no fuel, supplies, communications, or adequate direction. By the end of April all operations against the western Allies had ceased, while the last remnants of the air arm, a ragbag of units operating all types of aircraft, were scattered around northern Austria and Bohemia operating spasmodically against Russian forces until the final surrender.

Despite every possible disadvantage, it must be recognised that the men of the Luftwaffe's operational flying units fought fiercely and courageously to the bitter end, fulfilling a clear duty to their nation and to their personal codes of honour as professional fighting servicemen. The cost of their long struggle in human terms was grievous. From 1 September 1939 until 28 February 1945, the last date for which reliable records are available, a gross total of 44,065 air crew members had been killed, a further 27,610 were known to be prisoners or had been lost in unknown circumstances, and 28,200 had suffered serious or crippling wounds. The combined figures represented virtually the entire air crew force available to the Luftwaffe at the outbreak of war. The fates of the surviving Luftwaffe personnel in May 1945 depended entirely upon circumstance, in the main, their actual location at the point of Germany's unconditional surrender. For air crews,

particularly, the immediate future for a vast majority was imprison-
ment as the victorious Allies rounded up all and any personnel in
uniform. The more fortunate – the term is merely relative – were
captured, or surrendered to British or American occupation troops,
and were destined to serve relatively brief sentences before being returned to the bleak existence of civilian life in an utterly ruined Germany. The less fortunate – especially any commissioned officers – were
incarcerated in Russian prisoner or labour camps for many years; a high
proportion disappeared for ever in the ensuing years.

The vast material stocks of aircraft, engines, armament, and other
appurtenances of the Luftwaffe were, with rare exception, consigned
to the scrapheap. Examples of the latest German jet aircraft, guns,
rockets, radar and other technologically-advanced equipment were sent
back to Britain and the USA for study and possible use in future development, while Russian occupation forces gathered both men and
material of any importance for shipment to Russia.

If this legalised looting of Luftwaffe resources, both human and
material, was to a great extent a palpably human reaction from any
conquering army, it was at the same time an extremely short-sighted
action in certain aspects. A treasure-house of ultra-modern armament,
engine, and other facets – either in operational use or under development at that period – was destroyed or ignored; while some of the most
expert German scientists and engineers in the fields of modern aeronautical research were literally told that their long years of virtually
unequalled experience and accumulated knowledge were '. . . of little
or no value' by some British and American authorities. Inevitably, such
rejection led to many such invaluably knowledgeable men being driven
into the highly appreciative arms of the Russian authorities. Those few
visionary British officials who fully appreciated the future value of
such ex-'enemy' personnel to the postwar RAFs jet age were in the
event over-ridden by higher authority.

The stark lessons of recent history, particularly the eventual results
of the harsh treatment of Germany after the 1914–18 war, had clearly
not been learned by many of the victorious Allied authorities in 1945–
46. Even the golden opportunity for each of the main Allied air forces
to assess the success – or otherwise – of their strategic bombing offensives was not wholly implemented. While the USAAF almost immediately after Germany's surrender moved in some 1,200 personnel com-
prising the United States Strategic Bombing Survey 'team' to carry
out a properly organised scientific survey of (mainly) the effect of
American bombing operations; the RAF, tardily, despatched merely a

handful of 'observers' with relatively vague terms of reference for a
similar report on RAF Bomber Command's efforts.

For the RAF, as it took stock of its war effort, the war had claimed
a tragic toll. By August 1945, after Japan had surrendered to the
threat of a continuing atom-bomb offensive, the RAF world-wide had
suffered totals of 70,253 killed, 13,115 men made prisoner, and 22,924
wounded. Of these overall casualty figures, the men of RAF Bomber
Command had suffered the highest proportion, with 47,268 air crew
members killed, 4,200 wounded on operational activities, apart from a
further 8,305 men killed in non-operational accidents during training
et al. RAF Fighter Command had also sacrificed a high proportion of
its splendid youth, having 3,690 pilots or other crew members killed, a
further 1,215 seriously injured or wounded, and 601 prisoners of war.
Thus, the two major offensive commands of the RAF engaged in the
European theatre of operations had accounted for more than eighty
per cent of the RAF's entire war casualties. In this context, it must be
remembered that the term 'RAF' embraced a multitude of non-British
nationalities, and RAF Bomber Command particularly epitomised the
astonishing blend of differing nationals who flew operationally in RAF
bombers. Such men, volunteers from virtually every corner of the
globe, paid a high price for their willingness to bolster Britain's air
offensive against Germany. Of those bomber crew members who died
on operations, the Royal Australian Air Force (RAAF) lost 3,412, the
Royal Canadian Air Force (RCAF) 8,209, the Royal New Zealand
Air Force (RNZAF) 1,433, while a further 48 had come from other
countries. Thus, collectively, the 'overseas' contribution to Bomber
Command's overall losses was almost 40 per cent of those young men
who had died attempting to bomb Nazi Germany into submission.

The USAAF's 'late' entry into operations over Europe had meant
that the Eighth Air Force did not really contribute any significant
weight to the Allied bombing offensive until 1944 – some seventy-five
per cent of the bomb tonnage dropped by American bombers on
Europe were not released until *after* the Allied invasion of France in
June 1944, while its later 'shuttle-partner', the 15th Air Force, from
Italian bases, did not commence operations until late 1943. From
August 1942 until May 1945, the Eighth Air Force dropped some
715,000 tons of bombs, while the 15th Air Force, from November
1943 until VE-Day dropped slightly more than 340,000 tons. The
USAAF's dogged persistence with proving the efficacy of a daylight
bombing offensive proved expensive in aircraft and, especially, men, as
had the same form of bombing by the RAF during the early years of

the war in the air. Of the overall total of American airmen killed in the European theatre of operations, including those who died in accidents, non-operational flying, *et al*, amounting to almost 80,000, some 64,000 were men of the heavy bombers. Such a heavy cost might be argued to have been inevitable. The USAAF had almost no experience of conducting any form of *operational* bombing of *any* type prior to its entry into the European war, and little enough practical experience in the multi-faceted problem of operating heavy bombers in great numbers. Thus, suddenly to be transformed from a peacetime, well-ordered existence to a frontline, spearhead bombing force in full-scale war, facing a veteran, determined, well-equipped opposing air force, was a traumatic experience. To then adhere to a style of bombing operations already well-proven as inviting disastrous casualties was – at least – a daring decision. That the Fortress, Liberator and Marauder crews eventually triumphed was more a tribute to the courage and determination of the American crews and the ruggedness of their machines, than any true justification of their higher command's theories.

While the cessation of hostilities in Europe provided a momentary pause in the pace of air operations – much of May and June 1945 were weeks of untroubled operations by British and USAAF bombers acting as freight carriers for supplying much-needed food rations to European countries, and the retrieval of the many thousand of Allied prisoners of war – preparations had already been progressed for large detachments of operational bomber and fighter units eastwards to the Pacific theatre to prosecute the final assaults on Japan, and as re-inforcement for the projected seaborne invasion of Japanese soil in November 1945. The need for such additional air strength was nulli-fied by the dropping of atom bombs on the Japanese cities of Hiro-shima and Nagasaki on 6 August and 9 August respectively; six days later Japan surrendered. Peace was officially declared on 15 August, VJ-Day, on which date an advance element of the USAAF Eighth Air Force, equipped now with Boeing B-29 Superfortresses, was due to fly its initial missions against Japanese targets; while forward units of the RAF's 'Tiger Force' – the Bomber Command force detailed for Pacific operations – were finalising preparations for reception of the Lancasters due to arrive in the ensuing weeks.

The first few years of the post-bellum era were occupied by all Allied air forces in a swift but orderly reduction in strength and huge de-mobilisation of personnel wishing to return to civilian life. It was a period of logical retrenchment, during which scarce attention was paid to analysis and assessment of the results of the massive use of air power during the war years. To the multi-millions of men and women for whom the war had been traumatic and – in so many cases – a shattering of their previous lifestyles; any academic studies of war damage and strategic or tactical problems were the least in priorities. Of the main Allied nations involved in the aerial war, only the United States had made prior arrangement for any such postwar research, and their Strategic Bombing Survey team commenced its studies almost immediately after the surrender of Germany, while material and people were still 'available' and evident. Apart from the awesome material destruction starkly in evidence at every known bombing target, the team's prime concern was the recovery of Luftwaffe and industrial documentation. Only with such contemporary records could an accurate survey be made of the short- and long-term effects of Allied bombing on Germany's industry and population. Despite wide destruction or secretion of such documents by certain German authorities or individuals, it was found possible to assemble a virtual mountain of records and reports *et al* for the major part of the war, and certainly for the years 1939–44. The final months of the conflict in early 1945 were less comprehensive, a perfectly natural outcome of the rapid disintegration of Germany and its administrative services as the Allies squeezed Germany into submission from all sides. The only near-reliable records to be gathered covered most facets of January and February 1945, but the remaining weeks of the war left few indications from official sources of ultimate statistics.

The main points to which the researchers required answers fell into several categories. One was whether the strategic bombing had achieved its intention of ruining German industrial capacity to maintain the German military machinery; while a second sought to establish the degree of morale effect such bombing had on the German civil population's will to continue the war. A third, though of slightly less importance within the research terms of reference, was an investigation into the workings and policies etc, affecting the Luftwaffe itself. The results obtained in each of these specific avenues of enquiry produced some surprising conclusions; at least, many previously held theories by Allied air commanders during the war proved to be either wildly inaccurate or, at best, only part-correct.

The first subject, the bombing offensive's effect on German production capacity, was probably the most contentious. The RAF and the USAAF had basically employed two different styles and methods in bombing. While the Americans had steadfastly stayed with a policy of precision bombing of specific targets almost throughout their operations, the RAF, virtually from the outset of the war, had concentrated in the main on the principle of area bombing attacks against large-area objectives such as cities and the bigger industrial complexes. Only after 1943, aided greatly by a myriad of new scientific aids to navigation and bombing, and no less by the experienced guidance now available from Bennett's veteran Path Finder Force spearhead, did the RAF become truly successful in raiding precision targets.

From 1944 to 1945 the Bomber Command crews enhanced such precise bombing with many highly successful, destructive raids against one-off targets, yet the command's overall policy still clung to the area bombing emphasis almost to the very end of its operational offensive. Both policies had their place in the combined Allied air offensive, with perfectly rational arguments in favour of each form. What mattered in the ultimate analysis was whether each – or both together – had actually achieved the common aim; the defeat of Germany's ability and will to wage war. In this context both air forces had no quarrel; both aimed to reduce Germany's industrial capacity to a completely non-effective status and thereby cripple the enemy's fighting potential. The only real difference between the two Allied forces was *how* best this might be accomplished.

For RAF Bomber Command the protracted and bloody path to maturity as a heavy, strategic strike force had been a saga of frustration. At the outbreak of war the command was totally unequipped or practised for the role intended by the Air Staff, being in a transitory stage of converting from its peacetime, obsolete aircraft to promised four-engined, long range bombers. Its crews too were by no means sufficiently trained or experienced in their war priorities – 'live' bombing by night, navigation over long distances in anything but perfect weather conditions, self-defence by day against aerial opposition. The parsimonious financial budgeting of the RAF during most of the inter-war period had precluded adequate advances in the latest aircraft and equipment, and 'rationed' any form of actual bombing and gunnery training to a scandalously low level. Even the RAF's principal aerial bombs in 1939, mainly of the General Purpose (GP) type, were aged in conception and near to useless for their purpose of destruction. The one saving grace of that dismaying situation was the keenness – and courage – of the crews, who, though in many cases only too aware of their 'deficiencies' in equipment and practice, never failed to at least attempt to fulfil every allotted task, whatever the odds against them. At Air Staff levels an unjustified optimism about the command's abilities and potential destructive power led to a first year of attempted precision attacks on specified targets, often in daylight hours – and quickly resulted in a crop of casualties which accentuated the bombers inadequacies and faulty tactics.

The long-term hope for a force strong enough to deliver a true strategic offensive against Germany was to be frustrated until at least late 1943. In the interim the 'sleeping giant' gathered strength and increasing expertise, though at an alarming cost in crews and aircraft. By late 1941 the policy of general area attacks had been firmly adopted, while the disastrous tactic of despatching unescorted bombers by day had finally been abandoned. In 1942–43 the advent of new aircraft in reasonable numbers, fresh bombs, modern bombing and navigational aids, and a steady flood of freshly-trained crews from the Empire Air Training Scheme combined to offer renewed hope for propagation of the long-awaited strategic offensive; only to have such hopes diluted by continuing imposed diversions of some bombers to operations in support of such equally vital campaigns as the anti-submarine battle in the Atlantic.

From March 1943 to March 1944 Bomber Command finally mounted the start of an escalating night offensive in the terms of its original goal, a year in which it despatched a total of 74,723 aircraft on operations and suffered a gross total of 2,864 aircraft lost in action. This twelve months of intensified 'area attacks' did not, however, produce the immediate results hoped for by Harris and his Air Ministry superiors. Vast acreages of German city property were razed or ruined, many thousands of German civilians were killed, and no few established industrial complexes heavily damaged. Yet German civilian morale was never significantly depressed, while the overall effect on German war production was merely to force it to be much more widely dispersed. Indeed, German production output, particularly of aircraft, was steadily increasing by early 1944.

The greatest obstacle to the RAF's night bombers was the Luftwaffe's night defence system, including the vast network of flak batteries and searchlights, but especially the nightfighter force. British bombers throughout the war were always out-gunned and under-protected in relation to the heavily-armed *Nachtjäger*. From December 1943 to April 1944 alone German nightfighter crews claimed almost 1,200 RAF bombers shot down, while the annual totals of nightfighter victims in 1943 and 1944 (1,820 and 2,335 respectively) reflect the increasing success rate imposed on the invading night bomber streams over Germany. Tragic as such statistics were – each bomber carried an average of seven men in its crew – they represented an overall casualty rate of barely five per cent of bombers despatched; in itself an indication of the numerical weight of attack now being mounted by Harris. Interspersed with the main night offensive, Bomber Command had demonstrated its occasional ability to destroy a precision objective – the finest example of such precise bombing being the much-publicised Dams raid by 617 Squadron in early 1943 – and in early 1944 the command was called upon to divert a number of sorties to similar specific targets in the dual-purpose attacks against V1 bomb sites and the French transportation system. Though necessary for the build-up to the Allied invasion in June 1944, such diversions of bombing effort by Harris's command continued to dilute the potential weight of offensive which might have been applied to the strategic plan. Postwar critics of Harris's persistence with the area bombing ploy have almost always failed to appreciate the extent and effect of the many 'diversions' of his command imposed by higher command throughout his tenure as chief of the RAF's main offensive force. As Harris himself has stated : 'Over the entire period of the war only 45 per cent of the Command's whole effort was against German cities, so that in fact we were using for the main offensive a force which was not only less than one-quarter of the strength originally planned, but nearer one-eighth.'*

Clearly, having been saddled with the area bombing policy created by the Air Staff before his appointment as AOC-in-C, Bomber Command, Harris was never permitted to marshal his complete bomber strength to implement the policy – a situation which pertained until the end of the European conflict. As a realist, Harris favoured the area principle simply because he was well aware of the inability of his crews to accomplish significant precision bombing against any selective target – the means and methods for such tactics were not to become generally available until the final stages of the air war. Once the command acquired dependable navigational and accurate bombing aids and target-marketing methods, the pace and weight of Bomber Command raids increased swiftly; during the last three months of 1944 the crews dropped the weight of bombs on enemy targets at least equivalent to the total tonnage dropped throughout the whole of 1943. Only *after* the war was it possible to compare the Allied intelligence estimates of the effect of the bombing offensive with the actual results. Then, and only then, it was realised that the area bombing policy had by no means accomplished fully the rather optimistic evaluations made during the war. This under-estimation by the Allies was clearly evident when the matter of German aircraft production in 1944–45 was con-

* *Bomber Offensive* by Sir A. T. Harris, Collins, 1947.

sidered – in itself something of a shock to the American bomber staffs whose prolonged *selective* bombing campaign against Luftwaffe aircraft resources had been thought far more effective than was the case.

Probably the greatest individual success was obtained by the Allied bombers, principally the USAAF, in their concentration on destroying Germany's oil production resources during the final year of operations. There can be little challenge to the view that this particular objective was achieved in high degree and was greatly instrumental in bringing the German military machine to a grinding halt. It was not, of course, the only 'ingredient' of eventual victory, but was at least a deliberate bombing policy aimed against selective targets which produced most fruitful results. Though primarily a form of strategic offensive credited in the main to the USAAF's bombers, the RAF Bomber Command contribution to the 'oil plan' was not small. In his report to Hitler dated 19 January 1945 on the contemporary state of oil production, Albert Speer included the comment :

> . . . it has now been determined that the attacks which take place so often at night now are considerably more effective than daylight attacks, since heavier bombs are used and an extraordinary accuracy in attaining the target is reported. Consequently, even if during the first quarter of 1945 the repair work and plants are completely untouched, the theoretical production figures, which seemed possible in the last quarter, will not be reached.

Thus, in reality, it was necessarily a combination of the RAF's ever-increasing accuracy and mounting weight of attack by night – and in the final months by day – and the continuing determined daylight raiding by the men of Carl Spaatz's bombers which gained such results.

If such a combination of bombing attacks seems wholly logical to the casual observer, it should be remarked that in spite of the official declaration of the inauguration of a 'Combined Bomber Offensive' from late February 1944; the two main Allied bomber formations – the USAAF Eighth Air Force and RAF Bomber Command – were at no time a truly *unified* force, either in operational direction and control or, indeed, in pure policy. Moreover, Bomber Command throughout the war was a separate entity from the other forms of RAF offensive air formations such as Fighter Command and Coastal Command. While the USAAF Eighth Air Force embraced bombers and fighters under a single overall force commander, thereby automatically placing all operational effort and direction in a single channel of control,

Bomber Command's Arthur Harris had no direct authority over Fighter Command for necessary concomitant operational requirements. He could only 'request' necessary co-ordination of fighter or other forces for his bombing operations from other formation commanders of equal rank and authority; a circumstance which never entirely succeeded in producing 100 per cent unity. Such stubborn clinging by the RAF to its peacetime, traditional command structure is all the more questionable when it is realised that virtually every other theatre of operations during the war had demonstrated abundantly the efficacy of an interservice, integrated air-ground-sea command organisation; while the example of the USAAF's Eighth Air Force in this context was available in England. It might be added that the basic fact of a unified air control, linked necessarily to a true interservice co-ordination was not to be inaugurated in Britain's services until many years after the cessation of the European war.

In summary, the Allied fighter and bomber offensives throughout the war against Germany *might* well have been more successfully directed and employed towards the declared ultimate objective of demoralising and defeating Hitler's Germany, a view too often expressed in post-bellum years by 'historians' wallowing in the golden warmth of supreme hindsight and abundant archival evidence; yet no serious student of the bombing offensive in particular can justly deny the vital and decisive contribution, directly and indirectly, made by the bomber crews in the shattering of Hitler's vain-glorious phantasy of a 'Thousand-Years' Reich'.

Nor can any historian worthy of that description diminish the personal contribution to that triumph of arms of the bomber commanders Harris, Eaker and Spaatz. Rarely in the whole cavalcade of military history had such commanders had to bear such weighty responsibilities. And at no time had any other military commanders been called upon to commit virtually their entire forces to battle not just once but almost *every* night and days over many years. Such awesome decisions and weight of responsibility can only be borne by exceptional men, and in Arthur Harris the RAF possessed a commander of outstanding ability, fortitude, courage and decisive determination; a leader in the finest traditional mould for whom the young crews he despatched over Germany night after night held a respect and devotion given to few other men.

Whomever the commanders might have been, nevertheless the real victory belonged to the men who had to prosecute the actual war; in this context, the men of the bomber crews. To them must be given the ultimate accolade. Strategic or tactical policies may be argued, changed, or expounded by the gold-braided armchair 'warriors', but it was the young air crew members of the fighters and bombers who had to implement them at the sharp end of the war. Young in years – any man over twenty-five years of age was regarded often as an 'old man' by fellow air crews – they nevertheless displayed the courage of veterans as they voluntarily returned to the hell of operations over enemy lands time and time again. Their sacrifices were grievous, the very flower of a whole generation of splendid youth, yet they were never deterred. They had come from all nations of the free world, all walks of life, blending easily and readily in united comradeship to forge a weapon of warfare unprecedented in human history and unmatched in power. They had no part in the decisions to wage war, but had willingly placed their unfulfilled lives on the borderline of possible supreme sacrifice in order to regain the 'peace' lost to them by the machinations of their elder statesmen. Whatever academic debates may still be waged about the way they were employed, or the material results they achieved, the air crews had obeyed their orders without demur and to the very limits of their abilities. Their collective contribution to the victory is undeniable.

What of their defeated counterparts in the Luftwaffe? It is fashionable during wartime to denigrate the character and abilities of the 'enemy' – a ploy consistently exploited by the popular media and propaganda machinery of each opposing nation under the guise of boosting morale. It is also, albeit unwittingly, a grave error in psychological judgment; if an enemy is so 'inferior', technically and/or humanly, then it follows that little effort or courage is required to defeat him, thus such propaganda merely, if unconsciously, denigrates the fighting qualities of one's own fighting men. It is a view of the 'enemy' seldom encountered among the men who actually fought; they, and they alone, were best qualified to judge their opponents. Such was the case with the opposing air crews in the European war in the air. Only a fool or a knave underestimated his immediate opponent, and although the morale of the Allied crews seldom admitted to any feeling of inferiority in any sense, they always looked upon the Luftwaffe as a formidable foe. It was an attitude reflected within the German air force about the RAF and USAAF.

Born in the heady atmosphere of a revitalised Germany climbing from the ruins of a shattered economy to a new, bright prosperity, the new German air force was inculcated with an unquestioning belief in its superiority and strength. That it was structured in error as a purely tactical force, with little if any thought or effort devoted to any long-term strategical employment, has been discussed in earlier chapters. The undeniable successes the Luftwaffe achieved during the first year of the war boosted this image of invincibility, at least outwardly, and it was not until its patent failure to subdue RAF Fighter Command over England in the summer of 1940 that any of its crews or commanders were given serious pause in such airs of confidence. From late 1941 until the end of hostilities the Luftwaffe inexorably declined, despite brilliant spasms of momentary victory or air supremacy in particular situations. This decline became evident after 1942 as the twin hammers of the USAAF and RAF in the west and the Russians in the east began to increase the weight of their blows. By 1944 the Luftwaffe's effectiveness was overtly slipping away, with the one notable exception of the much-strengthened nightfighter defenders of Germany itself and the desperate operational effort of the Reich's day fighter force. By early 1945 the Luftwaffe was, for all its paper strength, a spent force. In its mere ten years' existence the Luftwaffe had known the very peaks of triumph and the degradation of utter defeat.

The causes of such a reversal of fortunes were relatively clear to many members of the Luftwaffe and objective 'outsiders'. They could be simply combined under the generic term 'personalities'. It was perhaps inevitable in the sort of totalitarian dictatorship which ruled Nazi Germany that the hierarchy would emerge as self-seeking individuals primarily and 'leaders' secondly. This was particularly so in the case of the Luftwaffe higher commanders during its relatively brief existence. The central figure was Hermann Göring, the air force's supreme commander throughout its entire operational career except for the final weeks of defeat. Until late 1941 when Hitler declared himself as the Commander-in-Chief of the Armed Forces, Göring had a virtually free hand in the conduct of the war being waged by 'his' Luftwaffe; during which time he saw his airmen achieve their greatest victories. His conduct of the pre-invasion assault against the RAF and English cities during the Battle of Britain and its subsequent night blitz gave the first indications of Göring's lack of strategic, even tactical knowledge in the context of air power. His failure to break the RAF in 1940 was also the beginning of a growing mistrust of the Luftwaffe by Hitler, who at no time ever fully understood the importance of air power, being wholly orientated mentally to matters relevant to the ground fighting of his armies. As an ex-infantry man himself, Hitler had no conception of the correct use or purpose of air power, regarding it as merely an adjunct to the army; a view which was to be emphasised as the war progressed in a series of disastrous decisions and directives affecting the Luftwaffe, its equipment, operations and direction.

The fact was that Göring, despite a steadily waning popularity after 1941 with both Hitler and 'his' Luftwaffe, remained in supreme command of the air force, and should thus have been able to exercise a firm guiding hand in the Luftwaffe's destiny in every respect. Had he done so, it is possible that the later stages of the aerial war would have assumed a greatly different complexion. Instead, jealous of his personal status, and at all times motivated by a survival instinct which gave ultimate priority to pure self-preservation, Göring became merely a filter for Hitler's increasing interference with all aspects, large and trivial, of the Luftwuffe. It was Hitler who ordered the cessation of night intruder sorties over England in mid-1941 despite their increasing success; who depleted the fighting firstline strength of the Luftwaffe prior to the Allied invasion of France by transferring large numbers of units to Russian front areas, and to Norway and Greece to prepare for imagined Allied invasions in these countries; and it was Hitler who deprived the Luftwaffe of the Messerschmitt Me 262 jet fighter by relegating this superb fighter to a *blitz-bomber* role at a time when full-scale production as a pure fighter might have given the Luftwaffe *Jagdgeschwader* a vastly superior weapon to meet the RAF and USAAF in 1944. These are but a few examples of the continuing interference in Luftwaffe matters which played so large a part in its eventual defeat. Had Göring asserted his proper authority and control of the Luftwaffe, as was his clear duty to 'his' Luftwaffe, things might well have been different in each case. Instead, Göring, ever-fearful of incurring Hitler's personal displeasure and thereby compromising his private status, demurred to Hitler's orders on every occasion, merely passing on his Führer's wishes and orders without qualification.

Among the many facets of Göring's mishandling of the Luftwaffe even in pre-war days was his constant suspicion of all or any other senior figures who might affect his personal authority or his close relationship with Hitler. As a result, he often appointed senior officers on a purely personal basis, men such as the World War One fighter ace Ernst Udet whom he persuaded to take over the Luftwaffe's Technical Services department. Udet, for all his devotion to flying and national popularity, was unfitted for any such task of such significant importance. Under Udet's aegis, for example, the policy for future equipment of the Luftwaffe was decided, and resulted in too much emphasis being placed upon standard aircraft types' production to the exclusion of many other promising or important designs which the Luftwaffe was to need during the war. Göring too was not above playing off one senior officer against another if it meant reducing any 'threat' – real or imagined – to Göring's personal position. In essence, Göring's self-interests clouded his interpretation of his responsibilities as the Luftwaffe supremo throughout the war. Combined with Hitler's misguided 'instinctive' interventions in many crucial facets of the air force's equipment and operational employment, these dual 'masters' of the Luftwaffe were the prime saboteurs of the air arm.

In the *Geschwader* of firstline units, the fighter and bomber crews fought bravely notwithstanding such lack of intelligent leadership at the helm. Whereas operational crews of the RAF and USAAF were given specified limitations to tours of operational flying and then 'rested' at intervals, no such respite was available under the Luftwaffe's terms of duty. Fighter and bomber crews remained on operations until death, crippling injury, promotion or some similar cause removed them from the front line. Many German fighter pilots saw virtually continuous operations from the outset of the war until its conclusion, interrupted only by spells of leave or hospitalisation and convalescence resulting from 'minor' wounds. By 1945 some of the highest-scoring *Kanonen* ('Aces' or 'Big Guns') – the so-termed *Experten* – had accumulated astonishingly high victory tallies as a direct outcome of such extended periods of operational flying; but had often survived being shot down five, six, even twelve times.

That they fought on to the bitter end was an indication not of any Nazi indoctrination, but of a code of honour and duty as professional officers. They deserved far better of their fanatical 'leaders'. Defeated in the air by the overwhelming superiority in sheer numbers of the Allied air forces in the end, they were in a sense defeated too by their own hierarchy. Courage alone was not enough.

Selected Bibiography

The plethora of literature already published about every possible facet of the 1939–45 aerial war is daunting to even the most avid researcher or reader. Therefore, in keeping with the purpose of this book as a panoramic general survey of that conflict, the following list is simply a personal selection of reliable reference works about the broader aspects of the European air war, with an occasional specific subject to lend authentic atmosphere to particular actions or phases of the struggle.

*

Bomber Offensive, MRAF Sir A. Harris; Collins, 1947

The Strategic Air Offensive against Germany, 4 Vols., Webster & Frankland; HMSO, 1961

Royal Air Force 1939–45, 3 Vols., Richards & Saunders; HMSO, 1953–54

RCAF Overseas, 3 Vols., OUP; Toronto, 1944–49

RAAF Official History, 2 Vols., J. Herington; AWM, 1954–63

New Zealanders with the RAF, 3 Vols., H. L. Thompson; WHB, NZ, 1953–59

Destiny can Wait, PAF Association, Heinemann, 1949

The Defence of the United Kingdom, B. Collier; HMSO, 1957

The Battle of the V-Weapons, B. Collier; Hodder & Stoughton, 1964

The Narrow Margin, Wood & Dempster; Arrow, 1969

Dowding and the Battle of Britain, R. C. Wright; Macdonald, 1969

Fighter Command, P. Wykeham; Putnam, 1960

Fighter Command, 1936–68, C. Bowyer; Dent, 1980

Blitz on Britain 1939–45, A. Price; Ian Allan, 1977

Pathfinder Force, G. Musgrove; Macdonald & Janes, 1976

2nd Tactical Air Force, C. F. Shores; Osprey, 1970

Photo Reconnaissance, A. J. Brookes; Ian Allan, 1975

Instruments of Darkness, A. Price; Kimber, 1967

Confound and Destroy, M. Streetly; Macdonald & Janes, 1978

Battle over the Reich, A. Price; Ian Allan, 1973

The Thousand Plan, R. Barker; Chatto & Windus, 1965

The Destruction of Dresden, D. Irving; Kimber, 1963

The Nuremberg Raid, M. Middlebrook; Allen Lane, 1973
The Rise & Fall of the German Air Force, Air Ministry, 1948
The Birth of the Luftwaffe, H. Schliephake; Ian Allan, 1971
Luftwaffe – an Analysis, Ed. H. Faber; Sidgwick & Jackson, 1979
History of the German Nightfighter Force, G. Aders; Jane's, 1979
The Luftwaffe War Diaries, G. Bekker; Macdonald, 1966
The First and the Last, A. Galland; Methuen, 1955
The Mighty Eighth, R. Freeman; Macdonald, 1970
The US Strategic Bomber, R. Freeman; Macdonald & Jane's, 1975
The Night Hamburg Died, M. Caidin; Ballantine, 1960
Big Week, G. Infield; Pinnacle, USA, 1974
Black Thursday, M. Caidin; Ballantine, 1966
The Greatest Air Battle – Dieppe, N. L. R. Franks; Kimber, 1979
Eagle Day, R. Collier; Dent, 1980
Fighter Pilot, P. Richey; Batsford, 1941
The Big Show, P. Clostermann; Chatto & Windus, 1951
Scramble, J. R. D. Braham; Muller, 1961
Enemy Coast Ahead, G. P. Gibson; Michael Joseph, 1946
A Penguin in the Eyrie, H. Bolitho; Hutchinson, 1955
Coastal Command at War, C. Bowyer; Ian Allan, 1979
The Mare's Nest, D. Irving; Kimber, 1964
V2, W. Dornberger; Hurst & Blackett, 1954

Index

Names

Arnold, H., Gen, 108, 109

Babington-Smith, C., Flt Off, 168
Bader, D. R. S., Sqn Ldr, 59, 77
Balthasar, W., Obltn, 57
Bär, H., Obltn, 205
Barkhorn, G., Obltn, 204
Barratt, Sir A., AVM, 36, 54
Bateman, M., Flt Lt, 153
Becker, L., Obltn, 82, 144
Bennett, D., AVM, 103, 214

Chamberlain, N., 19
Cheshire, G. L., Wg Cdr, 192
Churchill, W. S., 25, 62, 107, 118,
134, 140, 172
Coningham, Sir A., AM, 168, 173,
178, 189
Cotton, S., Wg Cdr, 157, 158
Cunningham, J., Wg Cdr, 85

Daladier, M., 28
Dale, Wg Cdr, 98
Dempsey, Sir M., Gen, 199
Douglas, S., ACM, 88, 90, 93, 118,
125, 133
Douhet, G., Gen, 34
Dowding, Sir H., ACM, 22, 40, 41,
46, 56, 59, 60, 66, 68, 69, 71, 72,
73, 75, 76, 79, 84, 88, 126, 158

Eaker, I., Gen, 107, 108, 109, 135,
141, 145, 218
Eden, A., 23
Eisenhower, D., Gen, 144, 168, 188,
206, 208
Ensor, P. S. B., Fg Off, 91

Esmonde, E., Lt-Cdr, 124

Falck, W., Major, 82
Franco, Gen, 18

Galland, A., Gen, 57, 66, 77, 95,
122, 123, 124, 128, 202, 204, 205
Gamelin, G., Gen, 54
Garland, D., Fg Off, 55
Gibson, G. P., Wg Cdr, 112, 113,
139
Gnys, W., Lt, 35
Göring, H., FM, 15, 17, 19, 21, 28,
31, 32, 52, 58, 60, 61, 62, 63, 64,
69, 70, 71, 72, 75, 76, 78, 79, 82,
83, 84, 86, 87, 91, 92, 93, 102,
117, 122, 128, 129, 131, 133, 136,
146, 156, 179, 204, 220, 221, 222
Gray, T., Sgt, 55
Guderian, H., Gen, 58

Harris, Sir A. T., ACM, 100, 101,
102, 103, 107, 108, 110, 111, 117,
132, 134, 138, 140, 141, 142, 143,
144, 145, 163, 168, 170, 177, 178,
183, 185, 186, 187, 189, 195, 197,
198, 200, 201, 202, 206, 207, 215,
216, 218
Heinkel, E., 16
Held, A., Fwbl, 46
Herrmann, H., Major, 136
Hill, Sir R., AM, 168, 169, 172,
173, 174, 178
Hitler, A., 16, 17, 18, 19, 20, 21,
23, 25, 26, 29, 30, 31, 32, 47, 48,
50, 52, 58, 61, 62, 64, 75, 76,
78, 80, 82, 86, 89, 91, 92, 102,
106, 117, 118, 122, 123, 126, 128,
130, 131, 138, 140, 167, 174, 176,

Lincoln, 99
Lingen, 97
Lipezk, 16
Littlehampton, 74
Liverpool, 86, 89
London, 37, 40, 41, 75, 76, 77, 78,
    83, 84, 85, 86, 87, 89, 169, 172,
    173, 174, 175, 200, 207
Lottinghem, 167
Lützkendorf, 200
Luxembourg, 54, 55
Lympne, 71

Maastricht, 54
Magdeburg, 183, 200
Maginot Line, 45, 50, 53
Manchester, 86
Mannheim, 146
Manston, 71, 74, 124, 171
Marienhe, 120
Martlesham, 71
Medmenham, 163, 166, 191
Metz, 199
Middle Wallop, 70, 71
Middleton St George, 98
Mimoyecques, 167
Mitteland, 207
Möhne, 112
Mortain, 197
Mourmelon-le-Grand, 37
Munich, 19, 20, 25, 31, 204

Nagasaki, 212
Newcastle, 88
Nijmegen-Grave, 199
North Coates, 152, 153
Nuremberg, 143, 144, 184, 209

Orpington, 174
Oslo, 165
Ostheim, 50

Paris, 60, 123, 186
Pas de Calais, 147, 170
Peenemunde, 139, 141, 165, 166,
    167, 168

Plymouth, 86
Poix, 91
Poling, 74
Pölitz, 200
Portland, 70, 71, 78
Predannack, 154

Rapallo, 15
Regensburg, 146, 147, 181
Rheims, 36, 208
Rochester, 71
Rotterdam, 50, 51, 52, 97
Rouen, 115
Rouen-Sotteville, 104
Ruhland, 200

St Eval, 159
Ste Foy de Montgomerie, 197
St Nazaire, 109
Salzburg, 205
Scampton, 39
Schaffen-Diest, 51
Schillig Roads, 38, 39, 46
Schiphol, 50
Schweinfurt, 146, 147, 148
Sealand, 71
Sedan, 55
Sevenoaks, 165
Siracourt, 167
Sorpe, 112
Sottevast, 167
Southampton, 70, 71, 78
Stettin, 183
Stuttgart, 147
Swanton Morley, 99
Swansea, 89
Swinemünde, 166
Sylt, 40

Tangmere, 74, 75, 85
Thames Estuary, 70
Thorney Island, 74
Tonsberg, 208
Torgau, 209
Toul, 196
Troyes, 56

Biggin Hill, 74, 75, 93
Birmingham, 86, 89
Blizna, 167
Bohlen, 200
Boscombe Down, 98
Bouillon, 55
Boulogne, 58, 77, 191, 192
Breda, 55
Bremen, 39, 101, 115, 184
Brest, 98, 123, 125
Brize Norton, 74
Brunsbüttel, 46, 124
Brunswick, 183
Bützweilerhof, 50

Caen, 91, 126, 192, 194, 196, 200
Cap d'Antifer, 192
Casablanca, 105, 107, 132
Castle Camps, 125
Calais, 77
Chartres, 126
Cherbourg, 192
Chiswick, 173
Cologne, 50, 101, 102
Colombelles, 200
Compeigne, 61
Conde Vraux, 54
Coventry, 86, 87, 101
Cracow, 34
Cranwell, 120
Croydon, 71, 74
Culmhead, 171

Danzig, 19
Debden, 125
Detling, 70
Dieppe, 126, 127, 128, 176
Dirschau, 34
Döberitz, 17
Dortmund-Ems, 207
Dover, 192
Dresden, 184, 207
Drem, 40
Dreux, 91
Duisburg, 98, 206
Dunkerque (Dunkirk), 58, 59, 60

Duxford, 77, 78

Eastchurch, 70
Ecury-sur-Coole, 38
Eder, 112
Eggebeck, 208
Eindhoven, 199
Equeurdreville, 167
Essen, 100, 101, 111, 132, 136, 144, 184

Farnborough, 74
Firth of Forth, 40, 41, 80
Ford, 74

Gosport, 74
Gotha, 182
Gravesend, 165

Hague, 50, 173, 174
Hamburg, 39, 134, 135, 136, 137, 138, 139, 140, 144, 180, 206
Hartford Bridge, 189
Harwell, 192
Hawkinge, 119
Heligoland Bight, 46
Hemswell, 46, 114
Heston, 158
Hiroshima, 212
Hornchurch, 75
Husum, 208

Isle of Sheppey, 70

Kenley, 74, 75
Kiel, 136, 166, 208

Lammermuir, 41
Le Bourget, 196
Le Havre, 98
Le Mans, 56
Le Touquet, 93
Lee-on-Solent, 74
Leuchars, 153
Leuna, 200
Leipzig, 183, 184

177, 180, 182, 184, 201, 204, 206, 217, 218, 220, 221, 222
Hohagen, Obltn, 204

Inskip, Sir T., 24

Jeschonnek, H., Gen, 52, 122, 129

Kain, E., Fg Off, 38
Kammhuber, J., Gen, 82, 83, 91, 102, 106, 129, 130, 131
Kingcombe, B., Sqn Ldr, 124
Kluge, von, Gen, 201
Kreipe, W., Major, 59
Krupinski, W., 204

Le Roux, J. J., Sqn Ldr, 196
Letchford, F., Sgt, 38
Leigh-Mallory, Sir T., ACM, 169, 178, 187, 188, 191
Lippe-Weissenfeld, Prinz zur, Major, 98
Ludlow-Hewitt, Sir E., ACM, 157
Lützow, G., Obltn, 204, 205

Malan, A. G., Grp Cpt, 59
McPherson, A., Fg Off, 38
Milch, E., Gen, 28, 122, 123, 128, 148, 180
Mölders, W., Haupt, 57, 122
Mould, P. W. O. Plt Off, 38

Park, Sir K., AM, 59, 76
Patton, G., Gen, 197
Portal, Sir C., ACM, 133
Priller, J., Obltn, 194

Raeder, E., Adm, 128
Rayski, L., Col, 29
Richthofen, M. von, Rittm, 122
Rommel, E., FM, 197
Rundstedt, von, Gen, 52

Salmond, Sir J., MRAF, 23
Scherling, Fwbl, 97
Schnell, 204

Searby, J. A., Grp Capt, 139, 166
Seeckt, H. von, Gen, 15
Simon, Sir J., 23
Smuts, J., Gen, 14
Spaatz, C., Gen, 178, 187, 200, 201, 217, 218
Speer, A., 138, 179, 217
Speidel, Gen, 32
Steinhoff, J., Obltn, 204, 205
Steventon, D. W., Flt Lt, 166

Tedder, Sir A., ACM, 178, 188, 197
Trautloft, H., Oberst, 77
Trenchard, Sir H., ACM, 23, 29
Tuck, R. R. S., Wg Cdr, 59
Tuttle, G., Wg Cdr, 159

Udet, E., Gen, 28, 122, 221

Vuillemin, J., Gen, 28, 44

Wick, H., Obltn, 57
Wodarczyk, H., Ltn, 194
Wood, Sir K., 25

Zemke, H., Col, 181

Places
Aachen, 184
Abbeville, 91, 93
Amiens, 91
Amsterdam, 50
Antwerp, 116, 199, 203
Arnhem, 199, 200
Augsburg, 181

Benson, 159
Bentley Priory, 67
Berchtesgaden, 208
Berlin, 17, 28, 75, 81, 97, 139, 140, 141, 142, 143, 144, 148, 167, 168, 182, 183, 184, 185, 186, 195, 198, 202, 205
Bethnal Green, 165
Bielefeld, 207

Turin, 65

Urville-Hague, 192

Vallo, 208
Vegesack, 109, 115
Veldwezelt, 55
Ventnor, 74
Vistula, 34
Vroenhoven, 55

Waalhaven, 50, 51
Waddington, 39, 98, 99
Walcheren, 201
Wangerooge Island, 208
Warnemunde, 16
Warsaw, 35
Washington, 108

Watten, 167
Wattisham, 46
Wick, 159
Wilhelmshaven, 38, 46, 109, 124
Wizernes, 167
Wembley, 159
Westminster, 78
West Malling, 74
Westkapelle, 201
Woolston, 78
Worthy Down, 71
Wyton, 38, 39, 46

Ypenburg, 50
Yvetot, 192

Zeitz, 200